THE MAKING OF MR. MAC

THE MAKING OF MR. MAC

A MEMOIR

Jim Maechling

PRECOCITY PRESS

This book is dedicated with great respect to the late Rev. Edward J. McFadden, SJ, vice-principal of Loyola High School in charge of discipline in our day.

Editor: Ruth Mullen
Creative Director: Susan Shankin
Designer: Barbara Garibay

Text set in Century Schoolbook

ISBN: 978-0-9987963-8-3

Library of Congress Control Number: 2020904322

Published by Precocity Press
Venice, CA

First edition. Printed and bound in the United States of America

CONTENTS

As I sat down to write, I had just filled out my affirmative RSVP to the sixtieth reunion of the class of 1960 from Loyola High School, Los Angeles. This convergence is more than sentimental coincidence, as the reader will discover. Loyola High School and its Jesuit ethos are the backdrop for Jim Maechling's engaging odyssey. The recurring names of lifelong friends in this story are those of Loyola classmates, myself among them. The friendships forged over those adolescent years were strong, intense, and lasting, even when the infrequency of personal contact was measured in decades. This memoir is a ringing endorsement of the indelible imprint those Jesuit priests and scholastics left on our hearts and souls and Maechling's amazing memory. Reading the manuscript was made bittersweet by the realization that those long-gone Jesuits could not enjoy the stories we retell over and over again with gratitude and affection about them and all that they gave us, perhaps unwittingly.

Maechling suggests his *apologia pro vita sua* (defense of one's life) when he cites Sir Thomas More's exchange with the overly ambitious Richard Rich in Robert Bolt's *A Man for All Seasons*:

> MORE: *Why not be a teacher? You'd be a fine teacher; perhaps a great one.*
>
> RICH: *If I was, who would know it?*
>
> MORE: *You; your pupils; your friends; God. Not a bad public, that.*

Maechling's is the anti-story to Richard Rich's ruthlessly selfish pursuit of wealth, power, and influence at the court of Henry VIII. Rich willingly sacrificed his conscience, his integrity, and his humanity for those treasures "that moths consume and rust destroys." These pages tell the story of a person who early on decided to "be a teacher," fully aware that he was sacrificing wealth, power, and influence for a life of purpose, satisfaction, learning, wisdom, and influence over the minds and hearts of generations of students. This is the story of a "great teacher," and when you read his story you will understand why he is held in such high regard by "his friends, his God, and his pupils." What Robert Whittington wrote of Thomas More in 1520 is apropos of Mr. Mac: "... a man of angel's wit and singular learning ... where is the man of that gentleness, lowliness, and affability? ... a man of marvelous mirth and pastimes, and sometime of sad gravity. A man for all seasons." As you leisurely read through the seasons of this man's life, you will find warmth, humor, tragedy, hope, and glimpses of our humanity at its best.

—*Stephen A. Privett, SJ*

Reverend Stephen A. Privett, SJ, is president of Verbum Dei High School (2018–present) in the Watts community of Los Angeles and president emeritus of the University of San Francisco, where he served as president from 2000 through 2014. He graduated from Loyola High School in 1960 and entered the Society of Jesus that same year. He is a graduate of Gonzaga University, and holds a master's degree from the Jesuit School of Theology and a doctorate from the Catholic University of America. He is author of *The U.S. Catholic Church and Its Hispanic Members* (Trinity University Press, 1988). He was elected to the Accrediting Commission, Western Association of Schools & Colleges (2010–2016). He has been a trustee emeritus of Santa Clara and St. Louis Universities and is currently a Trustee of Fairfield and Loyola Marymount Universities. He has received many other awards, too numerous to mention.

 | # REMEMBERING MY ROOTS

The heart that has truly loved, never forgets.

—THOMAS MORE

Harry

In 1905, the Lower East Side of Manhattan was crowded with immigrants. Men, women, and children from all over Europe survived in dingy, rundown tenements where extended families were crammed together in one- or two-room apartments like herring in a tin. Tenants descended to the crowded streets below on broken concrete stairways. There, vendors peddled all varieties of food, clothing, and cheap wares in the open market. In the harbor, Lady Liberty welcomed her visitors. The literate would take heart in the immortal words of Emma Lazarus:

> *Give me your tired, your poor,*
> *Your huddled masses yearning to breathe free,*
> *The wretched refuse of your teeming shore.*
> *Send these, the homeless, tempest-tost to me,*
> *I lift my lamp beside the golden door!*
>
> —EMMA LAZARUS, *"The New Colossus"*

For many, the journey was far from over. Some would make their way to Chicago to find dangerous, backbreaking toil in the stockyards and meatpacking plants owned by Philip Armour and Gustavus Swift. Their brutal labor struggles were well documented by writer Upton Sinclair in *The Jungle*. Other settled in the prairies of the Midwest where they farmed the fertile land as their ancestors had done "back in the old country."

Most of these immigrants came from European countries—Italy, Greece, Germany, Lithuania, Russia, and Ireland. They would feed the hungry furnaces of the burgeoning Second Industrial Revolution. The factory system had arrived along with the expansion of the railroads. Many Irish had the advantage of speaking English; it enabled men working in factories to rise from the lowly status of floor worker to foreman and women to obtain service employment in the homes of the wealthy.

Not far from the Lower East Side, a very different New York City existed—a world of wealth and privilege. This was the so-called Gilded Age, an era of big business, Wall Street tycoons, political machines like that of the legendary "Boss" Tweed, and corporate icons such as Andrew Carnegie of U.S. Steel and John D. Rockefeller of Standard Oil, nicknamed by former gas station owners as "Wreckafella." Wall Street investors J.P. Morgan and Cornelius Vanderbilt of railroad fame enjoyed their vast fortunes in palatial estates before the era of income taxes. While the rich millionaires in Upper Manhattan lived in regal splendor, immigrant women and men struggled to get by.

A teenage girl walked along the street wearing high-top black shoes and an oversized black coat that concealed the fact that she was pregnant. She made her way several more blocks to a tenement house, opened the door, and slowly climbed the narrow staircase several floors to the top. It was a private maternity hospital for unwed mothers. Several hours later, she gave birth to a baby boy. It was September 27, 1905. The birth certificate listed his name as Harry Philip Maechling.

Little is known about the first few years of Harry's life, which were spent in an orphanage. A few years later, as a toddler, he was placed on board one of the infamous "orphan trains." Founded in New York City by a well-meaning reformer in an era when there was no social safety net, the trains carried poor, homeless, and parentless children from cities in the East to the rural Midwest, where they would be adopted by families and put to work on farms. Stories have been written about the scams of profiteers and the indignities suffered by these children. The orphans simply hoped to be taken by a loving family into a real home rather than live on the streets. Sometimes they were asked to audition on a makeshift stage for their prospective parents, hence the term "up for adoption."

When the train arrived in New Orleans, Harry Maechling was adopted by an Irish Catholic woman and a US Army officer. The family of three moved to Douglas, Arizona, a small town on the Mexican border. The officer was part of the mission to capture the notorious Mexican outlaw Pancho Villa. When that campaign ended with Villa's death, he abandoned his wife and their adopted son. Young Harry and his single mother remained in Douglas. She worked as a maid at the local Gadsden Hotel. As a boy, Harry sold newspapers at the town train station and sometimes begged food from the sympathetic Mexican vendors who sold tamales to the travelers as they passed through the station. He formed a lifelong affection for the Mexican people and their culture.

Harry grew up to be a husky teenager. He found a steady job working in a copper-smelting factory for the Phelps Dodge Corporation. One day, a large automatic sledgehammer used for breaking up rocks of copper ore suddenly jammed and disconnected.

The huge metal hammer head slid forcefully across the factory floor, hitting Harry in the right foot and shearing off three of his toes. Labor unions were illegal in those days in Arizona. There was no such thing as workers' compensation or employee accident insurance. As an injured employee, he was no longer of use to the company and was laid off. As compensation for his misfortune, he was given twenty-five dollars.

Soon after, Harry attended Douglas High School. In spite of his slight limp, he became a starting guard on the football team. It was obvious Harry would never become a scholar, but his older and far more sophisticated English teacher was fond of him. When he failed a test on Milton's classic, she penned *"Paradise Lost* will always be lost to you" on his paper. Her first name was Mercedes. Shortly before he graduated, they had a love affair. It soon became the town scandal. Harry and Mercedes were married, and moved to Santa Barbara, California. Harry took a job as an appliance salesman and quickly discovered his natural talent for sales.

The early and middle Roaring Twenties were economic good times. Harry started a chain of appliance stores along the Pacific coast from Santa Barbara to Inglewood. He quickly became successful. He and Mercedes were happy and although she was frail, she became pregnant. Sadly, the baby died a few weeks after birth and was buried in the local cemetery. The couple had wanted a child for some time so they decided to adopt. They visited a Catholic hospital and orphanage in Arizona. There, they adopted a young boy they named Phillip, after Harry's middle name. Soon after, Mercedes became pregnant again. This time, she became very ill and died from uremic poisoning. On October 29, 1929, the stock market crashed and America was suddenly plunged into the Great Depression. Life for many Americans became dark, dismal, and often tragic. This was painfully true for Harry who suddenly lost his wife and his businesses, and was left to care for his motherless, two-year-old adopted son. It was an immense challenge for a young man in his twenties.

Mattie

Her name was Matilda Marie Knoebber. Her family called her Mattie. Born in Paxico, Kansas, in 1898, Mattie was the second youngest of the nine children of Hermann and Minnie Knoebber. Both of her parents were immigrants from Germany. They arrived in the 1880s and were processed through Ellis Island. William I and Otto von Bismarck's frequent wars of expansion motivated many men and their families to immigrate to America with its promise of fewer wars and greater opportunities. Hermann had been a successful shoemaker in Germany, a master craftsman supplying specialty boots for army officers, orthopedic shoes for those with deformities, and footwear for townspeople. He brought his cobbler's hammer with him on the long journey to America. This was evidence that he had a respectable trade and would not be indigent.

All the Knoebber children were bilingual. Faith and religion were at the core of their lives. This was true of many immigrants who took the risk of traveling across the Atlantic Ocean to the New World. The Knoebber family shared a deep Roman Catholic faith. They were devoted to the Church, the pope, and the clergy. Next to their church in Paxico was a tiny Catholic school. It did not teach beyond seventh grade. The parish priest forbade Catholic children to attend the local public school and threatened to refuse Holy Communion to them if they did. Mattie's only opportunity for higher education was to become a nun. She did not want to become a nun so her education ended that year.

Mattie grew up to be tall and attractive. She was a social person with a warm, friendly, and fun-loving personality. She loved to sing and play the piano. She was in her early twenties at the start of the Roaring Twenties. At one point she worked as a model for a clothing store in downtown Kansas City, Missouri. Despite the excitement of the big city, Mattie gravitated back to small-town Kansas. Her siblings had either married or moved away. Her brother John was a priest and her two sisters had become Benedictine nuns.

Sometime during the late 1920s, Mattie faced the crisis of her life. She became pregnant out of wedlock. Mattie took a "vacation" from her work as a secretary and accountant at the local Chevrolet dealership. She took a trip to Arizona where there was a more suitable climate for her "health problem." She gave birth to a baby boy and put him up for adoption. The child was left in the care of a Catholic hospital run by the Sisters of Charity. They were known for their tall bonnet headdresses and abundant kindness to downtrodden strangers. After her baby's birth, Mattie returned home to Kansas to live with her parents. She believed it was her duty to be her parents' caregiver for the rest of their lives.

The Sisters of Charity and Divine Intervention

Out of desperation over losing his wife and job, Harry returned to the convent in Arizona where he and Mercedes had initially found and adopted their baby boy. Sister Hyacinth was the nun in charge who greeted Harry and little Phil, who was almost three years old. She and Harry had a long and eventful conversation during which fate and God were designing a plan.

Events happened quickly. Mattie was given the news that her baby's adoptive father was now a widower. Harry sent a letter from Santa Barbara to Mattie in Wamego, Kansas, and it was soon followed by more letters and phone calls. They met in Chicago and Harry's apprehension at meeting Mattie for the first time disappeared when he discovered how warm and beautiful she was. After a brief courtship, they were married early one morning at the local Catholic church in Kansas by Mattie's brother, Father John. The couple quickly left on their honeymoon, heading west to Douglas, Arizona, to pick up their little boy, who had been living with his paternal grandmother. It was a long and difficult automobile trip from Kansas to California during the early years of the Great Depression. The roads were crowded with "Steinbeck's people" escaping the Midwestern dustbowl and drought, striving for a better life in the promised land of sunny California. The young couple stopped in Wichita, Kansas, for lunch. When they returned to their car, they discovered that all their luggage had been stolen, including Mattie's trousseau.

Little Phil's grandmother in Arizona had prepared him admirably for the moment of the newly married couple's arrival. The little boy was anxiously waiting to meet his "real mother." Fifty years later, he still recalled the moment with teary eyes: "Yes, I remember meeting Mom. I was absolutely thrilled to meet the beautiful lady in the yellow dress!"

Inglewood

There were no suburbs back then. Inglewood was a beautiful small town with tree-lined streets a few miles southwest of Los Angeles. Although Harry had lost his businesses during the Depression, he was determined to care for his bride and young son by taking any job he could find. He took a job as a forklift driver for the Great Atlantic & Pacific Tea Company. He loaded and unloaded freight stored in their large Long Beach warehouse. One morning, he went outside for a cigarette break. Suddenly, he heard a rumble and felt the ground begin to tremble. He instinctively ran and within moments the entire brick building collapsed into rubble behind him. Everything and everyone inside had been crushed. This was the devastating Long Beach earthquake of 1933. It seemed to Harry that divine intervention had touched his life once again.

Happy Beginning

I was born in the Stork Nest, a small maternity hospital in Inglewood, California, on December 18, 1941. It was eleven days after the Japanese attack on Pearl Harbor. The hospital bill came to sixty-nine dollars plus an additional five dollars for my circumcision. In those days, mothers were required to convalesce in the hospital for a minimum of ten days after giving birth. Because it was Christmas, the doctor made an exception and we were released early. We arrived home to my eagerly waiting family in a large white ambulance. My sister Mary later described how beautiful Mom looked in her elegant red silk nightgown and robe with me bundled in her arms.

World War II had just begun, although I was far too young to know about that. As soon as war was declared, it was obvious to Dad that there was no security in selling washing machines and other household appliances. Fortunately, the managers of the local Metropolitan Life Insurance Company needed a salesman. They knew Dad from his job at Aylsworth Appliance nearby and his reputation as a good salesman. When Harry told them he was looking for work, they offered him a position selling life insurance.

School Daze

At the age of six, I was excited about my first day of school. I was enrolled in the first grade because the local Catholic school did not have kindergarten. When that September morning finally came, I donned my uncomfortable school uniform for the first time: speckled blue and gray corduroy trousers held up by a brown belt, a light blue short-sleeved shirt, and a plain dark blue tie. It took me weeks to learn how to tie it. A few boys wore suspenders. They soon grew tired of being tortured by pranking classmates pulling and snapping them.

Our school was named after Saint John Chrysostom. Seventeen centuries earlier, he had been an important church scholar. He was distinguished by the title "Doctor of the Church." He was also the Bishop of Constantinople and a contemporary of Saint Augustine. Since we had trouble pronouncing the name Chrysostom, we referred to our school as St. John's, or sometimes as St. John's of Inglewood. Located on the top of a hill at a busy intersection, our school had a tired, dreary appearance. The old, broken Spanish tiles on the roof were reminiscent of an abandoned California mission.

Inside, the classrooms were crowded and noisy. Earlier that summer, my classmates and I had been unrestrained, running carefree and barefoot in the sun. Like many of my new friends, I hadn't had a care in the world. Most mornings, I would jump out of bed, pull on my jeans and T-shirt, and eagerly dash to the kitchen to wolf down cold cereal and orange juice. After a quick kiss goodbye to Mom, I would hop on my bike and race to meet my neighborhood buddies at the nearby park. We would play ball or cowboys and Indians, run races, or just see who could spit the farthest. If someone told what Mom called a "potty joke," we would laugh until our bellies ached. Then, hot, sweaty, and ravenous, we would scamper home for lunch. That scenario would start all over the next day.

Now we were sitting in desks with cowlicks slicked back and uncomfortable neckties, our bodies restrained by belts and new shoes that hadn't been broken in. Most of us had more energy than we could contain. It was released by much squirming, uncontrolled leg jerks, and rhythmic kicking of leather shoes against the metal legs of wooden desks that had been bolted down in straight rows.

Our first teachers were nuns who wore long black habits and starched white collars. Their heads were covered by black veils that partially covered the sides of their faces. To some students, these women looked foreboding, but their attire did not seem strange to me. Both of my aunts were Benedictine nuns who dressed similarly. Our teachers belonged to a religious order called the Sisters of Saint Joseph of Carondelet. They taught and administrated at many of the Catholic schools in our area of Los Angeles.

I loved my first-grade teacher, Sister Noreen. She was warmhearted, kind, and quick to smile. Her voice was soft but with just the right assertiveness. She told us stories to help us visualize scenes in the Bible. One day, Sister Noreen was giving us her explanation of death and the afterlife. She told us that everyone had to die someday and then they could go to heaven to be with Jesus. I raised my hand and asked, "Do even our mommies and daddies die?" She nodded affirmatively just as the bell rang for recess. The power of suggestion is enormous, especially for a six-year-old with an active imagination. I left the schoolyard and began running home. My mind was consumed by the frightening thought that my mother had died. Our house was six blocks directly down the hill and a quick turn onto a side street. When I got to our house, I continued running down our driveway to the back door, which I knew would be unlocked. I dashed to my parents' bedroom where my mother was sleeping. She woke to the sound of my panicked wails. She kissed away my tears and with a hug, my anxiety evaporated.

When the school bell rang for morning classes, we formed into two lines with boys in one and girls in the other. We placed our lunch pails on the floor in the long narrow room that led to the classroom. It was called the "cloakroom." The name was a vestige from schools long ago in harsher climates and had little relevance to the sunny suburbs of Los Angeles. Besides our lunch pails,

Sister Noreen also stored our school supplies there. The combined smells of paper, paste, and crayons in that narrow space is an olfactory memory that still remains with me to this day.

The schoolyard was a typical asphalt playground located between the school and the church. It had the usual attractions for kids: slides, monkey bars, tetherball poles, and a basketball court. There was also a drinking fountain. Once, the young Father Duffy, fresh off the boat from rural Ireland, playfully but carelessly slapped a kid on the back while he was drinking from the fountain. It chipped his front teeth. Father Duffy was one of thousands of immigrant priests to come to America from seminaries on the Emerald Isle. This was the period when the Catholic school populations were on the rise in American cities and priests were being recruited. Unfortunately, Father Duffy proved too much of a liability for the parish. His driving record was abysmal because the crowded streets of Los Angeles were far different from the lanes of Limerick where he rode his bicycle. Several years later, after I became an altar boy, I served at a funeral service at the cemetery where the clumsy priest crashed his car into the hearse.

I loved school from the start. To me, it was a warm, nurturing place that enabled us to grow and develop self-confidence. Learning for me was like my mom's potato pancakes, I just couldn't devour enough. Catholic schools in the forties and fifties were dogmatic and doctrinaire, but that never bothered me. My favorite subject was Bible history. Epic tales of the first man and woman, a talking snake, a man swallowed by a whale, and a burning bush that spoke with God's voice created exciting panoramic images in my mind.

At the center of it all was God. He was the Creator, hero, protagonist, and main attraction. His ten rules were carved on a stone tablet for us all to follow. These were the fundamental ethical laws of the Judeo-Christian tradition and they came directly from God Himself. They told us how to live our lives, and especially warned us that He was the one and only God. The message translated to me at my young age as "Stay loyal to me and don't hang out with those false gods or you'll be in big trouble." We knew He meant it because He could play hardball with little sense of humor. He had already kicked the first two humans out of His beautiful garden for eating that forbidden apple.

I was enthralled by these fantastic tales, which I took literally. I never questioned their veracity back then. I wondered why this all-powerful yet loving God was so harsh. He destroyed everyone in a wicked city called Sodom, except for one good man named Lot. Unfortunately for Lot's wife, she disobeyed God's command to not look back at the city. As a severe penalty for this simple infraction, she was instantly transformed into a pillar of salt.

I had no idea that there were other variations of Christianity besides Catholicism. I hadn't yet studied Martin Luther and the Reformation and the myriad denominations to follow. I loved to read the grand stories of the Old Testament: Noah and the Ark, Abraham and Isaac, Moses parting the Red Sea, and so many others. Sister St. Joan would read to us from the book called *The Lives of the Saints*. I wondered why so many holy figures were far less than holy in their earlier lives. I didn't understand what Saint Augustine meant when he said, "Lord, give me celibacy, but not yet."

As Catholics, we had saints you could rely on for almost everything. Saint Christopher would protect us on dangerous journeys. Saint Anthony helped find our lost holy medals or rosaries, and in modern times, car keys or cell phones. Of course, most of this was superstition, but "betting with the house" improved the odds if the saints were involved. There were enlightened saints like Francis of Assisi. He understood there was a higher value than simply enriching his father's "war chest." As depicted in Giotto's frescoes in Italy, he left town naked after giving his cloak to a beggar and his wealth to the poor. Saint Francis may have been one of the first enlightened Europeans regarding the humane treatment of animals.

I loved our nuns at St. John Chrysostom. My personal favorite was Sister St. Peter. She was my eighth-grade teacher and principal of the school. What we boys especially loved about her was that she was kind of a tomboy. She would join us during recess baseball games. Tall and sturdily built, she would step up to the plate, bat the ball, then run the bases with her veils flying. I would do anything to please her. One time she asked me if I would take up a new commission as the head of the Cleanup Committee. I thought this was a real honor and a bestowal of greater responsibility and prestige than I ever deserved. The next thing I knew, I was the only kid in the schoolyard picking up trash.

It's hard to overestimate the importance of the Catholic Church in the 1950s. It played a significant role in our young lives: our first confession, Communion, confirmation, and becoming an altar boy. All matters of importance seemed to revolve around the Church.

In Bible History class, we moved on from the Old to the New Testament and God's image began to improve. He gave the world His only son, Jesus, in an extraordinary act of generosity. The story of the life and death of Jesus was clearly taught as a testament to God's love for us. I became especially aware of the enormity of this around the Easter holiday and Good Friday. Lent was torture. When my parents asked what I was "giving up for God," I would try to get away with something like not changing my underwear or taking baths. They insisted that was not acceptable and I ended up promising not to eat candy for a month.

My perception of God from the New Testament was that He became more kind. Inexplicably, He had a Son who came to earth to help us. We humans badly needed a "spiritual upgrade" after endless millennia of war, perdition, and human sacrifice. God's Son was sent to earth to help bail us out from the penalty of our own corrupt human natures. I not only learned this information, but memorized it, as did all Catholic schoolchildren. It was spelled out clearly for us in *The Baltimore Catechism*. This book chronicled the rules for becoming a good Catholic. It explained who God was and that our primary purpose was to "know, love, and serve Him." Jesus was God's only Son and a third divine entity, the Holy Spirit, was created through their union. These truths had been passed down to us over two thousand years by the magisterium, the teaching authority of the Catholic Church. It began with Jesus and was passed on to the first pope, St. Peter, and all subsequent popes down to the present day.

I was okay with this information and did not challenge it until a difficulty arose one day in our seventh-grade church history class. Sister Mary Anne was teaching us about famous heretics. She drew a line on the chalkboard, starting at the bottom with Jesus. The line went up to the top of the board. She called it "the line of truth." She explained that various people and groups that strayed from the line were labeled "heretics." Near the top of the chalk line, around 1500 AD, she wrote the name Martin Luther. She then proceeded to explain why he was in error regarding church teaching. He had started a new church called the Lutheran Church and he was a heretic, too. Something didn't seem right to me about this explanation. I raised my hand to ask: "Sister, what if the Lutherans think they are on the line of truth and we're not?" She looked troubled but quickly recovered. Frowning, she said sternly: "That's ridiculous! Just follow the line."

Dad

We weren't affluent, but Dad made a good living. His hard work meant that we had educational opportunities, plentiful food, and a warm and loving home in which to grow.

Mom and my sister Mary always had dinner ready for the family at 5:30 p.m. That was when Dad came home for an hour. After dinner, he went out for a few hours to sell life insurance. Sometimes he would return around 9:00 or 9:30. He said he always sold the most insurance in the evening. That was because he could meet with both husband and wife and sell to them as a couple. One sales tactic was to ask the husband somewhere in the conversation: "Don't you love your wife enough to protect her from destitution in the event of your early death?" The deal clincher would be when he got out his actuarial tables and explained why a man tends to die earlier than his wife.

It was customary for Dad to tell stories about his work day at the dinner table. One evening he told a story about how he almost "blew it" with one of his clients. He was trying to sell Mr. Greenberg an endowment policy for his infant son. It's important to note that Dad sold a lot of life insurance in the downtown area of Inglewood. Many of his clients happened to be Jewish merchants on Market Street and they assumed he was a Jew. Dad's pitch was: "Greenberg, you should buy this policy. You put in a few bucks every month and by the time your boy is old enough for college, his education is paid for. I know, I have four kids myself." Mr. Greenberg asked an innocent question in response: "Where do they go to school?" This caught Dad off guard. He worried that if Greenberg learned he was Catholic it might kill the deal, but he didn't want to tell a lie. He replied: "Well, I have two sons who go to Loyola University, another son at Loyola High, and a daughter at Mount St. Mary's College."

Greenberg looked puzzled for a moment before he said: "So . . . you married a Catholic woman, huh?"

Selling Papers

Dad handed down his strong work ethic to his boys. I was six when I had my first job, selling newspapers on weekends in the summer with my twelve-year-old brother, John. We sold the afternoon daily *Herald-Express,* the *Los Angeles Weekly Mirror,* and the *Los Angeles Examiner* Sunday edition. The Sears department store was only a couple of blocks away from our home and I would stand outside, yelling "Zaminner-Times!" and "Extra, extra, read all about it." I wore a little apron that was dirty from holding the change I collected. Daily papers cost a nickel or a dime. I hadn't yet learned to make change for a dollar. I would leave the customer waiting on the sidewalk while I took his dollar bill and ran the length of the huge department store to find John, who was selling papers on the other side. He would make the correct change for me and I would run back.

On cold nights Dad would bring us our dinner in a metal pot. He was proud that we were working and would stay to watch with satisfaction as we devoured the warm chicken-fried steak on French bread. He took visceral pleasure in knowing that his kids were well-fed, unlike himself at our age.

Bosco

When my brother John entered high school, Dad got me a job working for his client George Schmidt. George had a large newspaper stand on the corner of Market and Queen. He was a friendly man with a terrific personality. His nickname was Bosco. Everybody who walked or drove by his newsstand would shout "Hiya, Bosco!" On weekends, the delivery trucks would leave huge stacks of thick Sunday papers, creating walls much taller than I was. By evening the papers would all be sold. Dad once told me that Bosco was so popular that he could be elected mayor of Inglewood.

Bosco's young adult son, George Schmidt, Jr., worked with us at the same newspaper stand. George was handicapped. At the time he was known as a "spastic." He was tall and thin, with a purposeful and somewhat jerky and uncontrolled manner of walking. There was something out of sync. One leg would stop short and the other leg would go long. Then he would catch his balance. George was a walking machine. I could hardly keep up with him. Bosco would send us all over the downtown district to put newspapers in his many racks. I don't remember having much conversation with George because he seldom spoke and it was difficult to understand him when he did. Occasionally, young people driving or walking by would make fun of George. It made me feel uncomfortable and embarrassed for him. Eventually I began to walk a few steps behind him.

Later, Dad told me that he had sold Bosco's life insurance policy and collected his weekly premiums. Dad admired him. He confided that Bosco sold newspapers primarily so he could be close to his son and look after him. That made me understand how all of those insults to George must have been painful daggers in Bosco's heart.

One day I decided to set up a newspaper stand of my own. It was a couple of blocks away from Bosco's. I hired a few friends to work with me after school. I dealt directly with the newspaper distributors and had several racks of my own. We were all about eleven or twelve years old and I was proud to be the boss. One day, I caught one of my employees, a slightly older and bigger boy than I was, taking money from a rack with his key. Even though I was intimidated by his size, righteous indignation took over and I yelled at him: "Hey, you're stealing! You're a thief!"

I wasn't sure what his reaction would be and was surprised when he started to cry. A sense of empowerment came over me. I was proud that I had stood up to him. Although he feebly apologized, I didn't feel I could trust him and told him to turn over his key; he was fired.

The Cheeseburger

As a Catholic, I was taught that the main purpose of my life was to know, love, and serve God in accordance with the rules of the Church. I had never really been tested until one chilly Friday Halloween night. I was walking along Manchester Blvd. on my way home and decided to try to sell the rest of my papers at a small diner. The aroma of sizzling hamburgers and French fries was overpowering. I sold my papers and as I was leaving, a waitress came up to me and said "trick or treat." She handed me a large, juicy cheeseburger, hot and fresh off the grill. I thanked her and walked outside holding the burger, my grimy hands stained black from newsprint and handling coins. Just as I began to take a delicious bite, I heard that little inner voice of conscience reminding me that it was Friday and I was Catholic. It was a mortal sin for Catholics to eat meat on Friday. If I sinned and then died before confessing, I would go directly to hell for eternity. I contemplated eating the burger and being extra careful not to get hit by a car on the way home, rationalizing that I just needed to make it to the next morning when I could confess to a priest. Then my slate would be wiped clean with minimal spiritual damage to my soul.

But a mortal sin was a mortal sin, whether it was murder, theft, adultery, or eating a cheeseburger on Friday. Having a mortal sin on my soul was an entry into the cavernous world of evil that I had never entertained. I knew I had often committed venial sins—everybody did that. However, a mortal sin was out of the question. I took the meat patty out of the bun and threw it to a stray dog. I rationalized that eating the bun alone, even with its meat juices, was merely a venial sin. Fear definitely won out over love that night.

Father John

Father John, my uncle, was a parish priest who was ordained in his twenties in Missouri. He lived well into his nineties and became a monsignor. As my mother's closest brother, he exerted an enormous influence in our lives. He was, without question, the family "superstar" and always our most interesting and entertaining guest. A truly colorful character, Father John had been a chaplain during World War II at a prisoner of war camp near Joplin, Missouri. Later, he was on the staff of the state mental hospital there.

I was the youngest and most loyal member of the family audience. I would sit at his feet, eagerly waiting for one of his stories. A skillful raconteur, he spoke five languages and made us laugh by imitating all kinds of foreign accents. One of his stories was about a patient named Blanche who continually repeated to herself and others that "I got my complexion in Montana." Another story was about a mental patient who was asked if he knew why he was in the hospital. "I don't know," the patient replied. "I guess it's because I like pancakes." Father John asked: "What's wrong with that? I like pancakes too." The patient replied: "You do? I've got a whole trunk of them in my garage!"

When I asked Father John why he became a priest, he said his initial motivation as a teenager was the opportunity to take his first train ride from Wamego, Kansas, to Columbus, Ohio. He described his first night in the seminary. He had arrived early and was alone in his dorm room. It was becoming dark and he had never seen an electric light switch before. Somehow, he ended up disassembling it and was later reprimanded by a strict old German priest.

After over a decade in the seminary, Father John was finally preparing for graduation and his ordination as a priest. His buddies had nicknamed him "Pax" after his hometown, Paxico. On their last night in the seminary, Pax and his classmates decided to have a small after-curfew party, with beer and leftover fried chicken from the kitchen. The location for this secret celebration was a small room reserved for a confessional and counseling for seminarians. It was strictly forbidden for any other purpose. The party was proceeding well until they heard the footsteps of the priest in charge of discipline on the squeaky steps of the stairs. The fear of expulsion loomed large. Just as the handle of the door began to turn, a quick thinker in the group said: "Father, for these and all the other sins I have committed, I am truly sorry." The door was not opened and the footsteps were heard retreating up the staircase.

When he visited, Father John would be our guest for an entire month. He was often accompanied by his friend Father Bill, who stayed at the nearby Hillcrest Hotel. After they celebrated Mass in the morning, we would all enjoy breakfast in our large dining room with platters of eggs, ham or bacon, potato pancakes, toast, and wonderful summer fruit. After breakfast, the two priests would grab their bags and head to the nearby golf course. They would return for lunch and afterward Father Bill would go back to his hotel and Father John would have a quiet hour in which to say his mandatory breviary (daily prayers).

Once I asked Father John how many people he had visited at their deathbeds. He replied that it was in the thousands. As a result, he'd concluded that the way a person approached the moment of death revealed much about how they had lived. Some reacted in anger over their fate, while others accepted death peacefully. He described two dramatic examples. One man died with his fist raised in rage, cursing God as he drew his last breath. The other was Father John's own father and my grandfather, Hermann Knoebber, whose countenance turned to one of joy as he said to his deceased wife, "I can see you now, Minnie. I am coming to you!"

The Walnut Box

Since the Middle Ages, Germans have been known for their woodworking artistry. Medieval artists such as Tilman Riemenschneider, the "Michelangelo of limewood," were said to have been so talented they could carve the Last Supper inside a walnut shell. Our family's master craftsman was Father John. As a priest, he ministered in rural areas of Missouri known for their forests of walnut trees valued by furniture makers. He crafted beautiful armoires, chests, and bookcases, as well as a dollhouse and miniature furniture for my sister, from this wood.

Father John created his own version of "Boys Town," a famous charitable organization for orphan boys, and taught woodworking skills to the many orphans there. They made and sold crucifixes, candleholders, and kneelers to Catholic churches throughout the area.

As a boy, I admired a beautiful walnut box on top of the armoire in my parents' bedroom. It contained their important documents. The lid of the box had an exquisitely carved rose and two overlapping inlaid initials, "MM." Since much of the furniture in our home had been made by Father John, I assumed he'd made this box as well. I thought the initials stood for my mother, Mattie Maechling. Sixty years later I learned the actual story.

After my mother passed away, I found the box in an old trunk that had ended up in my garage. Inscribed in it was the name "Stephan Millisich," an address in Austria, and the words "Camp Clark, Missouri, 1945." There were additional inscriptions in

German that I couldn't translate. I realized that the box had been made by a prisoner of war in the Missouri POW camp for German and Italian prisoners where Father John had served as chaplain during World War II.

I took the box to my friend Lis, the librarian at my school. She was from Austria and could help me translate the inscription. She told me that she would be traveling to her homeland later that summer. She agreed to try to locate the man who had made the box and, if he were still alive, deliver it to him.

I was thrilled when she was able to locate the ninety-year-old man living on the outskirts of Vienna. He remembered Father John well from his days as a POW at Camp Clark. It was Father John who had given him the walnut wood and the carving tools—a razor blade and some broken glass shards—which he said were illegal for prisoners of war. Stephan laboriously crafted the "kassette" as a gift for his fiancée in Austria. In 1945, at the end of the war, he was told he would not be allowed to take it with him. He was aware that the American camp commander was eyeing it covetously as a potential cigar box. To protect it, Stephan made a formal presentation of the box to Father John as a gift. The initials "MM" on the top that I mistook for my mother's were actually those of his soon-to-be wife, Maria Millisich.

The Trip to Mexico

When I was in the eighth grade, our family took a trip to Mexico City to visit my mom's sisters who were both Benedictine nuns. As we stepped off the plane, Mother Mildred, Sister Victorine, and many of the nuns from the convent greeted us with a red carpet, flowers, and a lively mariachi band. As the foundress of the Benedictine order in Mexico, Mother Mildred was their Mother Superior. She had a PhD in psychology and was an exceptional individual by any standard. In the 1930s, both sisters immigrated to Mexico from Atchison, Kansas, with the ambitious intent of providing Catholic education. They had limited funds but were aided by then-President Roosevelt's Good Neighbor policy.

Mother Mildred had business acumen. Through a Jewish-Mexican real estate agent, she acquired a beautiful colonial villa in downtown Mexico City. It was to be the new location of their convent. Shortly after the closing documents were signed, the agent was contacted by a government representative from Peru who wanted the property for Peru's new embassy in Mexico City. Because of their sizable offer, the realtor tried to renege on the contract by imploring Mother Mildred to exercise Christian compassion regarding his situation. Mother Mildred replied: "A deal is a deal and the future education of Mexican youth is far more important than your profit-making." She went on to say that if he didn't follow through with his agreement, she would expose him to the community for being a fraud. He said he was shocked at the obvious lack of sympathy from a woman of the cloth, to which she replied: "This is a business deal and has nothing to do with religion."

Sister Vicky had a warm and kind personality. She was the main caregiver for the nuns in the convent, particularly the younger novices. Her black Benedictine habit was hooded and she wore a long apron that started at her waist and reached down nearly to the top of her shoes. Its very large pockets contained an assortment of unconventional objects: string, scissors, safety pins, bandages, gum, tools, and even firecrackers, which she produced as a gift for my brother and me.

Xochimilco, with its fifty miles of canals and beautiful floating gardens, was our most memorable excursion. I had seen the movie *Captain from Castile*. It was about the conquistadors' long voyage from Spain to America and the betrayal and ultimate death of Montezuma. The musical score by Alfred

Newman captivated me. It glorified the long successful march of the Spanish across Mexico. In one scene, Aztecs came with gifts and warned the European intruders to stop and return to Spain. Cortés responded by destroying their sacred statues with cannonballs as they scattered in terror. That day, I felt like a conqueror myself as we floated along the canals and traced the path of the conquistadors to the Aztec capital of Tenochtitlan, the site of the golden throne and treasure room of Montezuma. Montezuma was ultimately tricked, taken prisoner, and executed. After contact with the Europeans, most of the indigenous people died from diseases such as influenza and smallpox, for which they had no acquired immunity and no remedy.

My favorite Mexican on that memorable trip was my aunt's smiling, energetic, and comical chauffeur, Alfonzo. He drove us through the maze of Mexico City traffic in a spacious black limousine. Like visiting foreign diplomats, we attracted people's attention wherever we drove.

After a long morning of Mexico City sightseeing, we would return to the convent, where Alfonzo would have his lunch and take a siesta. One day, as he napped peacefully in the shade of a nearby tree, John and I lit one of Sister Vicky's firecrackers. Alfonzo woke with a jolt as we ran as fast as we could to hide. He pretended to show anger by raising his fist at us while smiling and muttering in Spanish.

It was December 12, during the Feast of Our Lady of Guadalupe, the patron saint of Mexico. I was sitting in the basilica next to Mother Mildred. I gazed up at the inlaid gold ceiling, awed by its splendor. The gold had been taken from the Americas and crafted in Spain. I looked around at the faithful people, hundreds upon hundreds of them, hoping to be healed by a miracle. Many were crippled and on crutches, while others were crawling on bleeding knees. It was obvious by their ragged and tattered clothing that these people were destitute. I gazed up at the gilded ornate ceiling again, trying to make sense of this disparity. Finally, I asked: "Mother Mildred, how come the church has so much gold and money, while so many people are poor?" She looked at me with a soft and slightly sad smile. "Yes, it's true that they have nothing and the church is very wealthy. But if you took away their faith and hope in God, what would they have then? Their faith is what keeps them alive."

Holy Infant of Good Health

Catholicism has claimed many worldwide miracles over its two-thousand-year history. There were the miracles of Jesus and His apostles, Joan of Arc in the Middle Ages, Lourdes in France in the nineteenth century, and Fátima in Portugal and Medjugorje in Yugoslavia in the twentieth century, to name only a few.

Concurrent with our stay in Mexico City in the nineteen-fifties, the Benedictine nuns at the convent became involved with a religious phenomenon known as the Holy Infant of Good Health. The story began in 1939, when Lupita, a poor girl from the village of Morelia, was given a statue of the infant Jesus at her first Communion by her godmother. When she returned home with the statue, Lupita's sister, who was to have surgery the next morning, asked to pray with her. The sister held the statue to the tumor on her cheek while they prayed together and asked God for healing. When they awoke the next morning, the tumor was gone. This was the first of many miracles that occurred when praying before this image of Jesus.

At one point, Lupita's spiritual voice instructed her to contact the Benedictine order in Mexico City. Mother Mildred, my aunt, arranged for Lupita to stay at the convent and the statue was placed on the altar in the chapel for public observation and veneration.

In 1959, Mother Mildred traveled to the Vatican for an audience with Pope John XXIII. She personally gave him a replica of the sacred statue. He granted plenary indulgence to those who went on pilgrimage to the Shrine of the Holy Infant of Good Health in Mexico.

That same year, my close high school friend Fernando was in a serious auto accident. While driving his old Chevy to work one midsummer morning, Fernando was hit by a cement mixer truck. He was not wearing a seatbelt, as few did in those days. Fernando was thrown through the front windshield of his car and hurled across the street, where he hit his head on a concrete curb. That afternoon I received the news that he was in serious condition at Daniel Freeman Memorial Hospital. When I arrived, he was lying naked on a huge slab of ice with large fans blowing on him. They had drilled a hole in his skull to release the pressure on his brain caused by so much swelling. Fernando remained in a coma throughout that summer and well into the fall. Many of our classmates and their parents visited Fernando and prayed for him. When school began, we were involved in our studies and football, but we still went to the hospital on weekends to pray the rosary together in the hospital chapel. At football rallies in the Loyola gym, my friend Steve would stand up and shout, "Okay, you guys, let's cheer so loud we'll wake up Fernando!" It had been almost two months and still Fernando remained in a coma.

My mom had been in touch with Mother Mildred. One day a package arrived at our home from Mexico City. Inside was a small medal replica of the Infant of Good Health. It was said to have been blessed by Jesus during one of Lupita's mystical experiences with the statue. That evening Mom and I visited the hospital to pray for Fernando. Before we left, she fastened the medal to the bedsheet near his head. The next morning, we received a phone call from Fernando's mother. She had just been told by the nurses that Fernando woke up and said his first words in fifty-two days: "Where the hell is my orange juice?"

Later that year, Loyola High School held its annual fund-raiser. There was a raffle and the grand prize was a new Cadillac El Dorado. Fernando's widowed mother, a secretary with a small salary and many hospital and doctor bills to pay, won the coveted prize. I have often wondered whether the human hand played a part in what one might describe as "a Jesuit miracle."

 # A YOUNG SAPLING GROWING UP

For the greater glory of God.

—St. Ignatius Loyola

Loyola High School Entrance Exam

The first time I saw the campus of Loyola High, I was in the sixth grade. It was my older brother John's high school graduation. Two years later, I would be among hundreds of other eighth-grade boys from all over the city taking the entrance examination for admission. Loyola High is the oldest school in Los Angeles. It stands solemnly on Venice Boulevard between Normandie and Vermont, near Koreatown. A dramatic visual contrast existed between the stately campus and the surrounding urban area, a neighborhood of rundown houses, small businesses, cheap liquor stores, and a large cemetery.

That day, I was as unnerved by Loyola's imposing nineteenth-century neo-Gothic architecture as Harry Potter might have been on his first day at Hogwarts. There were statues of legendary Jesuit saints, such as St. Ignatius and St. Francis Xavier, on the huge lawn. The overall impression was of a small Ivy League college transplanted into the heart of urban

Los Angeles. The strange environment and a substantial fear of the unknown added to my tension on exam morning. I knew I wasn't alone in my apprehension when I noticed a traumatized boy nearby throwing up into a flower bed.

There were a few familiar faces and we waved or briefly said hello. These were guys from other schools that I had competed against in seventh- and eighth-grade sports. There was Ron from St. Jerome parish, Al from Visitation, Jim from Transfiguration, John from St. Paul, Bill from St. Joseph, and Pat from St. Augustine. It was surprising to see these outstanding young athletes competing against me on a scholastic examination rather than on a court or field.

The exam lasted all morning and well into the afternoon, with only one brief break. Every seat in the room was filled. We were proctored by a middle-aged, heavy-set, black-robed priest. He said little as he called roll and placed us in our seats in alphabetical order. The exam itself was administrated by the school principal, Father Saussotte, over the PA system. His style of speaking was strange because his every word was stretched into elongated syllables: "Goo-ood morning, gen...tle...men. My name is Faaather Souss...ootte. I am the prin...ci... pal of Loy...ooo...la High Scho...ool. Loy...ooo...la is not an ordin...ary high school. It is act...tua...ly a coll...ege pre...par...a...tory schoo...ol. The fine...est in the U... ni...ted...States. Pen...cils...u p! Turn to Part 1, Section 1. You ma...a ay begin."

There were hundreds of challenging questions in multiple subjects: vocabulary, reading comprehension, math, history, and English, including diagramming sentences. Bright boys from all over the city competed. Some of the Catholic schools had tutored their eighth-graders every Saturday morning for months before the test, using copies of previous exams. My grade school was not as fortunate. Only two of us tried out for admission to Loyola. Most Catholic boys in my area attended either the public high schools or Loyola's despised rival, Mt. Carmel, run by the Carmelites. I felt my future was riding on success on that exam. Loyola was already a legendary institution in my mind. I'd heard so many stories from my brothers, Phil and John. It was the only option I ever considered. But out of over a thousand applicants, Loyola accepted only a precious three hundred.

Every afternoon for the next couple of months, I said a prayer on my way to our mailbox to see if my acceptance letter was there. It was a major relief and a thrill of achievement when it finally arrived! Even at the young age of fourteen, I knew that something greater was in my future. I believed education was my golden ticket!

Over the years, I learned to appreciate the Jesuits' extraordinary system of teaching. They had a five-hundred-year tradition that went back to St. Ignatius Loyola and St. Francis Xavier at the time of the Counter-Reformation. This was the same order of educators who taught Descartes, Voltaire, James Joyce, and many other world leaders, writers, explorers, scientists, and statesmen over the years. I knew from the first day that I was fortunate to be part of this tradition.

Father Gilligan

Loyola was organized differently from most high schools. We stayed in the same classroom with the same thirty students and the teachers rotated to teach us their respective subjects.

Our first class was Religion. The instructor, Father Gilligan, was a friendly, smiling, overweight Irish priest, whose black robe and wide sash hung below his prominent potbelly. He put us at ease from the start. He made us feel it was always okay to talk to him, especially if we had any problems adjusting to our new school environment. A student asked if he wanted us to put the initials JMJ at the top of our papers, as we were accustomed to doing in grammar school. Those letters stood for Jesus, Mary, and Joseph. He replied "I've got nothing against the holy family, boys, but at Loyola we write AMDG at the top of every paper." I did not realize then how the meaning of those initials would influence the rest of my life.

Father Doyle

After Religion, Father Doyle, another friendly-faced, smiling Irishman, came in to teach English and Speech. I learned he was one of the football coaches. That immediately caught my attention because I wanted to try out for the junior varsity football team. One of Father Doyle's first challenging assignments was to memorize the poem "How Did You Die?" by Edmund Vance Cooke. I still remember the poem's first stanza:

> *Did you tackle that trouble that came your way*
> *With a resolute heart and cheerful?*
> *Or hide your face from the light of day*
> *With a craven soul and fearful?*

Having no sense of the metaphorical at age fourteen, I initially thought, because of the word "tackle," that the poem was about football.

> *Oh, a trouble's a ton, or a trouble's an ounce,*
> *Or a trouble is what you make it.*
> *And it isn't the fact that you're hurt that counts,*
> *but only how did you take it?*

Each one of us had to memorize the poem for homework and each one of us was to recite it in front of the class using proper diction. Father Doyle's main emphasis was elocution. If you spoke too softly or slurred your words, in a loud voice he would say: "Diction, boys! Enunciate clearly, please!" Over and over, he would repeat those words until they became second nature to us.

Father Conneally

Third period was Western Civilization, now called World History in most high schools today, taught by my favorite high school teacher, Father Conneally. The lessons began with the cavemen of Paleolithic times and continued up to the present, which at that time was the era of the Cold War.

This slightly eccentric, very brilliant priest walked into our classroom on that first day accompanied by four students carrying two huge eight-by-four chalkboards. These boards contained all the notes he would cover during his lecture. He frequently strayed from his lesson plans to tell us colorful anecdotes. Some were made up and reflected his sense of humor. For example, he described how the Behistun Inscription was discovered: "One evening, in ancient Persia, Gene and the boys were gathered around the campfire with their guitars, singing their old favorite, 'Stars Shining Over Good Ol' Sogdiana.' Suddenly, one of them noticed an enormous boulder with ancient inscriptions. Eventually, the cuneiform was translated and it connected the ancient Persians with the Israelites." Another time, he told how Howard Carter discovered King Tut's tomb: "He poked his candle through the massive entrance. When he was asked what he saw, he replied, 'Wonderful things!'" Father Conneally's fascination for his subject encouraged me to become a history major in college and graduate school. He inspired me to teach and study history for the rest of my life.

Father Pallas, SJ

Our fourth hour was Latin class with Father Ray Pallas. Our lessons were mainly memorization and repetition. Father Ray was a character. You never knew what he was going to do. He was Italian and there was something about his personality that later reminded me of the actor Peter Falk. Besides teaching us

Latin and drilling us on verb conjugation—*laudo, laudas, laudat, laudamus,* etc.—he loved to play "Gotcha." Sometimes during tests, he would write on the chalkboard, purposely turning his back to the classroom, tempting us to cheat. He would then quickly pivot on his back foot to face us, sometimes catching a slow-reacting kid looking at someone's paper. "Gotcha!" I wasn't quite sure why I was studying Latin because I didn't yet understand the meaning or purpose of having a classical education.

ROTC

During my high school years, we were engaged in the Cold War with the USSR. As teenagers, most of us felt there was little need for the military program at Loyola. But Army training was profitable for the school, so compulsory ROTC was implemented. The sergeants came across as oafs and buffoons, like characters from the old *Phil Silvers Show* on TV or the popular movie *No Time for Sergeants.* The concept of "military intelligence" was a humorous oxymoron that made our ROTC instructor a tempting target for pranksters. He and the fawning "kiss-ups" in the program—enthusiasts we derisively referred to as "RO Joes"—were locked inside the rifle storage room by a group of rebellious students.

Major Bloom had been a line officer in Korea and was in charge of our ROTC program. The federal inspection by high-ranking military officers was a big day, because our instructors' jobs were on the line. As cadets, we were told to have a haircut, press our uniforms, look sharp, and walk straight and tall. After snapping to attention, we were to remain in that position without moving until further command. Major Bloom pre-inspected us before the army brass arrived. "Attention! I said attention! What'sa matter with you guys? You're supposed to be standing smartly at attention. You're movin' around like bacon on a hot griddle!"

Most of us disliked ROTC, except for the RO Joes. They were bucking for leadership roles, perhaps admission to the military academies. One was a miniature Major Bloom martinet who had earned the title of Student Commander. He made numerous enemies by issuing demerits to anyone who didn't take his orders seriously. The morning of the federal inspection, one of his adversaries stole his hat, an essential part of the uniform of a properly dressed Student Commander. For the rest of the year when he walked by the ranks, students would call out, "Hey, Commander, where's your hat?"

Along with the uniform, you were given an unloaded M1 rifle. You memorized the drill commands: "Right shoulder arms! Left shoulder arms! Present arms!" and the most troubling for me, "Inspection arms!" For that maneuver, you were supposed to bring the rifle down to your waist; open up the bolt where the ammunition was placed; with a careful manipulation of your finger and thumb, let the inspector see the open chamber; and finally, with an agile move, close the rifle back up and end the inspection at attention with the gun butt on the ground, your right hand holding the rifle and your left hand smartly to your side. You were supposed to do this drill properly and quickly, but I usually failed because when I opened the bolt on my rifle, it often snapped back and jammed my thumb painfully in the chamber.

Every student in a competitive school like ours ultimately forms his own ethical code to survive. I respected the teachers and the subjects I was learning, but ROTC was a different matter. Our instructor, Sergeant Quarrels, was a strict, heavy-set, old-school army man with a southern accent. He used colorful colloquialisms we didn't understand. He called anyone he wanted to demean a "honyocker" (a country slang expression meaning loafer, rube, or simpleton). When it came time for him to give us an exam on the M1 rifle, I didn't prepare. I didn't care about the subject and didn't respect Sergeant Quarrels. We were given our tests in the old basketball gym while sitting on multilevel wooden bleachers. It was a bad seating arrangement for managing students during an exam. Sitting right below me was my friend Ken, one of the brightest guys in the class. From my vantage point, I could see everything on his test paper by just looking down.

The next day I learned that Sergeant Quarrels was more clever than I realized. He seemed to be in a particularly jovial mood. When I walked by him, he smiled. We sat on the bleachers in the same seating arrangement as the day before. He handed everyone's exam back with the exception of Ken's and mine, and addressed the class: "Before we go over the exam, I would like to congratulate Cadet Ken and Cadet Jim because they had the two highest test scores." There was applause. He continued. "Let's review the exam now, shall we? Question number one asks: Which answer is wrong? The M1 rifle is: (A) 30 caliber, (B) air-cooled, (C) 10 shot, (D) clip-fed, or (E) semi-automatic. Ken answered correctly. The answer is (C)."

Then Sergeant Quarrels squinted dramatically at my paper and then held it up to the light. After a pause, he said: "Mr. Maechling originally answered incorrectly with answer (D), but then it looks like he erased it and changed it to the correct answer, (C)." From that point on, I knew I was in trouble. I had changed my answers at least half a dozen times. He kept a straight face as he reviewed the entire exam. By the end, the whole class was laughing hysterically. The joke was on me!

Suddenly, his demeanor changed. He no longer looked like he was enjoying himself. He leaned toward me with a frown on his face. "Maechling, you are a cheater and a honyocker! If this were West Point, you would be expelled for violating the honor code. During tomorrow's class, you will not march with the rest of us on the drill field. Why? Because you will be standing on top of the wall along Venice Boulevard, between our school and Rosedale cemetery. Every thirty seconds during that entire hour you will loudly shout 'I am a gooney bird!'"

And so it happened. I was one of the first gooney birds, although others followed in my dishonorable footsteps. I served my penance for cheating. That following year I devised a plan to get out of ROTC. I met with Major Hirning, the band director, and begged him to let me join. When he asked what instrument I played, I told him truthfully that I couldn't play any, but was very interested in learning the percussion instruments. He assigned me to play the cymbals at varsity football games. My only task was to crash the cymbals at precisely the right moments near the end of the national anthem. When my sophomore year ended, I joined the varsity football team and my brief musical career in the band came to an end.

Father McFadden, SJ

Every Jesuit high school has a "Father Discipline." Ours was Father Edward J. McFadden. He was a short, red-haired Irishman from San Francisco, the son of a cop. He was also Loyola's vice principal. We called him "Clyde" behind his back. This irreverent nickname was borrowed from Clyde McPhatter, a popular 1950s African American R&B singer.

Our Clyde perpetually worried most of us and occasionally terrified some. When we walked down the main corridor of the school building, we wondered if he was watching us. He was the boogeyman. If Clyde was nearby, we immediately monitored ourselves for any infraction that might possibly catch his eye. If he was walking behind us, it felt like being followed by a police car. There was an omniscient Orwellian presence about him. Big Brother was always watching or listening, even when you were in class with the doors closed. There was a two-way sound system interfacing every classroom with his office. We dreaded hearing our name over the loudspeaker because that usually meant the penalty of "JUG" or worse. For years I thought those initials stood for "Justice Under God." Actually, they came from the Latin *sub iugum,* roughly translated as "under the burden or yoke," meaning the direct consequences for your wrong actions. JUG was a penalty of a minimum of ninety minutes of detention after school. It included a mandatory five-hundred-word writing assignment. Frequent tardiness, an unexcused absence, goofing off in class, rudeness, insubordination to a teacher, or even eating food in a prohibited area of campus were all infractions punishable by JUG.

I received JUG the first week of school. I was taking a self-guided tour of campus during the lunch break. I was eating an apple outside of the Bing Crosby Memorial Library when a black-robed Jesuit sauntered up to me. In a friendly voice, he asked: "Did you know that eating food is forbidden in this area?" I apologized and said I hadn't known. "Yeah? Too bad," he replied and took out a pad and a pen. "What's your name? Spell it." After writing my name, he said: "You had a brother or two who went here, right?"

For a moment I thought he might give me a break, but no such luck. That was my first JUG. Many more would follow. The next day I was required to meet after school in a specific classroom. It was crowded with other JUG recipients. Soon Father McFadden arrived. He appeared to be in a hurry and by the expression on his face, it was obvious that we were a personal inconvenience for him. With a piece of chalk, he scribbled the essay topic on the blackboard: "If there were no laws or rules to influence your behavior, how do you think you would act?" Underneath that, he wrote "NEAT!" in capital letters. When he was finished, a younger future priest, a "scholastic," arrived to proctor JUG and Clyde left the room.

Clyde made all the critical decisions involving discipline, whether it was JUG, or more serious punishments, such as suspension or expulsion from school. It seemed to us as though he regulated most of the other important issues in our daily lives, as well. Sixty years later, nearly every classmate I spoke with felt Clyde was at the heart of their experience at Loyola High.

A JUG essay was usually on a topic of social or ethical significance, such as "After a game, how should a Loyola gentleman react to provocateurs from a rival high school in the Carnation Ice Cream Parlor parking lot on Wilshire Boulevard?" Sometimes, a topic would be creatively challenging, such as "Describe life inside a ping pong ball," or "Explain why meatballs don't bounce in the desert." If you didn't take your essay seriously, couldn't come up with the required five hundred words, had messy penmanship, or made too many spelling or grammatical errors, you would be invited back to JUG again in the near future.

JUG was a serious deterrent to those of us who were athletes because it took priority over afternoon sports practice. If you missed practice during the week, you most likely wouldn't play in the Friday night game. It didn't matter whether you were a star player or not. Rules were rules.

During my junior year, I was suspended by Father McFadden for "inappropriate antics" while performing in a pep rally skit in the gym in front of the entire student body. I was standing on the stage in an overcoat impersonating the basketball coach of Mt. Carmel, our rival team, and reciting an original poem I had penned that included the term "half-assed." Out of the corner of my eye I noticed Clyde rapidly striding across the gym floor in my direction. He was waving his arms for me to get off the stage. The skit abruptly ended with his stern words: "See me in my office immediately!"

I was officially suspended from classes and sentenced to memorize and recite a lengthy poem. I spent that afternoon and the following morning in a coffee shop across the street from school, memorizing "My Last Duchess" by Robert Browning. My worst fear was that my parents would be notified of the suspension. That never happened. The next day, I made an appointment to see Father McFadden in order to recite the poem so I could be re-admitted to my classes. I went into his office and he acknowledged me with a nod, but didn't say a word. There was a literature book opened to the poem. He seemed preoccupied with another "more important" matter. He picked up the book, slammed it down in the middle of his desk, and said: "Recite it from the beginning." I began with the opening which I knew best.

> *That's my last Duchess painted on the wall,*
> *Looking as if she were alive. I call*
> *That piece a wonder, now . . .*

Suddenly his telephone rang and he began speaking to someone on the other end of the line. He glanced at me and motioned that I should continue reciting. He paced around his office, seeming far more concerned with his conversation than with my recitation. He often turned his back while I continued to recite. This allowed me to glance at the open book which was turned halfway toward me. I could pique my memory if I lost my place in the lengthy poem. Finally, I made it through and while still on the phone, Clyde nodded and waved me back to class. That afternoon, I thought the phone call he received was my lucky break. In retrospect, I think he was concerned about my grades and contrived the situation so I wouldn't miss class. It made me wonder about him. He was the head cop who terrorized us with his discipline and authority. Could it be that Clyde was actually a man of compassion?

Sometime later, during my junior year, I again faced Father McFadden in his office. Football season had ended, giving me more time to relax and socialize. One Friday night I drove with a few friends to attend a varsity basketball game. We were carrying contraband. One of my friends had stashed an unopened six-pack of Coors beer on the floor of the back seat. A Jesuit scholastic on parking lot duty approached our car as if to have a friendly conversation. He saw the beer, removed it, and told us to park. Nothing was said after that and we went on with the evening, hoping nothing more would come of it.

On Monday morning, as I was sitting in my first period English class, I heard the dreaded voice of Clyde over the speaker: "Will Mr. Mechling please come down to the vice principal's office?" He always mispronounced my last name and his tone sounded ominous. Father McFadden's office was on the main floor of the building. I arrived to find some of my Friday night beer buddies also sitting on benches outside his office. The first thing I noticed when I entered the office was a large painting of the Golden Gate Bridge. On the corner of his desk was the incriminating six-pack of beer. He had a Cheshire cat expression on his face. "Notice anything familiar in here, Mr. Mechling?" It seemed obvious that my second suspension was about to be handed down.

The son of a San Francisco policeman, Clyde maintained his suspicious attitude and demeanor most of the time. If there was any irregularity in our appearance, he would call us on it. My friend Jocko is a case in point. Jocko loved to bait people and then smile at them with his characteristic "shit-eating grin," like actor Jack Nicholson's smug self-satisfied grin in *One Flew Over the Cuckoo's Nest* when he ruffled Nurse Ratched's feathers. Guys from other schools sometimes took umbrage at his sarcasm and retaliated. He would often come to school on Monday with scrapes and bruises from his weekend scuffles. One Monday, the ever-vigilant Clyde asked: "Where did you get those bruises?" Jocko replied: "Uh, I slipped and fell in the shower, Father." A couple of weeks later, it was the same scenario. Again, Jocko came under scrutiny, this time because of his purple and puffy cheek. When Clyde walked past him in the hall, he stopped, stared at Jocko's face, and said wryly, "Slip in the shower again? Maybe you should consider taking baths instead!"

As the years went on, our fear of Clyde gradually diminished, although his enforcement of the rules never lessened. When we were upperclassmen, he became more approachable and affable. He would tell us personal stories and laugh with us. It was then that I learned he had a wonderful sense of humor and a keen Irish wit. One day after school, a couple of my senior classmates and I joined him while he walked across campus on his rounds of inspection. At the main building, we walked downstairs and entered the large latrine-lined room in the basement. All four walls were covered in graffiti. As he looked around, he said to us with a twinkle in his eye: "I occasionally come down here to check out public opinion. If I notice frequent pejorative references to a certain character by the name of Clyde, I know I've been getting my message across." We had been very careful not to call him by that nickname within range of his hearing, for fear of retribution. It came as a surprise that he knew who our reference to Clyde was, all along.

The Rams Band Disaster

As a teenager, I assisted my brother John when he took over for our older brother Phil as the manager for Johnny Boudreau, the conductor of the Loyola University band. Boudreau also conducted the Los Angeles Rams band. As compensation, John received field passes, which meant we could enjoy every game at close range. As assistant to the director, once the music for the pregame was decided, his job was to go to the bandhouse, find the specific music for each song, and file it in a folder according to each instrument. John had joined the Marine Reserves and had compulsory duty one weekend. There was a Rams game that Sunday and I gladly substituted for him as band manager. It turned out to be a disaster! I wasn't aware of the critical fact that there were three different arrangements of "The Star-Spangled Banner." Consequently, I put different renditions of the music in each band member's folder.

As was the custom, the armed forces marched with their flags to midfield at halftime. The well-known voice of halftime master of ceremonies Paul Picerni announced: "And now, ladies and gentlemen, Johnny Boudreau and the Los Angeles Rams band will play our national anthem. Will you all please rise?" With the downbeat of the conductor's baton, a long, confusing cacophony of musical sound immediately ensued. A feeling of panic came over me when I realized what I had done. To my relief, the band members instinctively figured out what had happened, found the same key, and pulled it together. The next time I saw Boudreau, he glared at me, but said nothing about my clerical error.

Rebels with a Cause

To me, growing up near Los Angeles, the Coliseum was an exciting, magical place. That iconic stadium provided me the opportunity to observe America's greatest professional football players at close range. Because my older brother and I worked for the Rams band director, we had free access to the games through the back gate of the tunnel. This was before the National and American leagues merged and the Super Bowl was created. When the Rams won the NFL championship game in 1951, the team featured star players such as quarterback and football hall-of-famer Bob Waterfield, who was married to the bombshell actress Jane Russell, Elroy "Crazylegs" Hirsch, and the future all-pro quarterback Norm Van Brocklin, often referred to as "The Dutchman."

In the latter part of the fifties, the Baltimore Colts captured my interest. Their lineup of superstars left me, an aspiring high school football player, in a state of awe. My favorite pregame activity was hanging out in the enormous Coliseum tunnel, rubbing elbows with these behemoths as they stood quietly during the playing of the national anthem. The players would lean up against the huge concrete walls that led down into the stadium, sometimes shutting their eyes, psyching themselves up for the bloody battle ahead. These modern-day gladiators were literally my biggest heroes at the time. I can still visualize legendary quarterback Johnny Unitas, bruising fullback Alan Ameche, and right halfback Lenny Moore, who looked like he was wearing spats by the unique way he taped his ankles. There was left end Raymond Berry, who always seemed able to get into the clear, and left tackle Jim Parker, the largest man I had ever seen. He was once described as an "apartment building." On defense were "Bulldog" Art Donovan and the rugged Gino Marchetti, whose tackles were likened to "running into a tree trunk in the dark." Gene "Big Daddy" Lipscomb was the second largest man I had ever seen. Even at six feet two and two hundred and fifteen pounds, I'd look at these giants and wonder how anyone could block powers like them.

One time on the field during a game, I noticed one of my new Loyola High School friends, Ralph, sitting at the empty end of the team bench. When I asked him how he acquired a field pass, he said: "The same way you did, from Johnny Boudreau." I learned that Boudreau was Ralph's great-uncle. The previous year, Ralph's family had moved to Los Angeles from San Francisco. Their new home was located in a new suburban tract not far from where I lived. When I asked him how he liked LA compared to San Francisco, he replied, "Not bad, especially lately. We heard that in LA we could see movie stars. It's true! In the alley behind our place they're making a movie. I think it's called *Rebel Without a Cause.*"

Later that week, I went over to Ralph's house after school. We climbed a tree in his backyard and watched the film crew shooting a scene with James Dean. I owed Ralph big time for the opportunity to observe the young film sweetheart Natalie Wood, wearing a blue cashmere sweater, acting in one of the scenes. I repaid Ralph for this unique memory by including him in an escapade with my brother John: stealing an official NFL football inside the Coliseum during a game. Ralph wanted to participate and was not worried about getting into trouble with his great-uncle. In those days, when an extra point or a field goal was kicked, the football would usually land near the back wall of the stadium. When that happened, a stadium official would retrieve it for the next play. Before someone thought of putting up nets behind the goalposts, it wasn't uncommon for the ball to fly into the grandstands. Usually, a lucky kid would recover it. I never understood why the kid would get a police escort out of the stadium . . . however, I would soon learn!

It was the Pro Bowl game of 1957. For post-season and exhibition games, the crowds were slightly smaller and the rules were more relaxed. My brother John had devised a complex plan where we would snatch and keep one of those authentic NFL pigskin footballs inscribed with "The Duke." John's plan was based on some finely calculated assumptions. He would stand next to the game official stationed behind the goalpost, and catch the extra point ball himself before it reached the grandstands. Then, he would heave a long pass to me at the sidelines. My job was to run out of the stadium carrying the ball. This was a long run, more than the length of the field, then up the steps of the stadium, and under the Olympic torch. From there it would be an easy walk through Exposition Park to Menlo Avenue where John's car was parked. I was supposed to stash the ball safely in his car and re-enter the stadium through the tunnel with my field pass. It was a daring caper, and was to be carried out under the unknowing nose of our boss, Boudreau.

Finally, a touchdown was made and the extra point kick was good. John made a terrific leap in front of the stadium wall and caught the ball. He threw a perfect long pass to me on the sidelines and I caught it. With Ralph on my left, we began running. Ushers and spectators were laughing. I yelled to Ralph, "Hey, we did it!" and flipped him the ball. I was worried that a security guard might stop us but we made it without a hitch. As we sprinted up the steps toward the torch, Ralph tossed the coveted pigskin back to me. When we reached Exposition Park and slowed down to catch our breath, I saw a swarm of inner-city kids following me. There was no doubt what they wanted, so I began running again. I yelled to Ralph, thinking I could pass him the ball, but he was out of earshot. I was tackled right then and there. As I hit the ground, the pack tried to pry the ball from my grasp. There was punching and kicking as I held on to the football as long as I could. It finally popped out of my grasp, and another kid caught it and ran. The mob chased after him. I felt dejected as I picked myself up and slowly limped back into the stadium looking worse for the wear. I didn't see Ralph the rest of that afternoon. I figured he didn't want to risk guilt by association in case his uncle had seen everything and was still watching us. John was playing it cool. Not looking at me, he asked: "Well, did you get it? Did you put it in the car?" I replied: "Yeah, I got it. I got the shit beat outta me!" Realizing our brilliant scheme had failed, he snarled, "What do you mean? You screwed up! You should have run it straight to the car!" At that moment the realization hit me that I had been the expendable partner in my brother's *Mission Impossible*.

Getting Fired

The summer after my freshman year, I was hired as a busboy at the Ontra Cafeteria in LA, along with some other classmates.

Our job was to pick up the dirty dishes and utensils and carry the trays over to a central window. There was a Hispanic guy named José who emptied the trays that came on conveyor belts and then distributed the items to designated areas to be washed. One day during a busy lunch hour, I carried a full tray of dishes into the sorting room and noticed several busboys standing there with amused looks on their faces. José was not visible, but we could hear his frightened and frustrated "Santa María! Santa María!" coming from behind the stacks of dishes piled high on the broken conveyor belt. At that moment a busboy started singing his own version of "The Star-Spangled Banner": "José, can you see by the dawn's early light?" That got a huge laugh from my dad when I repeated the incident that night at the dinner table. What happened to me a few weeks later was not a laughing matter.

My boss frequently drank in his office and was usually in a bad mood. With two weeks to go before the end of summer, I was looking forward to my sophomore year at Loyola. I knocked on his door to give my two-week notice that I would be leaving. I was astounded by his reaction. He growled, "You are worthless! Why don't you leave right now? You're terminated!" Not understanding his vehemence, I said, "Excuse me, sir, I don't know what you mean by terminated." He yelled, "It means you're fired! It means you're shit-canned, kid. Get outta here!" I was in a state of shock. This was a seminal moment regarding my character. Jim Maechling, the son of H.P. Maechling, the hardest-working man in the whole town, had been fired! It gave me little comfort to learn that some of my Loyola classmates had also been fired that same day when they gave the bosses their notices. I never told my parents. Every morning for the next two weeks I packed my lunch and football gear in my backpack, walked to Centinela Park, and spent the day exercising and practicing wind sprints in preparation for the high school football season.

The following summer, I found a job at a furniture manufacturing plant through a friend of Dad. I learned some not-so-acceptable Spanish that summer from my friend Renaldo, who was from Cuba. One day I accidentally knocked over a heavy keg of nails that landed on his foot. His response was to howl "Chingate tu madre!" ("Go f*** your mother!") However, in spite of the painful foot he suffered because of my clumsiness, we remained friends.

By the end of summer, with two weeks to go, I nervously went into my employer's office to give my notice. Unlike my previous boss, he was friendly and more approachable. To my relief, his response was "Thanks for letting me know." Two weeks later was my last day. At closing time, he came out of his office and announced, "I can use one of you guys for part-time work to come in and clean up every Saturday. I'm gonna pick the hardest worker." He pointed at me! Ah, sweet redemption! I was exonerated. I would no longer think of myself as a failure in life.

Jocko

When it came to being funny, Jocko ranked number one among our peers. During a class lecture, he would do a silent routine with his fingers, imitating the mating ritual of two aardvarks. This would invariably cause me to laugh and get in trouble for disrupting the class. Jocko was always inventing practical jokes and "screwing around." As a teenager, he had a knack for imitating ethnic dialects. One time he phoned the exclusive, restricted, and segregated Los Angeles Country Club. Doing his best imitation of Amos 'n' Andy's beloved Kingfish, he said, "Say, uh, me and a couple of brothers wanna have a little party for Sugar Ray at your place. Kin you put dat together fo' us?" We listened on the extension phone and thought it was hilarious. The club official stammered while trying to come up with an excuse. At that time, I viewed the *Amos 'n' Andy Show* through a different lens than today. I loved the raw talent and humor of it and thought it was no more demeaning to African Americans than *The Beverly Hillbillies* was demeaning to Southern whites.

Another time, Jocko called the same country club using his best Asian accent: "Herow, is this the R.A. Country Crub? I would rike to apry for membership." The polite voice on the other end replied: "I'm sorry, sir, our manager is out of town. If you could call back next week?" Then Jocko raised his voice and said: "Why you arays say call back next week, call back next month? Pretty soon I too old to pray golf!" This was another prank involving racial stereotypes that we thought was hilarious and innocent fun at the time. Because we were taught by the Jesuits to regard all men as our brothers, we never thought of these antics as any more harmful than when Jocko would imitate one of us in a humorous way. Looking back, few of us were culturally sophisticated then. Loyola was our world and it was not segregated physically or intellectually. We would become more aware of the scope of racial bigotry after we graduated and stepped into the "real world."

Dave

Dad was skeptical of my friend. He thought Dave was "girl crazy" and a bad influence on me. Dave was movie-star handsome, what we called a "chick magnet." It wasn't just his good looks and his baby blues that girls were attracted to. He radiated sexual energy. We guys saw Dave differently. He was an instigator who liked to "stir up the pot." He loved the challenge of conflict and initiated it every chance he got.

One evening, two weeks after football season was over, I was riding "shotgun" in Dave's car. Our friend Bill, who later was admitted to the Naval Academy, was sitting in the front seat between us. Dave pulled into the parking lot of Tops Drive-In in Inglewood. A group of guys from a car club were watching us as we drove by them. Dave grinned with an inviting smirk and extended his middle finger toward them in full view. Back then, we would have said "he flipped them the bird." Immediately, a swarm of black leather jackets converged on us, smashing Dave's front window with a baseball bat. They proceeded to hurl broken glass in our direction. Dave and I jumped out of the car and started punching our adversaries. Bill remained in the car and covered his face to avoid the flying shards. Finally, the police arrived and put a stop to the ruckus. They considered this a routine incident by unruly teenagers and after interrogating us, let us go. Dave and I were both bleeding from facial cuts and bloody knuckles. Bill was unscathed.

I wasn't an aggressive person except on the football field. Why then was I so ready without a moment's thought to jump out of that car to help Dave? I can only say that I felt a fierce sense of loyalty. Although the Jesuits would have condemned the fighting, loyalty was a virtue they drilled into us and it became our mantra.

Over the decades, Dave has said that I saved his life that night. Although that's an exaggeration, it has boosted my self-esteem to know that an LAPD officer credited me with saving his life.

Steve

Steve and I became friends during our freshman year at Loyola High. Steve and his brother John lived with their parents on a beautiful street in the Hancock Park area of Los Angeles, not far from Wilshire Boulevard and what was then called "Miracle Mile." Steve's father had a successful advertising agency and his mother's family owned extensive agricultural properties in

California. At fifteen, I was not yet aware of the socioeconomic differences between my friends' circumstances and my own.

That changed when I was invited to my new friend Steve's home one weekend. It had a breakfast nook designed to look like a diner. I was surprised to be handed a menu by sturdily built Alberta, their African American full-time housemaid. We had no maid and no menus. We were expected to eat whatever food was placed in front of us. Alberta was warm and sociable. I made a point to butter her up, not only in order to get extra helpings of the delicious food she prepared, but also because I loved the way she expressed herself.

When Steve and I were discussing our respective English class essay assignments, he went to a filing cabinet in his room and pulled out his composition that he had filed under E for English. I was impressed at how well-organized he was. I had only seen filing cabinets in banks and my dad's office before that.

Steve's parents were generous. During the summer, they invited me to stay a few days with them at their beautiful summer home on Balboa Island in Newport Beach. I went water-skiing for the first time in the nearby bay. One evening, as I entered their dining room for a second helping of roast beef and mashed potatoes on their buffet, I could hear Steve's parents playing Scrabble with their friends in the living room. I overheard his mom say: "You should get that one, Jack. You were an English major." He wittily replied: "No dear, I was an American lieutenant." I remember thinking that I had never heard clever, sparkling conversations like that between my parents. Steve's parents were college graduates. Mom had only completed seventh grade and Dad had barely graduated from high school.

Steve was a spirited teenager at Loyola. He was an officer in the Pep Club and the head cheerleader, or what we called "Yell King." He was very bright, did well in his advanced classes, and usually acted with more maturity than many of us. He had a highly developed set of values. At graduation, it did not surprise me that Steve, his older brother John, and a handful of other classmates entered the Jesuit Novitiate in Los Gatos, California, to become priests. I envied them for their ability to make such an important life-changing decision. I knew I was not mature enough to do that at age eighteen. Over the following year, I visited these friends to see how they were getting along at the novitiate. During my first visit, I thought that their personalities had not changed much from high school. Over the years, most of these classmates, except for Steve and John, left the Jesuit order. I am proud that these remarkable men remained, and respectful of the dedicated service they have given others for most of their lives.

LA Fifties Jazz

Los Angeles in the fifties was a terrific place to grow up as a teenager. Unlike today, I could safely hitchhike across the city to Loyola High. On my way home one day after football practice, a driver let me off at the corner of Adams and Western in front of the old Watkins Hotel. I immediately became aware of rich and mellow jazz music coming from the open glass doors of a nightclub with "Rubaiyat Room" etched on the front panels. A group of black musicians was rehearsing before the evening show. I quietly went inside and sat down at a table in the very back, trying not to be noticed. The room had an unfamiliar smoky odor. I didn't realize until over a decade later, in the late sixties, what it was. The musicians continued to jam as if they weren't aware I was there. I watched and listened through the smoky haze to the smooth, energizing music.

I was to return several times after that. I would sit alone in a corner, mesmerized by the wonderfully rich, "juicy" sounds the jazzmen generated in that room. Sometimes one of them would nod and smile to make me feel welcome. There were advertising placards on the walls for Marv Jenkins and Les McCann. I didn't know then that both men would go down in history as greats in the world of jazz. All I knew, as a teenager, was that they were so good I wanted to hear them play again and again.

Football

Football season began the week after school started. As a freshman, I decided to try out for the junior varsity team, which was a bit of a gamble. I wasn't intimidated because I was a pretty big kid. Growing up with two older brothers, I was accustomed to physicality. My brother John was six years older and my rival when we played one-on-one basketball in our backyard court. We would frequently go in for dinner with blood from scrapes on our limbs and shirts. The junior varsity coach, Mr. Valenti, was also our English teacher. We were to participate in a drill to determine who would make first string, as opposed to sitting on the bench or "riding the pine," as it was called.

We were told to match ourselves with another player roughly about the same height and weight and to face each other with approximately ten yards between us. Upon hearing the coach's whistle, we were to smash into our opponent and drive him to the ground. A feeling of apprehension came over me when I saw my opponent was Ricky, a lean, mean-looking Mexican kid from the inner city. I knew he came from an area of town that was known for gang violence. I also knew that he carried a switchblade in the pocket of the immaculate white suit he always wore. Ricky and I made eye contact. He smiled at me with a quizzical sneer, as if to say: "You aren't really stupid enough to tangle with a honcho from the barrio, are you?" This was a defining moment. My dream of becoming a football star and getting a scholarship to Notre Dame was riding on this. I felt like Spartacus in the arena, waiting for the kill. At the cue of the coach's whistle, I lunged at Ricky with everything I had, including forearms, fists, and elbows. I caught him by surprise. He was on the ground with blood on his mouth and I was standing above him. I gestured to help him up but he refused. I made the starting team while he sat on the bench and eventually quit the team. Whenever we crossed paths at school, I made a point to smile and extend friendliness toward him, but he would barely nod in return. For a while the fear that he might retaliate made me uneasy. The switchblade he carried haunted me. Ricky was expelled by the end of the year due to poor grades and cutting classes.

By junior year, we had a change of coaching staff when the school hired two great young coaches who had played football at UCLA. We changed to single-wing formation, which was a fundamentals-based, "grind it out" ball control power offense, affectionately described by legendary coach Woody Hayes as "three yards and a cloud of dust." We didn't know it then but this was the beginning of a Loyola High football dynasty that would last for decades. Our new coaches were good at teaching the techniques of our new system. My favorite was Don, the line coach. Before a game, he would help me tape up my fingers, while softly asking: "You gonna kick some ass out there for me tonight, Tiger?" He made me feel like a gladiator. I was so charged up by game time, I would have run through a brick wall for him and Loyola.

It was 1958. I was a junior, and it was the week before our first game. The coach announced the starting roster and to my surprise, I was not only starting tackle on offense but tackle on defense, as well. This was a huge responsibility and I wasn't sure I could handle it. The significance of it really sank in on game day at the pre-game rally in the gym, when I stood with the team in front of our cheering student body. This filled me with such pride and burning resolve. The game had escalated in my mind to almost spiritual, even historical, dimensions. It had become something equivalent to the First Crusade or the Battle of the Somme. That night we suffered a close loss to Santa Barbara High, a tough team that had been favored. I don't think I ever exceeded that performance in any future game. When athletes speak of "playing in the zone," that was me that night.

Before practice the following Monday, the whole team watched a 16 mm film of the game. Coach gave our effort a mixed review but then said: "It's worth showing this movie because one guy played his heart out. Keep your eye on number seventy-five." That was my number! When he rolled the film, I saw myself tackling the opposing team's runner on the opening kickoff. I was everywhere that night on both sides of the ball. On offense I made some leveling blocks that sprang our runner for long gainers. The coach ran the projector back and showed the play a second time. I was so inspired that night that when they punted, I broke into their backfield, lifted up one of their half-backs who was trying to stop me, and hurled him directly into his own punter.

That same year we played a night game against Pius X, a Catholic school named after one of hundreds of popes. It was their ball at midfield. We were on defense. On my right was my teammate and friend, "Big Rich." Their offense came up to the line and the quarterback began barking the signals. I had a gut feeling the play was coming my way because before the snap I noticed their right guard preparing to lunge at me in order to drive me to the right. Most linemen acquire an instinctive reaction to apply counterforce in the opposite direction, which I did. I crashed into their fullback's knees at a low angle right at the line of scrimmage. His knees were driving and one of them hit me squarely in the mouth. The whistle blew and the opposing team went back into their huddle. I got up and felt a sudden jolt of sharp pain in my mouth as I breathed in the night air. Instinctively I put my hand to my mouth and could feel the bloody gap where my front teeth had been. I turned to Rich and yelled: "I think my teeth got knocked out!" He saw my bloody face and shirt and immediately signaled for a time-out. I trotted off the field to show our coach. He looked at me and nonchalantly said: "Get a bunch of cotton from Louie (the manager) and get back in the game!" We won the game and that was it. After the game, the coaches came up to me and patted me on the shoulder. Then, while smiling, both pulled out their dentures. "Welcome to the club, Jim," they said in unison. They both had played on championship UCLA football teams a few years earlier.

Apples were being handed out as we boarded the bus. When they got to me, I heard somebody say, "Better make it applesauce!" The most difficult part of that evening was returning home to my family. Mom never went to my games because she couldn't bear to see me get hurt. Dad rarely attended because he worked Friday nights selling life insurance. Mom was already in bed and Dad was sitting in his chair reading the paper. He asked how the game went. I tried to speak in such a way that my upper lip would conceal the gap where my front teeth had been. A few years earlier, Dad had spent thousands of dollars for braces on the teeth that were now lying somewhere near midfield in Rancho La Cienega Stadium. "Good, Dad. We won. I guess the bad news is that I kinda got injured a little bit." He got up and looked at my mouth. All he said was, "Oh God! You'd better see Dr. Daly tomorrow morning."

Dr. Daly had graduated from USC dental school and was our family dentist. As he looked in my mouth, he asked, "Was your dad there to see this?" By this time, the pain was intense and I was beginning to feel sorry for myself. "No, Dad never goes to my games because he's out selling life insurance on Friday nights!" I must have sounded whiny and pathetic. He indignantly responded by saying: "What? Wait a minute! You're upset because your dad doesn't go to your games while he's working and you're playing? Listen, sonny, your dad is the hardest-working man I know. Do you have any idea how he busts his ass every day and night so you can go to that rich boys' school, get a great education, and play a game?" I momentarily forgot my self-pity and remembered how Dad diligently left every morning and went out again in the evening after dinner to sell insurance.

The humbling lecture was over and in a stern voice, Dr. Daly ordered me to open my mouth because it was time for him to get to work with his drill.

The dozens of photos he took of my damaged mouth and missing front teeth eventually made it into a dental magazine. They were a factor that helped influence the California Interscholastic Federation to require mandatory mouthpieces for all high school football players. You might say I lost my teeth to save others.

In the spring semester of my junior year, I was strongly considering running for student body president. I thought it would be a great honor to hold that position at a respected school like Loyola High. Also, it could help me in the area of college admissions. I heard through the grapevine that the only other probable candidate was another football player, my friend and teammate Pete. Pete was highly intelligent, scholarly, and trustworthy. He also had a certain polish that I lacked. On the other hand, I figured I might be able to beat him with my personality if I positioned myself as the grassroots "people's candidate." I had already played some behind-the-scenes politics by privately seeking endorsements from some of the popular senior athletes. To make sure it was okay with the school administration, the week before declaring my candidacy, I scheduled a private conference with Father McFadden to ask what he thought of the idea. His response was quick, decisive, and brutal. "No! You won't be running. You don't have the grades for it. You are already captain of the football team and there are a lot of conferences and meetings that go along with being student body president. The fact is that you're going to have to work very hard next year on your grades for college admission. That's it." The finality of his words was devastating. I knew there would be no chance for appeal. I was reminded of the sarcastic joke about democracy in a Jesuit institution being a contradiction of terms, i.e., "The student petition has been rejected unanimously by a vote of one to nothing."

I went from his office straight to the empty school chapel. It was a good place for comfort and reflection. After a while, my thoughts turned to football and I remembered a game we had played earlier that year. It was the game that would determine whether or not we would compete for the league championship. In the last thirty seconds of the game, Loyola was ahead by a few points, but our opponents had just connected on a long pass. They were on our two-yard line. After the huddle, they lined up and their quarterback started barking the signals. Sure enough, I could feel their guard blocking me. I knew their big fullback was right behind him and charging hard. I was standing up too high when I caught him on the goal line. Because his knees were driving, I was leaning backward and ready to fall with him into our end zone for what would be their winning touchdown. This all happened in seconds, but at the moment, it seemed like slow motion. Suddenly a powerful force behind me crashed into my back and forced me out of the end zone and into the ball carrier, knocking him down to the ground. That "powerful force" was Pete, our middle linebacker and next year's student body president. He saved the game.

The last game of senior year, we played valiantly against Mt. Carmel, but in the closing seconds they scored the final winning touchdown. They kicked off to us in what is called "garbage time." For the losing team, the only reason for the last play was to vent angry feelings of aggression against members of the winning team. I picked the wrong guy to vent mine. He was their big fullback and linebacker on defense. I didn't know that he was a transfer student from Hungary and had fought in the Hungarian Revolution of 1956 against the Soviets. Since he had been throwing Molotov cocktails at Russian tanks two years earlier, I doubt he had any serious fear of me. As their team came running toward us, I saw what looked like a smirk on his face. I wanted some payback and decided to take out my disappointment with a vengeful lunge at him. He sidestepped me like a seasoned matador and as I hit the ground, he kicked me in the face, hitting the bridge of my nose. Both of my eyes quickly turned into black-and-blue shiners. I spent the next few seconds temporarily blind while listening to Mt. Carmel fans cheering their victory. That was my last game.

As graduation drew near, many of us began making our choices regarding which college to attend and what course of study to pursue. I went to Father McFadden's office with my new syllabus from Loyola University. I was unsure of what to choose for my major. Without hesitation, he grabbed my syllabus, turned to the History Department section, and signed his name on the page. That important life decision regarding my higher education was decisively made for me in an instant and I have never regretted it.

 # GOING OUT ON A LIMB

I alone cannot change the world, but I can cast a stone across the water and create many ripples.

—MOTHER TERESA

College

The transition was easy for those of us who went from Loyola High to Loyola University. The location, however, was quite different. The university campus was not nearly as awe-inspiring. In fact, it was shabby. Located on a hill overlooking Hughes Aircraft Company and a strip of Pacific Ocean beach in Playa del Rey, it had only a few large buildings, such as Bellarmine Hall. Many of our classrooms were corrugated metal Quonset huts built in the early forties during World War II. Despite the uninspiring environment, we realized that our education was not about the bricks and mortar. Its value was in its tradition and the superior caliber of its professors. These were the areas in which the Jesuits excelled.

Father Cyclic

One of my first college professors was the eccentric Father Cyclic. Three times a week we crammed into one of the overly warm and rundown huts for his two-hour psychology lectures. Father Cyclic had emigrated from what is now Croatia. On the first day he warned us that to succeed in his class, we had to "fuckus." After a few minutes of confusion, we figured out that he actually meant "focus." His thick accent was problematic for us all. "Today vi vill tawg abot the skeen zenzes," he said. Seeing our puzzled faces, he pinched the skin on his arm and shouted: "You know—the skeen, the skeen!"

I learned an important lesson in Father Cyclic's class. At first, I tried to take down every word he said in my notes. When I would review them later, they had little meaning to me. The student next to me would spend the entire class drawing vines and flowers around his notes, which consisted of only about seven to ten key words out of the entire two-hour lecture. Once, after our tests were handed back, I noticed his grade was an A, as usual. Mine was a C or a B at best. I asked him, "What is your secret?" He thought for a moment. "I don't know. I guess I just really, really listen." To listen carefully and retain the words that represented the key concepts in a lecture was a revelation. My grades improved after I stopped taking copious notes and applied his example of listening more carefully.

Father Azber, SJ

Our philosophy teacher was Father Azber. Most of his exams were essays, but occasionally they were in a multiple-choice format. After one particular multiple-choice exam was returned, I realized there was a problem with my grade. I had received a C, but when I compared my answers with a friend who had a grade of B+, I noticed we had marked the same correct answers.

After class, I approached Father Azber with both exam answer sheets and said, in a friendly manner, "Father, there must've been a clerical error here. Please compare my friend's answer sheet with mine and you'll see what I mean." He studied them both for what seemed like a long time. Then he turned to me and said, "Even though you did have the same answers, in your case they were not what you meant."

My immediate reaction was "How in the hell do you know what I meant?" Subjective grading on an objective test didn't make sense, but I bit my tongue and let it slide. Perhaps he had some Byzantine grading system that was "a priori" or superior to any logical systems currently in use. I knew this wasn't a person with whom I could reason.

One day a couple of my friends and I were driving to campus and saw Father Azber walking by himself in our direction. I pulled over to the curb, rolled down the window, and shouted, "Hi, Father! We're heading back to campus. Would you like a ride?" A strange expression came over his face. He looked at us as if we were muggers and began to scream at the top of his lungs: "Get out of here!" In fact, it sounded to us like one long word: "Geooowowofffhere!" We quickly waved goodbye and sped away from our strange philosophy professor.

Doc Sullivan

Dr. Frank "Doc" Sullivan was one of the most charismatic and unforgettable professors I had in college. His enthusiasm for teaching affected me the rest of my life. He was passionate about exploring ideas, books, and films in depth. He was often late for his next class because of his willingness to talk with any student who approached him with a question. This lovable, eccentric Irishman carried books, old film reels, and papers around campus in a knapsack on his back and wore an alarm clock on a chain around his neck.

Although I was a history major, I took so many English classes from Dr. Sullivan that I earned a separate minor in English.

One class I enjoyed in particular was Motion Picture Film Analysis. Doc Sullivan had personal friendships with celebrities like actress Rosemary DeCamp and director John Farrow. They sometimes visited his classes unannounced and we could interview them. During his film course, he would frequently rewind the projector and replay the same scene multiple times to point out small details. We watched Audrey Hepburn and Gregory Peck cross paths in the same scene from *Roman Holiday* at least a dozen times. This taught us to see what a film was expressing visually apart from the dialogue. We often discussed the deeper levels of meaning of poems, books, plays, and films.

Dr. Sullivan was a role model for me of what teaching at its best could be. During class one day, we were discussing what made a film humorous and laughing at retelling some of the funnier scenes. Suddenly he stopped and said: "Can you believe I actually get paid for having fun like this?" Several years later, when I was considering a profession, I remembered those words, along with my father's insightful advice: "Find a job you love and you'll never work another day in your life!"

Father Ed Burke, SJ

Father Ed Burke was a brilliant Jesuit priest and everyone's favorite philosophy professor. He taught a course called Philosophy of Man. We were surprised to learn that he was a personal friend of Father McFadden, our legendary "Clyde" at Loyola High. Father Burke was so multifaceted that he could be lecturing on an abstract philosophical point and quickly burst into song, using the lyrics from a Broadway musical to reinforce his point. We loved learning from him and treasured his insights. Some of us even considered switching our majors to philosophy. We were disappointed when he left the Jesuit order to accept a philosophy lectureship at UCLA. This did not deter some of his devoted students from visiting him at his apartment in Westwood to continue learning from him and hearing his insights on modern philosophers such as Nietzsche and Sartre. They were listed in the *Index,* a list of books that we Catholics were forbidden to read.

One evening decades later, my wife Jeanne and I traveled to San Francisco to visit Ed. We treated him to dinner on Fisherman's Wharf. I asked him how he was able to make such interesting connections between Broadway musicals and abstract philosophical concepts while he was lecturing. He responded: "I'm not sure, but my psychotherapist once told me that I am either blessed or cursed with rich associational patterns." Many years later, when I received word from a friend that Ed was gravely ill in the hospital and wasn't expected to live, I wrote to him:

Dear Ed:

Yesterday I received the sad news of your illness. I simply need to let you know how much you have meant in my life. I have had some wonderful, outstanding teachers at Loyola High and Loyola University. Then there was Father Ed Burke. The title of "Father" was and is quite appropriate because you were an intellectual and spiritual father to so many of us back then and over the years.

You were the first teacher who inspired us to consider life's monumental philosophical and theological questions. The cliché about a teacher never knowing where his influence stops is so appropriate in your case. This is actually my fiftieth year of teaching. No other instructor ever influenced my teaching vocation as you did. At first I tried to imitate your style until I realized I couldn't. I needed to create and develop my own teaching personality. I think another cliché about teaching is also valid: Ultimately, a teacher teaches himself who he is and what his core values are. If so, then your gift to us was one of the richest blessings of our lives. I'm taking heart regarding your situation because of my belief in the existence of the afterlife. Once a student asked me what I thought the afterlife would be like. I related my conception that we would need recollections of familiar people and places in order to relate to our new ethereal surroundings. The lobby of the Fairmont Hotel on Knob Hill in San Francisco immediately comes to my mind. As a kid, my dad used to take our family there on trips whenever his company would have award banquets. I would crouch behind the sofas in their large lobby and watch the happy people entering through the shiny brass revolving door. They would be arriving for weddings or family reunions, smiling, laughing, greeting, and hugging each other. Personal memories will always vary, but for me that's what heaven would be like.

So, Ed, I won't say goodbye to you. Instead, I'll see you at the Fairmont.

Much love from your student forever,

Jim Maechling

Pledging

If you were a fraternity pledge in the early nineteen sixties, you were at the mercy of the actives, who were considered your superiors. In the Greek tradition, my role as a subordinate pledge was to be unquestionably obedient to any of their personal requests. One evening my buddy pledges, Jocko and Al, and I had been ordered to buy pizzas. As we sat parked outside Scarpellino's Pizza on Manchester Boulevard, we masterminded a plan in retaliation for our semester-long humiliation.

"Nos gusta muy, muy, muy caliente!" we told the Spanish-speaking man behind the counter. "We like it very, very, very hot and spicy." When the actives bit into what appeared to be a delicious, gooey, cheesy pepperoni pizza, they choked, coughed, spit, and gulped their sodas. With watering eyes and croaking voices, they ordered us to eat the remaining pizza as punishment for our insurrection. We refused, but we were to painfully suffer the consequences later that evening. It was Hell Night, the last night of hazing before we officially joined the fraternity. The actives were waiting for us.

We were taken to a deserted parking lot near campus. A smiling active carrying a large paddle with holes in it approached me. Horace and I had been teammates on the Loyola High varsity football team two years earlier. In a friendly way, he asked, "Wanna trade swats, Mac?" I hoped the bond of team loyalty we'd previously shared would diminish the severity of the punishment that I was about to face. If so, I wondered if I should hit him softly, hoping for a reciprocal response. I chose to take a more middle path and hit him with a somewhat modest stroke of the paddle. "Assume the position," Horace demanded. As I bent over, the impact of his swat propelled me forward five or six feet, resulting in radiant burning heat across my buttocks. It felt like sitting on the burner of a hot stove.

After our punishment, we instinctively made our way to Al's house. It was nearby and we needed to recover from our experiences. We entered and quickly ran to his bedroom. Jocko immediately pulled down the back of his trousers and showed us his seriously wounded derriere. It was covered in purple and red welts and bleeding abrasions. There was an element to Jocko's personality that aroused antipathy among some of the actives. They liked him but he always let them know that we chose them and not the other way around. The punishment Al and I received was light compared to that of Jocko.

Al was so shocked at the severity of Jocko's injuries that he yelled for his mother to come render medical assistance. By the time she arrived, Jocko's natural sense of modesty had forced him to pull up his bloody trousers and announce: "I don't want your mom to look at my sorry ass!" I was not able to sit comfortably for several days but Jocko's bashing was so severe he had to stand during classes and meals for the next three to four weeks.

No Swimming Allowed

John was one of my closest friends in high school. He was very loyal and our friends all agreed that if we ever got into a fight, he would be the best person to have by our side. He radiated courage and integrity. We nicknamed him "Marlboro Man," not because he smoked that brand of cigarettes, but because he projected a rugged outdoorsman image.

In the early spring of our freshman year in college, John invited Al and me to drive with him to Portland, Oregon, to watch our team play in the NCAA regional playoff games. It was midmorning when we arrived in Hilt, California. We parked by the side of the road and walked down to the nearby Klamath River to stretch our legs. It was a cold winter day and there were chunks of ice still floating on the nearly frozen water.

John seemed to enjoy a challenge and I thought this was a good time to put him to the test. "John, would you dive into the river for five bucks?" He shook his head no. "How about for ten bucks?" "Okay!" he replied, and immediately stripped down to his underwear and dove into the icy river. Al and I were dumbfounded that John had accepted my challenge. We were even more surprised when we heard the "bleep, bleep" of an approaching police car.

The officer pulled up, parked, and got out. With a big grin, he asked: "Did you gentlemen know that it's against the law to go swimming in the river without a permit?" He pointed to a large No Swimming sign. "No, officer, we sure didn't," John said respectfully. He was standing in his dripping underwear and shivering uncontrollably. The policeman looked at John and laughed. "Whew, that's a real cold one, ain't it! Bet that woke ya up!" He pulled out his ticket book and asked John for his driver's license. John handed it to him and then hastily pulled on his dry clothes and shoes. The police officer instructed: "You boys are gonna have to go see the judge. Lives just down that street there. Second house on the right. The brown one."

Sitting in an old rocking chair on the front porch was a large man wearing a heavy plaid hunting jacket. He was whittling a piece of wood and there were shavings around his booted feet. He was rather portly and had a broad friendly face. He reminded me of the actor Burl Ives. He invited us into his home and led us into a large open kitchen. "Get a ticket? Okay, let's see it," he said as he motioned for us to sit at a large battered pine table. It was nicked with dents and semi-covered by a checkered green plastic cloth.

John handed the ticket to the judge, who glanced at it and started to chuckle. "Good Lord! We get a lot of these swimming tickets during the summer, but not many this time of year!" He leaned toward John and looked him in the eye. "You must be one frozen trout!" He called to his wife in another room. "Babe, you'd better get these half-frozen boys something warm to drink!" A matronly middle-aged woman with gray hair, wearing jeans and a sweater, walked into the kitchen. She greeted each of us individually by shaking our hands. She poured us each a cup of coffee from a pot sitting on the back of an old-fashioned stove and then proceeded to prepare breakfast. Soon we could smell sizzling rashers of bacon and the aroma of fresh coffee brewing. I gazed through the doorway to their living room. It looked cozy. I could see a worn old armchair with an interrupted knitting project draped over its arm, a brick fireplace with a neat pile of chopped wood stacked nearby, and a wall with bookcases filled with what I presumed to be law books.

As we were eating, the judge turned to John with a question: "So, why'd you dive in, son?" John hesitated. I had the feeling he was trying to protect me. The judge said, "Let me make it easy for you, son. Were you dared?" In the casual and friendly surroundings, I felt safe enough to come clean with the truth. I blurted out, "I did it, sir. I dared him with a bet of ten dollars." The judge continued to look at me as he said, "I charge you gentlemen with violating ordinance 1151, which forbids swimming in the Klamath River in a non-designated area. That'll be ten dollars. Please pass the salt." I got out my wallet and handed the money to the judge, who folded my ten-dollar bill and slipped it into the pocket of his overalls. He continued to exchange pleasantries with us. "So, where are you boys headed?" Al responded quickly, "We're driving to Portland for a basketball game tonight. Our college, Loyola University, is in a playoff game."

After shaking the judge's hand and thanking his wife for her hearty breakfast, we drove off with light hearts, knowing we had just shared a unique experience.

Nesbitt's

In 1960, Loyola was the only all-male Catholic University in the Los Angeles area. For us, this meant facing four years without daily association with the opposite sex. We figured the best way to have interaction with girls was to invite them to our campus for shared activities. Loyola was surrounded by five Catholic women's colleges: Mount St. Mary's, Immaculate Heart, Marymount, and two nursing schools. Our campus was centrally located and convenient for various social events and programs.

As a sophomore class officer, I was in charge of the freshman orientation program held during the first week of school. Writing and producing that program turned out to be great fun, particularly during the planning stages. Several weeks before school started, I invited a few of the funniest guys I knew to collaborate on a sketch that was a takeoff on Prohibition during the Roaring Twenties. Over several evenings, we created a skit that was both funny and entertaining. Based on the popular television series *The Untouchables,* it included legendary gangsters like "Pretty Boy" Floyd, "Baby Face" Nelson, and of course, their nemesis, Eliot Ness. Our friend Joe was Italian and perfectly cast for the lead as Al Capone.

We recruited thirty girls from the nearby colleges to dress as flappers and dance the Charleston on our stage. The day before the show was to take place, I received a formal message from Father Kelp, our strict, conservative dean. He had recently banned the Twist and other popular dances involving "pelvic gyrations." His clear directive regarding our show was: "Any reference to the consumption of alcohol on our stage is strictly forbidden. If you do not comply, the show will be canceled immediately!" That afternoon our disheartened cast assembled for the final rehearsal. It wasn't clear to any of us how to rewrite our entire script on such short notice. Jocko, our resident quick thinker, came up with an idea. He said: "Why don't we just go with what we've got but every time we get to the words alcohol, liquor, or booze, we pause, do a 'nudge nudge wink wink,' and everyone on stage will simultaneously say 'Nesbitt's.' The audience will know what we mean anyway!" Nesbitt's was a popular orange soft drink at the time. This fix saved the show!

"Let Jock Support You"

Before the start of basketball season our senior year, I made an appointment to meet with the Dean of Students, Father Kelp, SJ. I wanted to talk to him on behalf of my friend Jocko. The purpose was to get permission to put Jocko on the ballot to be elected head cheerleader, or "Yell King," at the university. Our problem was that the deadline to become a candidate had passed by a couple of days. "Father, I really believe Jocko can help our school spirit. Let's face it. We don't have a great basketball team this year. I know I'm not the first person to say that. We need to get more people out to the games. I've known Jocko for six years and I believe he will rev up our team spirit. Also, he can entertain us, even if we're not winning!"

Father Kelp had a somber personality and wasn't much of a risk-taker. However, he was sympathetic in this case and consented to let Jocko enter the election slightly after the deadline.

The next step was to advertise Jocko's candidacy. We started the task of making flyers and signs. We came up with what we thought was a clever slogan: "Let Jock Support You." We printed out the flyers and spent the afternoon posting them around the campus. Unfortunately, Father Kelp didn't share our humor. The next day I received a stern lecture from him and was told to immediately remove the signs. Jocko won the election anyway.

Civil Rights and the Cuban Missile Crisis—1962

Unlike students at Berkeley or other progressive universities across the country, few of us had much political awareness of the national or international issues of the day. We were far too absorbed with our studies, sports, and parties to care about what was going on in our nation or the world. One day, I read an article about a young white student by the name of Jim Zwerg, who attended Beloit, a Christian college in Wisconsin. A year earlier, he had ridden on a bus with the Freedom Riders during one of their daring demonstrations in the South. This was a particularly dangerous fight against segregation because in many of these cities, the FBI, local police, and the Ku Klux Klan were working together to stop the protests. In 1962, Zwerg was viciously beaten by a racist mob in Montgomery, Alabama. He was a white man who had decided to put his life on the line by shielding his black friends waiting inside the bus while he tried to plead with the violent mob to disperse. They nearly beat him to death, breaking several vertebrae. After reading about his sacrifice, I felt in awe of his courage on behalf of social justice.

When I was a sophomore in college, the most dangerous threat to my carefree existence came in October 1962. One evening, President John F. Kennedy appeared on national television to announce that our U-2 planes had taken photos over Cuba showing that the Soviet Union was building missile silos on the island. We knew that a missile with a nuclear warhead had the capacity to destroy any major city in the Eastern United States. In that broadcast, he told us that the US Navy would respond with a blockade of ships around Cuba, which he called a "quarantine." A later broadcast went on the air while we were readying for the weekly Saturday night party at the fraternity house. Soviet ships carrying missiles were within a few hundred miles of our blockade. JFK declared that if they tried to penetrate it, they would be met with our "full-scale retaliatory response."

To our stunned group, it seemed like nuclear war was imminent and this might be our last night on earth. Pat "The Youth," our fraternity social chairman, came in carrying a keg of beer and set it down on the floor in front of our anxious group. He calmly said, "I guess the only decision right now is this: Do we party or do we pray?" Someone in our group said, "Can I have a beer while I think it over?" That was it. The party began immediately and raged on through the evening. A few couples remained quietly affectionate in the shadows, expressing tender goodbyes.

Very early Sunday morning, groups of penitent partygoers made it back to our nearby campus to attend the 6:00 a.m. Mass and fervently pray for world peace. A few days later, church bells rang out all over the nation. We were relieved to learn some of the Soviet ships had turned around and were heading back to Russia. Our prayers had been answered!

Although we did come close to a nuclear showdown, Kennedy avoided Armageddon. He achieved this through back-channel negotiations carried out by his brother Robert. JFK chose not to respond in like manner to the threats of Khrushchev, demonstrating that he had become a skilled diplomat. He agreed to remove our nuclear weapons from Turkey, directly south of the Soviet Union, in exchange for the Soviets turning back their warships headed for Cuba, loaded with nuclear warheads. This alarming near-confrontation also led to an arms treaty with the Soviet Union that permanently banned nuclear testing in the atmosphere.

Just for Medicinal Purposes

During my college years, I began to realize how different my parents were from each other. For example, I never saw Dad sip a beer. He had reached legal drinking age during the 1920s when Prohibition was the law. I don't think Dad actually acquired a taste for alcohol. Mom had grown up in a partying German Catholic family and her father made the family's wine and beer.

Mom was a delightfully social person. I was proud to introduce her to my friends in high school and college. Sometimes she would entertain them with her singing while performing on our grand piano. The only time I remember seeing Mom a little tipsy was at a wedding, but she had a hard time getting to sleep without her "nightcap." Often my college buddies Jocko, John, and Al would drop by and we would gather around our kitchen table to review before an exam. Sometimes we witnessed Mom tiptoe in, open the cupboard and pour herself a "tall one" from the bottle of Colonel E.H. Taylor bourbon, add a splash of water, and tiptoe out. If she noticed us observing her, she would smile and say, "Excuse me, boys. This is just for medicinal purposes." In unison, the guys would reply in a singsong, tongue-in-cheek manner: "Oh, sure, of course, Mrs. Maechling!"

In her later years, Mom combined her "cocktail hour" with her nightly prayers. The sweet memory of her softly saying her rosary while sitting in her favorite living room chair remains with me. "Hail Mary, full of grace, the Lord is with thee . . . (sip) . . . Blessed art thou among women . . . (sip) . . . Holy Mary, Mother of God, pray for us sinners . . . (sip)."

Dee McCarthy

In my freshman class at Loyola University, there were many friends from high school with whom I'd already bonded. Name recognition was definitely a factor in my yearly election as class officer. One new friend I made that first year in college was Dee. He had been a star basketball player at an inner-city high school. He was also one of the very few African Americans at the university in those days.

Dee and I were in the same English class and I vividly recall our eccentric professor, Dr. Sullivan, taking roll the first morning. When he came to Dee's name, he said, in his usual exuberant manner, "Ah, finally, an Irishman! Is Mr. McCarthy here?" There was a long silence, indicating that McCarthy was either absent or had dropped the course. "Ah, no McCarthy today, atall atall?" Suddenly Dee stood up and in his smooth baritone voice, said: "I'm here, sir, but I am not Irish!" Dr. Sullivan looked surprised when he saw that Dee was an African American, but quickly recovered. "Well, nobody's perfect. We won't hold that against ya, lad!"

Dee always seemed comfortable "in his own skin." This may have been because he realized his own innate self-worth, or because as time went on, he knew we all thought of him as one of us. He was confident and comfortable speaking in front of our class during discussions and always expressed himself in a soft-spoken, dignified manner. Over the years our friendship grew.

Once he invited me to a party at his home in the inner city of Los Angeles. My date was a pretty, red-haired, freckle-faced Irish girl. When we arrived, Dee and his girlfriend, Trudy, were out buying party supplies. It was disturbingly obvious that we were the only white people there. It was a good reminder to me that Dee experienced the same awareness of being in a minority every day.

My date and I sat alone in a corner while the others talked, danced, and generally ignored us. When Dee and Trudy returned, the crowd became more friendly and couples approached us and introduced themselves. A handsome black man wearing a stylish sports jacket came over to us and in a gentlemanly manner, asked if I minded if he danced with my date. I looked at her and she nodded affirmatively. Afterward, he returned with her, bowed, and kissed the back of her hand, suavely saying in a voice like honey, "Stay as sweet as you are." I knew he had borrowed his phrase from the title song of a recent Nat King Cole album. It was obvious my date was impressed by his charming and debonair manner because she blushed. Seeing her reaction, I filed "stay as sweet as you are" in my memory bank as a useful line I might try sometime in the future.

Except for attending meetings, I was rarely involved in fraternity business because I was busy with student government and needed to keep my grades up. One aspect of the fraternity that bothered me was the blackball system. I disliked the fact that behind the veil of anonymity, an active member could deprive a classmate from membership. I thought this custom fostered cowardice.

Dee was invited to join our fraternity after many of my friends and I had already joined. He was a tremendously likable person, a great athlete, and our friend. I was never concerned that he would be blackballed. Then information came to us from some of the southern chapters of the national fraternity organization saying that their segregation rules strictly forbade the membership of "Negroes." Some of our members worried that Dee's membership would be problematic as a result. The issue of extending an invitation to Dee was escalating as our cause célèbre.

The hero of the hour was our fraternity chapter's chaplain and faculty moderator, Father Zack Taylor, SJ, an easygoing but strong-willed Jesuit priest. He wrote a powerful letter to the national fraternity organization saying that if our school's black students were not admitted, not only would Loyola University sever ties with the national fraternity organization, but it would also encourage the other twenty-seven Jesuit universities in the US to do the same. I never spoke to Dee about it. The irony was that he and Trudy were getting married that summer and he had no plans to join the fraternity anyway.

A practical joke was played on me that following September by a fraternity friend whose nickname was "Stretch." He was a tall, blond athlete from Cincinnati who played on our basketball team with Dee and was also the starting pitcher on our baseball team. A few days before the school term began, Stretch trotted up to me on campus and said, "Did you talk to Dee? He's been looking for you. You know he and Trudy got married last summer and they're looking for an apartment closer to school. He wants to ask you about renting one of those apartments behind your house that your dad owns." A decade earlier Dad had converted the vacant space behind our house where we once played football into a three-unit apartment building to supplement our family income.

I drove home thinking: "Well, this is it. The civil rights issue has finally arrived literally in our own backyard. It comes down to a decision Dad has to make. He's fair and certainly not a racist but all the other tenants in our apartments are white. Some of them might not be happy."

We lived just a couple of blocks west of Prairie Boulevard. In the sixties, Prairie was the dividing line between the black neighborhood of Morningside and Inglewood, which was mostly white. As the line moved west over the years, our area became a real estate battleground rife with racial tension.

When I got home, Dad was finishing his lunch. Mom gave me a hug and quickly left when she saw the concerned expression on my face. "Dad, one of my friends got married last summer. He and his wife are looking for an apartment near college. Do we have a vacancy now?" Dad replied: "Not at present but we could have a vacancy in the near future. A couple might be moving back East in a month or two. Not sure yet." Then I told him that Dee was a Negro and on the basketball team at Loyola. "He just married his longtime girlfriend over the summer. How would you feel about them renting one of our apartments?" He replied: "Not great. If our other tenants moved out, it would be a big hit financially. We might have trouble re-renting the unit. I'd rather not take a risk on that."

I tried to think of another card to play. "So, Dad, what about equality? Human rights? Those values that I've been taught in Catholic school for most of my life? What about those principles?" Raising his voice, he said, "Whose rights, theirs or mine? Am I expected to risk giving up a pretty good chunk of our financial security for them?" I did my best to come up with a compromise. "What if the other tenants met them and said they're not opposed? They're a nice young couple." His reply was, "I would be okay with it as long as it didn't affect our income."

It was midafternoon when I got back to the university. I saw Dee walking into the back door of the gym. "Hey Dee, I talked to Stretch this morning and he told me you and Trudy got married. Congratulations! He also said you're looking for an apartment near school. I asked my dad about one of our apartments and he said if the other tenants agreed not to move after they meet with you, it would be okay." Dee looked puzzled, then began to laugh. "You got had, man! That damn Stretch, what a bullshitter! Last summer Trudy and I got our own place in Lemert Park. As for Inglewood, we don't wanna move near anybody that don't like us. What if we have kids? We don't want to deal with that prejudice bullshit."

My talk with Dad had given me a dose of reality. I began to understand that in spite of my friendship with Dee, there was still a real separation between us. It was a social division Loyola couldn't fix. It saddened me to know Martin Luther King's "dream" was far from coming true.

Father Tetzel

Father Tetzel was a good teacher with a broad knowledge of European culture, particularly music. However, during my final year of college, he became my nemesis. Our differences were not academic; they had to do with the location of a statue. It was a tradition for the senior class to present the university with a farewell gift. A previous class had gifted a bench that was positioned on the north cliff of campus overlooking the city and the ocean. Another gave a stained-glass window for the chapel. As senior class president, it was my responsibility to represent the Class of 1964's gift to the school. My gift idea was a marble statue of our mascot, the Loyola Lion, to be placed on a pedestal outside of the Lair, the main cafeteria and social gathering place. Even though a large marble lion carved in Carrara, Italy, and shipped to California would be expensive, my classmates liked the idea and approved it right away.

At the same time, Father Tetzel wanted his project, a religious statue of the Holy Family, to be placed at the very same spot. The only other option was an obscure site in front of a dorm. Because of this conflict, Father Tetzel and I had a battle to win over public opinion. We each wrote articles for the student newspaper explaining why our statues deserved the more visible spot. His argument was that as a Catholic university, we should prioritize the more spiritual icon. My position was that Loyola needed its own centrally located mascot, comparable to USC's iconic statue of "Tommy Trojan." There was no voting. It was decided by the administration in our favor because of the fact that each class member had already donated seven dollars to cover the cost and to have his name engraved on a brass plaque at the base of the statue. Father Tetzel was outraged at this decision. When the lion finally arrived from Italy, he was quoted in the school paper: "Maechling's lion is the perfect symbol for the senior class, sitting on its derriere." Other critics complained that the lion was not a manly symbol because it was missing its genitalia.

Most of my classmates were pleased with the lion's appearance but were disappointed not to see their names on the plaque. It simply read "Class of 1964." It turned out that over four hundred name engravings would have cost more than the statue itself. Over the years, the lion became a leading symbol of Loyola University (now called Loyola Marymount University). I was especially proud of it in the 1980s, when it became the gathering place for our grieving student body when Loyola's star basketball player, Hank Gathers, died tragically of a heart attack on the court in front of a large crowd in the gym.

The next time I spoke to Father Tetzel was in 1966 in front of the professors in the History Department at Loyola University. It was my oral examination to determine if I were qualified to receive a master of arts degree in history. As I was leaving the house that morning, Dad approached me with the ritual joke he always used to loosen me up on major exam days. "Good luck,

Jim. Remember, you've got your dad's brains." We always smiled when I gave my standard reply: "I know, Dad. That's what I'm worried about!"

I was definitely nervous that morning because I had learned that my first interrogator would be Father Tetzel. This was my Inquisition and Tetzel would be my Torquemada. He looked at me smugly as he said: "Good morning, Jim. My first question is in one of your subject areas: Ancient History. How many men would you estimate fought in the army of Pausanias at the Battle of Plataea on the Attican Peninsula in 479 BC?"

I saw a few raised eyebrows and I knew he wanted to derail me at the very start. I also knew it was imperative to keep cool and stay composed. I tried to speak almost nonchalantly. "I'm not sure. I doubt anyone could be, considering that there were no population statistics then. It would surprise me if there were over ten thousand soldiers." The questions from the rest of the professors were more in keeping with the traditional master's examination.

Afterward, I was asked to wait outside the room while they decided my fate. When I returned, they stood, applauded my success, and shook my hand—even Father Tetzel. I was now a full-fledged master of history. I was thrilled. To celebrate, I went straight to the beach and jumped into the ocean. While body-surfing, I wondered how my new degree would affect my future.

4

BRANCHING OUT

Tell me, Muse, of the man of many ways,
who was driven far journeys.

—HOMER, *The Odyssey*

Journey to Reality

It began with a letter to a Jesuit priest in India. During the last semester of my senior year, my friend Pete told me over a beer of his plan to enter law school that fall. When he asked about my plans, I admitted to being uncertain. Wondering if I wanted law as a profession myself, I'd cut class a few weeks earlier to visit the university library, where I browsed *Black's Law Dictionary* for two hours, waiting for an inspiration that never came.

Pete mentioned that he'd met a Jesuit missionary priest while touring in Rome the previous summer. The priest had told him that he was returning to his mission in a rural village in northern India. The romantic notion of a journey to India before settling down to a permanent career began to take hold in my mind and I asked Pete for the priest's address.

The next day I wrote to Father Guidera:

January 15, 1964

Dear Father Guidera,

*I am a twenty-one-year-old senior at Loyola University
of Los Angeles. In a few months I will receive a bachelor
of arts degree with a major in history and minors in
English and philosophy. I have become aware of you and
your mission through my friend Pete, whom you met in
Rome last summer.*

*After graduation in June, I plan to seek employment
on a ship from the port of Los Angeles to Asia and specifically India. After disembarking, I plan to travel by train
to your school in Bihar, India. I would like to meet with
you to determine whether or not I could be of service to
your mission. I would endeavor to learn the language
spoken there and would be willing to serve in any capacity you think might be needed. For twenty-one years I
have been given love, security, and material comfort.
I hope I am one who has much to give others.*

Sincerely,

*Jim Maechling
Inglewood, California*

Within a few weeks, I received a reply from Father Guidera:

February 25, 1964

*What do I think of your idea? Having been in the States
last year for the first time in fifteen years, I can appreciate what you are willing to give up for this adventure.
It takes guts to even suggest it and will take a lot more
to go through with it. During your days at Loyola, I am
sure you have picked up a few solid principles and that
you work at practicing your faith. I presume you are*

Catholic, although that would not be a requirement. Give me a week or so to think over all the angles before I can give you a definite green light. There are a few difficulties that might have to be worked out. The main obstacle would be obtaining a visa to get you into India for any length of time. If this problem is solved, I think all others can be solved. I will write you again in the near future . . .

His letter sounded encouraging and I began to get excited. However, within two weeks I received official notice from the Jesuit missionary headquarters in Baltimore that " . . . the Jesuits will neither obtain a visa nor take any responsibility for Jim Maechling in India."

Eventually I got over my major disappointment when I realized that the Jesuits' reasoning was sound. Why would they risk their delicate status in India on behalf of a kid who was looking for an adventure? I was now on my own. I wrote a second letter to Father Guidera, explaining that I was determined to travel to India and hoped to be of service in any capacity. I assured him there would be no contract, commitment, or obligation on either side.

Departure

On the day I left for India, Mom was bravely trying to conceal her worry and tears. Dad took me aside. Speaking in a thoughtful, measured, and concerned manner, he said: "Jim, if you get in any trouble or need money, please don't call home. Think how it will upset your mother. You know how she worries. If you need help, please call one of your brothers. Anyway, I know you can take care of yourself!" Those words might seem pretty cold to some, but I didn't take it that way. Actually, it was the greatest confidence booster he could have given me. His belief in me was empowering. I felt it during the entire journey and for the rest of my life. This was my rite of passage into manhood.

That evening in the early summer of 1964, I left home for the port of Los Angeles and boarded a freighter bound for Japan. The previous week, I had been hired as a deck boy by Westfal-Larsen, a Norwegian maritime company. As I boarded the ship, I carried an old leather suitcase packed with my worldly belongings. My jacket pocket held my seaman's papers, passport, and a wallet containing seventy-five dollars.

It was sunset as the HMS Ariel pulled anchor, accelerated away from the docks, and crossed beneath the Vincent Thomas Bridge. I was shaking with exhilaration. I had been planning this for months through letter exchanges with Jesuits, even though they formally refused to take any responsibility for me. Now that I was actually on board, an overwhelming sense of the present moment's reality swept over me. That evening, as we began to cruise the Pacific toward Japan, I stood on deck next to the guardrail, gazing down. For several minutes I allowed myself to become mesmerized by the effervescent blue-green water churning below. I tilted my head back to observe the starry sky. I had never had such a powerful feeling of closeness or connection to everything around me before. It was a spiritual awareness that inside of this seemingly timeless moment, God was truly with me. I felt an extraordinary combination of peacefulness and power simultaneously. I boosted myself up on the guardrail and sat, slowly alternating my view of the endless ocean below and the infinite universe above, until eventually I was jarred back to reality by the angry voices of officers demanding that I get back down on deck.

A few years later, while reading Steinbeck's *The Grapes of Wrath,* I came across this passage in which the preacher, Jim Casey, speaks about being alone in the hills: "Sometimes I'd pray like I always done. On'y I couldn' figure out what I was prayin' to or for. There was the hills, an' there was me, an' we wasn't separate no more. We was one thing. An' that one thing was holy." I easily related to his words because of my own pantheistic experience that first night at sea. What happened on that journey remains indelibly etched in my memory. Each new impression pulsated with the power and shock of a first experience.

The HMS Ariel delivered scrap metal—mostly demolished cars from numerous Los Angeles junkyards—to Japan. Japanese companies converted the junk for use in various new technologies. Transistor radios, televisions, and ultimately VCRs fueled Japan's escalating postwar economic boom. My job as a deck boy was scraping rust on the huge double-level deck. The freighter's noisy vibrating engine rattled everything that wasn't nailed down. After a few days, I became used to it. My two younger American coworkers were both high school dropouts and runaway teenagers. They were nice kids with huge personal problems. John, a tall, lanky kid with red hair, had impregnated a teenage waitress in the restroom of a Winchell's Donut Shop in Long Beach. He confessed this early on in our journey and admitted feeling guilty for not taking responsibility for the mother and their future child. He was hiding in this monotonous, dead-end travel loop back and forth between Japan and the United States. One of the muscles in his right eyelid involuntarily twitched, always followed by a short sniff through his nose as a "knee-jerk" response. He frequently fondled the brown leather strap that he wore on his wrist. My other coworker, Eric, told me he was eighteen, although his voice still cracked when he spoke and his pimpled face seemed pubescent. He revealed that he had been sexually molested as a child by his mother. He had been forced to grow up too fast and wasn't sure how to adjust.

The problems of these kids were well beyond any stretch of my imagination. I was four years older, with a college degree. My education came from books and lectures and theirs came from the school of hard knocks. I was surprised at how open they were with me by sharing their difficult real-world experiences. One day John asked me: "What kind of stuff do they teach ya in college?" I told him that it depended on what you majored in and what courses you took. I said that I had studied mainly history, English, philosophy, and religion. He wanted to know what I had learned from it all. This was a profound question that no one had ever asked me. I began to generalize, so he could narrow his focus. "Well, like how the earth got here, how life got here, and how we got here. Any thoughts?" It surprised me that both of my new friends were enthusiastic to voice their opinions. Eric began recounting the biblical tale of Eden that his grandmother had read to him. John was skeptical of the story. "How do we know that ain't a buncha made-up shit?" "We don't," I said. "Have you guys ever heard of a guy named Charles Darwin?"

For the next three weeks we huddled together, scraping rust as we crossed the enormous Pacific. Talking helped pass the time and ease the monotony. I was teaching them what I had learned in my Western Civilization and Cultures course. When we came to the topic of Greek drama, for Eric's sake I carefully avoided mentioning the story of Oedipus Rex.

This first teaching experience gave me a sense of satisfaction. John and Eric seemed genuinely interested in learning new ideas and constantly asked questions. The incongruity between my life and theirs became raw in its transparency and I was reminded of the blessings God had already given me.

The voyage across the Pacific seemed endless, although it actually only took about three weeks. The lashing sound of waves became monotonous. Often the weather was gloomy or rainy. When it stormed, a harsh white bolt of lightning sometimes illuminated the gray clouds angrily swirling above. On other days, pure uninterrupted blue skies stretched seamlessly across our field of vision. When night arrived, the moon would glow and the sky came alive with millions of sparkling stars. At such times, I would stand mesmerized at the rail. Again, the ocean, the sky, and my prayers melded into one and the same entity.

Some nights I stayed in my cabin rereading *The Caine Mutiny* by Herman Wouk. I had found a copy in a pile of books published in English in the ship's lounge. It had been one of my favorite books as a teenager and rereading it now gave me the comforting feeling of home.

While on deck one morning, I could see a tiny trace of land in the foggy distance. It was a small Northern Japanese island. The words of Columbus's lookout man in 1492 came to mind: *"Tierra! Tierra!"* Land! The island grew as we advanced. I could see the lush trees and plants, verdant and welcome after weeks of only seeing the blue of the sky and the ocean. The lyrics from Rodgers and Hammerstein's *South Pacific* began to play in my head as the island began to disappear in the distance . . .

> *Bali Ha'i may call you . . .*
> *Here am I, your special island . . .*

The next morning we arrived and docked in Kure, a small port in southern Japan. Our purpose was to unload cargo. While showering in the crew lavatory, I was surprised to see a naked Japanese woman in the stall next to mine. She walked over to inform me that her services were "reserved for officers only." I had never encountered a prostitute before and was shocked by her brazen nonchalance. I hadn't realized that the officers and some crew members had "regulars" who came on board when the ship docked at certain ports.

The steward paid me for my services with several thousand yen, amounting to about a hundred dollars. When I opened my duffle bag that night at the Kure YMCA, to my surprise I discovered an envelope. Enclosed were twenty-five dollars, John's leather wrist strap, and a note: "Hope you can do some good in India. If you ever get to the Lucky Dragon in Kobe, please give this to Yoshiko with my love."

I traveled by train to Kobe and over the next week searched the huge harbor looking for a ship bound for India and a waterfront bar named the Lucky Dragon. On my left wrist, I was wearing the leather strap that John had given me for Yoshiko. It was a hot day and I wanted some relief. I came upon a bar and as I opened the door, a burly Japanese man barred my entrance. He curtly said, "Sorry, you can't come in, Asians only!" and slammed the door in my face. I walked away in righteous indignation. I had never encountered racial prejudice personally before. It was something of a shock.

Suddenly there it was, right in front of me: The Lucky Dragon. Hot and thirsty, I walked into the cool and dimly lit bar and ordered a cold bottle of Kirin beer. A Japanese woman immediately came up to me and asked if I wanted to buy her a drink. I declined and told her I was looking for Yoshiko. She pointed to a table in the far corner where another "drink hustler" was entertaining a group of sailors. They were laughing and engaged in spirited conversation. When I finished my beer, I walked over to Yoshiko's table. As soon as she noticed me, I took off the leather wristband and handed it to her. "This is from John McDonald. He asked me to give it to you with his love." She took it, curtly thanked me, and quickly turned, continuing her conversation with the sailors. That was it. I felt sorry for John. He had told me he was in love with her and she didn't appear to care about him. Once he had paid for her services, she had quickly forgotten him.

The next day, I learned that another Norwegian ship bound for India would arrive in port the following week. I went to their office, showed my papers, and was immediately hired. I was relieved because I had been in Japan for nearly three weeks perusing English newspapers and going to waterfront bars hoping to learn of a ship whose destination was India. If I failed to find one and my tourist visa expired, I would be considered an illegal alien and sent to a detention camp in Okinawa.

That afternoon I decided to relax and take in a movie. I sat alone in a movie theater watching *The Sound of Music* with Japanese subtitles. As a kid, I loved all the musicals by Rodgers and Hammerstein. The film reminded me of home, our values, and everyone I loved. Tears blurred my vision. I was already homesick and deeply lonely after only five weeks.

With a few days to spare, the next day I took a train to visit Hiroshima. I arrived at the station and sat down on a bench at a bus stop to look at a city map. A Japanese woman sitting nearby was holding a tiny sleeping baby in her arms. It looked to be no more than a month old. I couldn't help admiring the doll-like perfection and serenity of the child's face peeking out from the blue blanket. Suddenly the sleeping eyes opened wide to the loud hissing air brakes from a nearby bus. The cherubic face instantly became red and distorted. Little legs and arms began thrashing. His toothless mouth opened and a loud wail filled our space. I was surprised when the woman pulled out her breast and pushed it to his cheek. Soon the harsh cries softened as he instinctively nuzzled and latched onto her nipple. With loud snuffling sucking noises, he became immediately comforted. Breastfeeding a child in public wasn't considered acceptable back in the US. Japanese society seemed so naturally practical and down-to-earth, unlike our own culture with its Puritan influence.

Later that day, I visited the Hiroshima Peace Memorial Museum, located near the site of Hiroshima's ground zero. I was shocked at the exhibits that demonstrated the horrific effects of the bomb that had obliterated most of the city. A large chunk of concrete was on exhibition. Human shadows of children on their way to school were etched into the stone, frozen in time at the split second of their disintegration from the atomic blast on that August morning in 1945. Nearby, two women were weeping and hugging each other. One appeared to be an American and the other Japanese. In one room, a two-ton steel door stood twisted and squashed like an empty soft drink can. Schoolchildren dressed in uniforms were lined up at a glass display case full of watches frozen at 8:15 a.m.

Suddenly a middle-aged man walked up to me. His face was so scarred and disfigured it was painful to see. Trying to express his own experience, he pantomimed a falling bomb and a blinding flash, and pointed to his face. Then he mimicked a silent scream of horror. I didn't know how to react. All I could think to say was: "I am so sorry this happened to you." For years I put that experience out of my mind, but it returned several decades later when I was looking at *The Scream* by Edvard Munch in an art book. It conjured up the image of that Japanese survivor of the atomic bomb. I remembered touring the Davis-Monthan Air Force Base in Arizona with my brother Phil when I was nine years old. It had been a thrill to sit in the cockpit of the *Enola Gay,* the B-29 that dropped "Little Boy," the first of the two atomic bombs detonated over Japan that ended World War II.

HMS *Hosanger*

The HMS Hosanger was good news. Not only would it take me to India, but I was promoted from scraping rust as I did on my first ship. Because I could use a typewriter and read and write in English, the international language, I was hired as one of the Chief Steward's two private secretaries. His other secretary was a Norwegian blue-eyed blond named Hika. Her job description was unclear. She didn't dress provocatively, but it was obvious that underneath her starched uniform, the secrets of fertility were in abundance. The only other female on board was a large woman in her forties. She resembled a Russian Olympic weight-lifter and worked as an operator in the radio shack. She was never friendly and seemed to view me with suspicion.

The steward was an easygoing, middle-aged, gray-bearded officer. He wore white uniform shorts and spent a considerable amount of his time sipping bourbon and napping in his cabin. My duty was to inform port directors of our cargo and order our ship supplies, such as aspirin, toilet paper, soap, mangoes, and cases of liquor. I would do this by telegrams to ports ahead such as Singapore and Manila. There was plenty of idle time for writing letters and socializing. The ship hauled industrial metal rods, gigantic spools of steel cable, and various metal tools. We docked briefly at ports in Southeast Asia—Jakarta, Bangkok, and Singapore—but we were not allowed to leave the ship.

Hika had the habit of punctuating her speech with laughter. Her every verbal response contained a giggle. She was bilingual, like most of the crew, but I was never quite sure how much of my conversation she was comprehending. As the days went by, I became aware that she particularly laughed at the risqué jokes some of the sailors would tell her. Since I had been raised to respect girls at all times, I never spoke that way to any of the girls I knew in Catholic school. I soon realized Hika was quite different.

A few nights out of Japan, the weather in the South China Sea was ramping up into typhoon proportions. Quickly the sky and ocean turned dark and ominous. Lightning cracked overhead and within a few seconds the rolling boom of thunder reverberated from the sky. I hung onto the rail and looked down at the violent ocean waves. I was in awe of the untamed power of nature and my own fragility and insignificance. At first there were a few experimental drops before the black clouds unleashed a torrent of water, driven by howling winds strong enough to push me away from the railing. Rain fell in gushes that slammed into my face, stinging my eyes. I could taste salt from the ocean spray. A seagull crashed to the deck and lay motionless.

We were ordered to go below deck and strap ourselves into our bunks. Once below deck, I stopped by the laundry closet to get an extra blanket and towels. I was surprised to see the voluptuous Hika. Without a word, she pulled her uniform over her head and threw it on a shelf. She wasn't wearing any underwear. At that moment I gained a fuller understanding of her secretarial responsibilities. Suddenly, we were thrown up against the wall. Then we were catapulted in the opposite direction. The ship's wooden beams shuddered with loud creaks above and below us from the heavy wind and fury of the turbulent sea. We were tossed about in a flurry of blankets and linen. The ship's pitching from the enormous waves was becoming a serious problem. Hika giggled nervously as the vessel began tilting at a sixty-degree angle. We were rolling in dirty laundry that now covered the floor. Inside the narrow closet, the prospect of a possible sexual odyssey was clearly doubtful under these conditions. The ship pitched and rolled heavily in the relentless swells. Every few seconds we would experience weightlessness, followed by a loud thud of the bow plummeting back down into the water. Finally, it became obvious to Hika that we were in a dangerous situation and with difficulty she managed to find her dress and pull it over her head. I crawled back to my cabin, strapped myself into my bunk, and quietly lamented the dirty trick Mother Nature had just played on me.

The next morning the ocean was as still as a millpond, in sharp contrast to the savage typhoon the night before. The sun just peeked above the horizon, causing red streaks in the sky. Gulls and albatrosses squawked as they circled overhead. I saw the dorsal fins of a pod of feeding orcas breaking the surface nearby. They were causing a school of silver fish with winglike fins to leap and glide over the water in an attempt to escape.

Madras

Finally, we landed and docked in the southeastern city of Madras, India, now called Chennai. For months, I had worried about whether I would be legally permitted to enter India without a visa. It turned out I was lucky because the captain had taken a liking to me. He was curious about my American background and education. When he learned the purpose of my journey, he concluded I was naive and became paternalistic. He was accurate. I was a young idealist holding on to a faith in myself and a noble purpose. At first, he tried to dissuade me from disembarking in India. "India is a desperate place," he said, "not a good place to visit. It is dangerous because of the poverty and there are bad people here." When he realized I was determined, he helped me by cleverly terminating me from the ship's employee roster so I could be classified as a passenger. He then paid me five hundred Indian rupees, which amounted to about one hundred and fifty dollars, and bribed the customs officials for my tourist visa with a case of Bombay Gin. I was admitted without a problem and free to travel wherever I wanted in India for a year.

My feeling of elation did not last long. I stepped out of the port area's immigration office into a street caked in filth. It was crowded with men, women, and children of all ages. Their brown skin was leathery from the relentless sun and their shoeless feet appeared chalky from dust and grime. Their gaunt bodies were partially covered in dirty rags and their eyes looked lifeless. The faces wore looks of hopelessness and resignation. I averted my eyes and walked quickly away from the dock area.

As I headed down a narrow alley, a stomach-turning odor of rotting meat hit my nostrils. I bit my lip to keep from breathing through my nose. At first, I thought there was a dead animal lying on the ground. As I came nearer, I discovered it was the partially clad decaying human corpse of an old man. I stared at him briefly before turning my eyes away for fear of retching. I was forced to step around the horrible mass that had once been a living human being. I walked away as quickly as I could, trying to regain my composure. Later, I learned the dead man was most likely an "untouchable," a name given since ancient times to those born into the lowest caste, class, or rung of society.

I walked several miles into the city where the scenery began to improve. There were clean sidewalks, greenery, and elegant British and French colonial-style homes. Occasionally, I would cross paths with nicely dressed pedestrians who acknowledged me with a smile. One man greeted me by bowing with his hands together as if in prayer and saying the word "Namaste." I asked him if he spoke English and he replied, "Yes, how can I help you?" I asked if he happened to know if a Jesuit Catholic college by the name of Loyola was nearby. He told me that it wasn't far and gave me walking directions. I continued on as the neighborhood gradually made way for rows of hedges and taller two- and three-story French colonial-style buildings with tall porticos and wide balconies.

Soon I came to a large gated property with a sign above the entrance that read Loyola College. I was directed to the office of a Jesuit priest by a groundskeeper and entered the old, stately building. I walked down a long hallway to an open door of an office where a man sat behind his desk. He wore the collar of a priest and was illuminated by the light from a window behind him. I would learn much later that he was one of the most famous Europeans living in India. At the time, I knew nothing of this smiling, soft-spoken man who seemed curious to know who I was. He wore dark-rimmed glasses and his face was thin and sinewy. His eyes reflected a combination of intelligence and kindness. He was a French Jesuit priest by the name of

Father Pierre Ceyrac. He invited me to sit and I told him about my determination to reach India, my long sea journey, and my plans to volunteer as a teacher at an American Jesuit school in the north.

Remembering the cautionary words of the Hosanger captain that morning about India's dangers, I asked Father Ceyrac what he thought of the Indian people. His answer was: "Zay are a beautiful peeple!" With a twinkle, he added, "Tomorrow, I vil show you."

He arranged a room for me that night in the college dorm and I was told I could dine as his guest in the large dining hall. For the first time, I enjoyed freshly made Indian chapatis and bowls of kaali daal, a delicious lentil dish. I was not prepared when I took a small bite of an Indian Tezpur chili pepper they called "pickle." It immediately brought tears to my eyes and burned my mouth and throat. These were far hotter than the jalapeño peppers I was familiar with back in California. I learned they were ranked on the Scoville Heat Scale as among the hottest peppers in the world.

The next day Father Ceyrac took me on a brief tour of a slum in the poorest part of Madras, where his latest humanitarian program, the Tondiarpet Projects, was located. It consisted mainly of small homeless shelters on the side of the road which housed the poorest of the poor families. I carried bags of food, which he gave to some, giving Indian coins to others. Before we left the area, he asked me if I would be interested in working there with him and his team in the "T-Projects." I thanked him and told him I was honored, but I wanted to meet the American Jesuits I had previously contacted at a school in Jamshedpur in the north. This was true...but privately I knew I didn't have the courage to work in such poverty and filth. I was in a state of culture shock.

The Train to Jamshedpur

The next day, I walked into the city and booked a train ticket from Madras to Jamshedpur. I sat down on a rickety bench outside the station to wait. As I looked down, I realized that although I had said goodbye to Father Ceyrac, I hadn't left his slum behind. The dust and poverty still lingered on the soles of my sandals and in the recesses of my soul.

My train was grossly overcrowded. It was pulled by a locomotive that belched black soot into the sky. The soot also blew through the open windows and into the faces of the passengers, causing coughing and hacking throughout the car. People sat anywhere they could find a space, including in the aisles. Some even perched outside on the rusty metal steps with their bare feet, chalky from dust, dangling over the side.

I was one of the fortunate passengers who had bought a ticket and arrived at the station early. From my window seat I gazed at the rural landscape as we pulled away from the outskirts of Madras. An elderly Hindu man sat next to me. His face was painted with ashes and he had large brass rings in his nose and ears. I was horrified when he spat what appeared to be blood that splattered on my sandaled feet. I learned later that it was actually juice from the betel nuts he was chewing.

Over centuries, the British had become masters at connecting India by trains that stopped at numerous small stations. A porter came down the aisle to ask if I wanted to order food to be delivered at the next stop. I ordered what I thought was a meal similar to a chicken dinner. When we stopped at the next station, the food tray was served promptly along with a cup of tepid tea. I had just taken a forkful of rice when two sorrowful-looking children standing outside on the platform stuck their tiny crippled hands through the open window. They appeared to be about six or seven years old and were crying "Saab, saab," a respectful word meaning "sir." When I saw their miserable condition, I completely lost my appetite and handed them my virtually untouched plate of food. They placed it on the ground and continued to plead with me for money. I gave the little ragamuffin of a girl a few coins just as the porter yelled at the children to back away. With a loud metallic screech, the train's brakes were released and with a lurch we began to move. Later, I learned that there were begging syndicates all over India. Tragically, these children had been purposely maimed in order to appear more pathetic and win greater sympathy, resulting in more money for their masters.

When I finally arrived at Jamshedpur, I walked to Loyola School. The American Jesuits greeted me warmly, although they weren't expecting me and had no idea who I was. I told them about my correspondence with Father Guidera. They could see I was exhausted and hungry. After a meal, they led me to a tin Quonset hut with a cot. Exhausted, I slept through the afternoon, evening, and well into the next day. After finally waking, I made my way to the office, where I was greeted by Father Greg Norman, SJ, whose title was "Father Minister," and Father Larry Hunt, SJ, the school principal. They took me to their empty dining room where I ate warm chapatis filled with potatoes and peas while we talked. This was my employment interview. When I told them about my educational background, they offered me a teaching position on the spot. As fate would have it, their regular high school history teacher had become seriously ill the previous week and had returned to his home in southern India. When they learned I majored in history at Loyola University in Los Angeles, they hired me for the entire term to teach world and Indian history. These men would become my colleagues and dear friends. This was my initial exposure to the teaching profession. I loved it from the first day. My students were Hindus, Muslims, Sikhs, Jains, Parsis, Jews, Buddhists, and Christians of all denominations. I was assigned to teach ninth and tenth grades.

During the first months, Father Hunt would occasionally stroll into my classroom to observe. On those occasions, I would lecture, but also would ask him questions using the Socratic method. Playing offense rather than defense was a good strategy I had learned from football. When I would call on him, Father Hunt usually knew the answers, but once or twice he struggled. At one evening supper, he sat down next to me and said with a smile, "You were a little tough on me in your class today, Jim. I majored in English, not history." He understood I was a novice, having never taught before, but I never felt my job was on the line. I was made to feel included and part of their Jesuit community. Years later, after I returned home, Father Hunt wrote a letter of recommendation for me. It helped me land a great position at a high school in Palos Verdes where I would teach for the next fifty years.

There were other young and friendly Jesuit priests on the staff. One was Father Joe Curry. He had a handsome face in spite of his crooked nose. He had broken it twice while playing rugby in college. Father Joe loved competitive sports. He and I played tough one-on-one basketball like I did at home with my brother John. He became a dear friend.

Father Norman was in charge of the physical well-being of all the Jesuits and lay volunteers, including me. He was the one who decided that I should be eating in the community dining room with the Jesuits. He hoped this would protect me from dysentery and other ailments caused by unsanitary handling of food sold in many of the restaurants and food stalls in the city.

Father Dineen was an energetic and very funny Irishman. His quick smile radiated warmth. Even when he wasn't smiling, his eyes were. They crinkled and shone. He laughed easily and loved telling jokes, many of which you wouldn't expect to hear from a priest. I remember being surprised when he told this one at dinner one evening: "A guy walks into an ice cream parlor in Glasgow and behind the counter is a cute-looking Scottish girl. He asks: 'What flavors have you got?' She replies in a thick brogue: 'Rassssspberry, strrrrawberry, and orrrrange.' He says: 'Hey, I really like the way you roll your Rs.' She replies: 'Ya oughtta see me with my high heels on!'"

Overhearing dinner conversations among the Jesuits gave me insight into their teaching philosophy and methodology, which had been extraordinarily effective worldwide since the Reformation. Long before "team teaching" became popular in public schools, the Jesuits were doing it. Over the course of the day, the priests would each teach different subjects to the same students, which meant they all were familiar with the same students. While at dinner, one priest would say: "I think Ashok is getting a bit too big for his britches. What do you think? Maybe we should lean on him a little." The next day would be difficult for Ashok. However, it would help him learn the virtue of humility.

The boarding students were mainly younger Anglo-Indian kids who had been abandoned after the British left. I thought they were funny and cute, especially when they would come to me to tattletale on each other. "Suh, suh, Rodney is playing the fool, suh."

One of my favorite students was a bright and energetic Bengali boy by the name of Surrunjan Batterchargi. He loved that I called him "Surrunjan Battery Charger." These kids who lived on campus had study hall every evening; Father Hunt and the other priests would tutor them after dinner. The strong and resilient love that these Jesuits gave the boys through their teaching, counseling, and parenting was obvious to me. Bonding with my Indian students came easily. Most of the instructors taught in the formal lecture style of the British tradition. My more relaxed approach came across as original.

India had gained its independence from the British Empire only sixteen years earlier. These boys were brimming with national pride. It was palpable. They admired Americans because we had won our independence back in 1776. When we studied the British Raj, I dressed up like a British general, complete with a pith helmet and riding crop that I borrowed from the beautiful Imperial-era British Beldih Club across the street from campus. Its colonial-style building featured a stately reading room, bar, and dining room. There were fields for polo and cricket matches on its grounds. In class, I would imitate a stodgy imperialist who believed God intended the British Empire to rule India. When I pointed at them with the crop and sang in a British accent, "Rule Britannia! Britannia rule the waves!" my students would burst out with loud boos and delighted howls. They loved learning about the conflict, especially when their new country came out on top.

A month later, I mentioned to a few of my colleagues that I had met the legendary French Jesuit Father Pierre Ceyrac on my first day in India and worked with him in Madras. They were astonished. I hadn't realized that he was so famous and revered. As a young priest, Father Ceyrac had been inspired by Mahatma Gandhi and Jawaharlal Nehru to work among the Dalits, or untouchables, the poorest of all Indian people. His first successful project was in the former French colonial city of Pondicherry. He and his students built roads and houses in Cherian Nagar, an area that was home to at least twenty thousand Hindus, Muslims, and Christians. In 1969, he established a cooperative farm system that provided thousands of villagers with food and jobs, helping over two hundred and fifty thousand people across southern India. In 1980, Father Ceyrac left India at the request of Father Arrupe, founder of the Jesuit Refugee Service, to help thousands of Cambodians entering Thailand to escape from the

Khmer Rouge. When he returned to India in 1992, the city of Madras had been renamed Chennai. He began a new program called "Open Hands," to provide orphans and impoverished children with shelter, food, health care, education, and love and emotional support. In 2004, well into his nineties, Father Ceyrac came to the aid of fishing villagers affected by the 2004 Indian Ocean tsunami. The last years of his life were spent back where I met him at Loyola College. He died at age ninety-eight and was posthumously awarded the French Legion of Honor in 2005.

Ratan

Ratan and I met during my first week of teaching when I was introduced at a faculty meeting as the new history instructor. I had already met most of the Jesuits, but not many of the sixty lay teachers. I greeted them one by one and shook their hands. Ratan was near the end of the line. She was tall and slender, in her mid-twenties, and wore her dark hair pulled back tightly in a bun. She was wearing a white silk sari embroidered with gold thread. I reached out my hand to shake hers, but she didn't reciprocate. She simply smiled and said: "Hello, my name is Ratan. I teach third grade."

Ratan means "jewel" in Hindi. She was of Parsi ethnicity. Her ancestors had emigrated from Persia (now Iran) in approximately 650 AD to avoid persecution by Muslim invaders. Parsis had made considerable contributions to science, industry, and the military and formed a wealthy class in India. As the faculty meeting continued, Ratan and I caught ourselves glancing at each other and quickly turned our eyes away.

A week later, I was invited to a faculty picnic at a beautiful local park. It had an aura of timelessness. Interspersed among the ancient banyan trees were statues of Hindu gods and goddesses, mostly nude and in erotic poses. I had to force myself not to gawk, while my colleagues simply took these ancient works of art for granted. Arriving teachers brought baskets of various Indian foods, arranging their dishes on blankets in the center of a circle. Ratan arrived with her friend Julie, and the two women immediately sat down beside me, giving me a chance to interact with Ratan and to study her face at close range. Her skin was considerably darker than mine. She had been educated at the local Jesuit college. Julie was dating my new friend, a Bengali teacher of English.

Just as we began to eat lunch, an elderly blind man with a cane slowly advanced toward our picnic blanket. He was virtually naked. Two quick-thinking faculty members got up to redirect him. Their tone was cordial as they spoke to him in Hindi, gave him food, and guided him toward the park pathway. We continued with lunch as if nothing had happened. Later, when I expressed curiosity about the man, I was told he was a *sanyasin,* a spiritual pilgrim who had given up all worldly comforts except for food and water. He was a wandering beggar now, a *sadhu* who relied on the generosity of others. In this final stage of his life, his goal now was to learn his dharma, the essential meaning and purpose of his life, before it ended and he was reincarnated.

As the school year continued, I would often take strolls around campus. I wanted to learn more about Ratan and would pass by her classroom. A couple of times she invited me in to talk to her students. She wanted them to hear "American English," which was different from the British English she taught her students. We became friends to the point where we felt comfortable teasing each other. I would purposely mispronounce her name, calling her "Rotten." She referred to me as "the lanky Yankee."

One weekend Ratan invited me to meet her parents. They lived in a stately home in a wealthy area. As I entered their living room, my eyes were immediately drawn to a shrine in a wall. It resembled a miniature fireplace with a gold screen enclosing a burning flame. Ratan told me that its purpose was to honor the Zoroastrian deity Ahuramazda, the god of light and goodness. This deity was in perpetual conflict with Ahriman, the god of darkness and evil. This ancient dualism predated and directly influenced the Abrahamic religions of Judaism, Christianity, and Islam.

Whenever I called on Ratan, her parents would greet me in a friendly way in the foyer and then disappear so we could take walks in their garden or listen to recordings in their library. Ratan had a natural wit and sense of humor. We shared a fondness for books and plays, particularly Broadway musicals. Her favorite song was "America" from *West Side Story.* Our mutually favorite play was *My Fair Lady.* She was impressed that I had committed to memory many of the lyrics of Lerner and Loewe, Rodgers and Hammerstein, Bernstein, and Sondheim. We discussed themes, characters, plots, and subplots. Ratan had a background in literature and was excellent at analysis. She once pointed out that Rodgers and Hammerstein wrote tentative love songs such as "If I Loved You" and "People Will Say We're in Love" for the first act in order to move the plot. Once I asked: "What do you think our song should be at this point?" She laughed: "I don't know. Maybe you'll have to write it."

Over the year, our friendship became romantic. Our faculty friends knew of our growing relationship, but they were discreet. Friday night was movie night. The administration rewarded the staff by showing fairly recent films like *Pillow Talk,* which featured popular actors Rock Hudson and Doris Day, in the small school auditorium on their 16 mm Bell & Howell projector. Men and women did not sit together unless they were married. Ratan would sit on the far left side of the faculty women's section and I would sit on the far right side of the men's section. That would provide us the opportunity to hold hands in the darkness.

For most of that year I was never completely alone with Ratan. The rest of my social life was at dances and parties held at the Beldih Club across the road. Some of the most attractive girls there were Anglo-Indians. Many were fair-skinned blonds who wore makeup and saris with a bare midriff. Unfortunately, when the British left India in 1948, they were the mistresses or daughters left behind. They were considered to be at the bottom of the social strata and looked down upon by polite Indian society.

Occasionally, I would meet an Anglo-Indian girl at a dance and ask her for a date, and she would accept. Being an American was a definite advantage. All I had to say to break the ice was, "Have you got any Beatles albums?" They would frequently brag about friends or relatives with wealth and social status in the UK but when I walked them home, I saw they often lived in the poorest, shabbiest parts of town. I was nervous about my personal safety as I walked back to school.

The teachers at Loyola, particularly the Jesuits, encouraged me to enjoy my social life. They appreciated my long journey as a volunteer to teach there. Once, after my only suit had been stolen, a Jesuit friend even loaned me his old civilian suit to wear to a dance.

The real action for guys my age took place in the big cities like Calcutta. Once, some American Peace Corps volunteers who worked on a farm on the outskirts of town invited me to go with them to Calcutta for the weekend, suggesting we might acquire some inexpensive hookers. That sounded like an interesting adventure, but I declined. A previous commitment required me to stay on campus that weekend; I had promised to perform for students and staff at the faculty talent show. I had memorized and was prepared to deliver the song "(Ya Got) Trouble," from *The Music Man* by Meredith Wilson. The show went well. From the corner of my eye, I noticed Ratan smiling and clapping for me in the audience.

It was very fortunate that I didn't go to Calcutta because my Peace Corps friends contracted syphilis that weekend and were forced to go to a local Catholic hospital to be administered penicillin injections by the nuns who were nurses there.

Many evenings I would sit alone in Father Hunt's office typing letters to family members and friends. He generously let me use his old manual typewriter and smoke his cigarettes. Smoking was a habit I had picked up my last year in college, after I was no longer an athlete. American cigarettes were expensive. Father Hunt smoked an Indian brand called Charminar. They tasted terrible and often had small pieces of wood mixed with the tobacco. I typed single-spaced letters home, filling up every corner of each aerogram. I tried to describe everything I was observing and experiencing. I carefully edited whenever I wrote to my parents, so my mother wouldn't worry. My college friends received the more entertaining posts regarding my private life. In those, I would describe the parties and dances, and the few dates I had with the Anglo-Indian women. I avoided any mention of danger, illness, or loneliness. I never mentioned Ratan to anyone.

Trying to Beat the Heat

India had two seasons: hot and wet and hot and dry. The monsoon season began in early June, and lasted for roughly four months through September. Following that was a comfortable period, then it became hot and dry. During monsoon season, the atmosphere over the vast Indian Ocean and Arabian Sea siphoned up enormous amounts of water. It proceeded to travel over India in the form of wave after wave of dark clouds that deposited incredible amounts of pelting, unceasing rain in a very short amount of time. The weather predictions on the radio were amazingly accurate: "The monsoon season will arrive Tuesday of next week at 1:15 p.m. and it will rain for fifty-six minutes."

Once the rain stopped, the heat would pull the moisture out of the earth and it would become steamy and sticky. I recall buying a postcard and watching it immediately bend and go limp in my hand from humidity. Insects, especially mosquitoes, increased exponentially at this time. Large swarms of bugs would cover the streetlights and lanterns in the evening, darkening the streets. The insects would fly into your eyes, ears, and hair. The Jains, followers of an ancient religion with similarities to Hinduism, were strict vegetarians and believers in nonviolence toward all living creatures, including insects. They wore masks over their mouths to protect the insects from accidentally flying in where they would ultimately die. If they saw an ant on the sidewalk, they would carefully step around it.

The temperature during the hot and dry season would start in the low hundreds and escalate a degree or two each day, sometimes reaching 115 degrees Fahrenheit. The humidity was unbearable. During those times the school schedule would change to start at 6:30 a.m. until noon with no break. Noon Mass was usually said alone by Father Hunt in the chapel, and occasionally I would serve as his altar boy. After lunch everyone would nap. We were so exhausted from the intense midday heat that no one could function productively. I would nap in one of the basement classrooms because my tin Quonset hut had become an unbearably hot furnace. You could actually fry an egg on its surface. Some nights I would take my cot and mosquito netting up to the roof of the school to sleep. A mosquito net was a requirement. One of the most annoying sounds was the buzz of a pesky mosquito that had slipped inside the net.

There was a small tube-style radio in my hut. Most stations broadcast in Hindi with occasional English-speaking news and music programs. One show I enjoyed was *Letter from America* narrated by Alistair Cooke on the BBC. On one lucky occasion I picked up the American Armed Forces radio network. They were broadcasting the USC vs. Notre Dame football game from the Los Angeles Memorial Coliseum. It was a close game between my two favorite teams, and I was completely riveted. Since I had worked in that stadium as a kid, the cheers and commentary were familiar sounds that transported me home. Right before the end, the radio reception went out and I had no idea who won.

Some nights, I would lie back and listen to the haunting sounds of Indian music. I had never heard anything like it before. I felt as if I were living on a distant planet. Instruments like the sitar were completely foreign to me. For the first time, I heard the intricate ragas of Ravi Shankar, a man George Harrison of the Beatles later praised as "the greatest musician on the planet." Ironically, over forty years later, that same Ravi Shankar pulled up in his chauffeur-driven limousine and knocked on the front door of my home in Redondo Beach, California. He was stopping by to pick up our young grandson, who was visiting us. Shankar was on his way to meet with our son-in-law, who was part of a team making a documentary on his life and music.

The Lingam

Sometimes after school or on weekends, my colleague Phillip Alencherry would act as my tour guide. We would ride bikes around the city. Jamshedpur, often referred to as "the Pittsburgh of India," was a prosperous industrial city and headquarters of the huge Tata Steel company.

Alencherry was a slightly older man from southern India and a well-respected English teacher. One day we stopped for a break. He pointed across the street to what looked like a small outdoor temple and said: "You might want to take a look because that temple is famous. I'll stay here and watch your bike." He seemed slightly embarrassed.

I entered through a gate enclosed by a wire fence. Inside was a statue of a Hindu deity in the middle of the tiled floor. The statue was several feet high and phallic in nature. I remember thinking, "My god, could that be a replica of a penis?" Just then, two Indian women entered through the gate behind me. I stepped aside, and they went up to the statue. With heads bowed, they began to pray in their native Hindi. Afterward, they touched the top of the statue while rubbing their stomachs.

Father Rocky

During one winter holiday, I was fortunate to experience the India of Rudyard Kipling. The Jesuits knew I wanted to see rural India and they gave me a train ticket out of the city to visit a missionary priest. After a long ride, the train stopped in an extremely remote area bordering the jungle. As I stepped off, a muscular, rugged-looking man in his late thirties greeted me with his hand outstretched. He was wearing a T-shirt and dirty jeans, and introduced himself as "Rocky." We proceeded to hike to his community and school. I only knew the jungle from movies and books. It turned out to be more of a wilderness than I ever imagined.

Rocky had a machete on his belt. At times he used it to cut through the dense, thick undergrowth, which produced loud squawking and the sound of beating wings as the birds in the trees overhead scattered into the sky. As we plodded along, I could hear monkeys hoot and shriek nearby and was startled to see a wild boar in the brush ahead. It looked at us suspiciously, then snorted and quickly scuffled out of sight. It was extremely humid and hot. Sweat was running down my face and neck and my shirt clung uncomfortably to my chest and back. Occasionally we would come to wet ground that was impossible to step around. It smelled of rotting vegetation. As it squished over my sandaled feet, I realized how naively unprepared I was to venture through a jungle without hiking boots.

After squeezing through a stand of bamboo, we came to a river. At the water's edge, Rocky said, "Time to take off your pants and shoes. Leave your undershorts on and hold the rest of your belongings over your head. We're going to cross here."

With trepidation I slowly followed him into the murky river that was nearly waist high and about eighty feet wide. The bottom was slimy and I cringed, wondering what the creatures were that I could feel nibbling at my bare feet and ankles. I saw a water snake slither away out of the corner of my eye. I was glad to be wearing my shorts. The force of our movements caused fish to briefly arc in the water as they swam away in fright. I was relieved to finally reach the riverbank. I dumped my backpack on the ground in preparation to dress and was shocked to see blood running down my leg. Rocky handed me a bag of salt. Evidently, he had experienced a similar situation in the past and came prepared. He said, "Pour this on and it will detach." I shuddered at the sight of the leech's glossy black body, already bloated from feeding on my thigh.

We walked a short distance to a clearing with some thatched-roof huts plastered with dried cow dung. This was Rocky's compound. Later that afternoon, he asked me if I would like to teach his students. He took me to a small classroom hut and introduced me. He told them in their native language that I would teach them English. They spoke Ho, one of India's lesser-known eight hundred dialects.

When he left, I taught my first and only ESL (English as a second language) class. I tried everything to get the students to respond to my questions. I took off my watch, held it up, and asked: "What is this?" There was no response. There was a map of Asia on the wall. I pointed to India. "What country is this?" No response. I continued to struggle. Finally, a small boy stood up. With a beaming face, he said, "I have dog. My dog name Kalu." After that my problem was solved. I would point to an object and students would repeat the word in English. The first half of my lesson was teaching them nouns. When I changed to teaching verbs, I became more animated. I would run around the front of the room and say "run." The boys would get up from their rickety desks and run around with me, laughing and repeating the word. Getting them to settle down was not easy. When Rocky returned, the scene was chaotic, but he had a smile on his face and said, "Good work, Jim."

Rocky was also the village doctor. The next day we walked to a gathering place of the natives. He handed me a small German tape machine with recordings of Ho-speaking people from another village. He told me to rest and listen to it while he went about his work giving inoculations of penicillin. Soon, a small, curious crowd gathered around me. They seemed bewildered at first, then astonished. Before long they were poking each other and laughing. When Rocky returned, I told him I was confused at their reaction. He explained that they were expressing their amazement and wonder at how "those tiny people could be living and talking inside that box."

On Christmas Day, Rocky and I visited the modest dwelling of a Church of England Episcopalian missionary family. They were sponsored by their small parish in Britain and lived in a humble cottage next to a small chapel. The chapel also housed their church school. They were poor, but shared the Christmas gift box of food they had received from their parish back home. We dined on canned beef, applesauce, and potatoes and rutabagas they had grown in their garden. I declined when their children offered to share their Christmas present of "lollies" with me after dinner. I was touched because I knew how rare and precious the candy must have been to the children.

Father Rocky and I had some memorable talks. On our last evening, I wanted to tap into this dedicated priest's wisdom and experience. By then, I had come to admire him a great deal. He had been my tour guide, host, friend, and advisor. I asked him about his personal life before and after becoming a priest. I told him I was considering the priesthood, but was still uncertain if that was my path. Rocky asked me how I saw myself, perhaps ten years in the future. I closed my eyes to think. "You know, it's hard to look that far ahead, but when I think of getting older, I see myself being married and having a family around me, something like the one I have with my parents and siblings." He looked at me and said: "That's a great way to go. I think you just answered your own question." It was as simple as that. On the train ride back to Loyola, I thought of Ratan. I was eager to see her again.

Darjeeling

With a week of winter vacation left, I took a long, slow train ride up to Darjeeling to see the Himalayas and Mount Everest. Over twenty-nine thousand feet above sea level, Everest extends farther into the atmosphere than any other peak in the world. Darjeeling had a spellbinding Shangri-La feeling about it. It was beautiful, ancient, and remote. You could see Everest far in the distance. Much nearer was Mount Kangchenjunga, the third-highest mountain, just a few hundred feet shorter than Everest. It was so high you had to stretch your neck backward to see its peak.

While touring Darjeeling, I walked by what appeared to be a small museum. I opened the heavy oak door and went inside. There were many old photos on the walls that depicted the first successful climb of Mount Everest in 1953, as well as previous expeditions that had failed and resulted in the deaths of climbers. In the center of the room was a large plaster model of the Himalayan range.

A stocky middle-aged Asian man sat at a table. Hanging above him was a large painting of a mountain climber wearing an oxygen mask. I asked him: "That wouldn't happen to be you, would it?" He smiled, nodded, and said, with a slight British accent, "Would you like a tour?" This man was none other than the world-famous Nepalese-Indian Sherpa, Tenzing Norgay. In 1953, he and Sir Edmund Hillary of New Zealand were the first humans to scale the highest mountain on earth.

The plaster model of the Himalayas included small replicas of all nine Everest base camps. We walked around the model as he explained its story. He asked me if I had any questions. "I've read that there are arguments over which man made it to the summit first. Was it you or Sir Edmund?" He pointed to the photo. You could see it was an extremely sharp climb until about the last few hundred yards. There, the snowy terrain sloped gradually up to the summit. With a wry smile, he answered: "I carried that poor Kiwi and our baggage for the last three hundred yards. That was my last favor for the British Empire!"

We chatted a little longer while sipping the most delicious tea I've ever tasted. When I told him I was teaching at Loyola in Jamshedpur, he told me his children all attended the Jesuit school in Darjeeling. I stayed that night at the college in a little room that had a couple of small electric heaters. I slept with my coat on despite turning them to the highest setting.

Theft Hits Home

It felt good to return to Jamshedpur. I had made friends there and I wanted to be with Ratan again. Upon returning, I discovered the lock was broken on my Quonset hut. Thieves had stolen my dress shoes, shirts and ties, and my only suit. Fortunately, I had taken my passport and money with me on my trip north.

Finding a tailor to make a suit for me was not difficult. The challenge was the shoes. They had to be custom made. With a pencil, the shoemaker outlined my foot onto a sheet of leather.

He crafted shoes by hand, much like my grandfather did in Germany in the nineteenth century. I was pleased with how my new shoes looked and felt when I tried them on. Unfortunately, after wearing them a few times, I felt disappointed. Every step I took produced a loud, annoying squeak.

I was surprised when the Jesuits told me they thought the robber was probably an untrustworthy servant. I had gotten to know the servants fairly well and they were amiable. That is, except for one, a man named Nohas. A month before, he and I had a negative encounter in the Jesuit dining room. Even though the British had left India in 1948, the tradition of having tea and crumpets still remained. One afternoon, I sat down at the main table for an afternoon snack and a cup of tea. The dining room was empty. As I was being served, Nohas approached me with a concerned look on his face. The corners of his mouth were turned down, which I thought made him look pompous. "Do you know you are sitting in Father Minister's chair?" he asked in a somewhat challenging tone of voice.

Nohas was tall and middle-aged. He wore an impeccable white, hip-length Nehru jacket and cap. His black handlebar mustache was waxed and curled up on the ends. He was the head servant, and had a strong sense of priority. He knew that Father Minister was not only his boss, but superior to the other Jesuit priests and lay volunteers like myself. It had never been pointed out to me that there was a specific dining room seating arrangement. For some reason his question rankled me that day and I curtly replied: "Well, I don't see him sitting in it! Do you really think he cares where I sit?" The next time I returned to the dining room, there was a small "Reserved" card at that seat. Nohas rarely smiled at me after that and when he did, I thought he seemed smug. Although I had no evidence, when the Jesuits suggested the robbery was an inside job, I couldn't help but think of the time I had been rude to him.

Divinity in a Shoebox

The day after I discovered the theft of my clothes, I received two packages from my parents. One was a shoebox filled with divinity, my favorite Christmas candy as a child. It was a kind of meringue fudge flavored with vanilla. The only Indian candy I had tasted was made from condensed milk flavored with honey. I didn't like its unfamiliar flavor. British Cadbury chocolates were available, but they were very pricey and not within my budget.

It was the custom at the Jesuit holiday table for each faculty member to bring a treat to share at tea time. I had contributed nothing and the holidays were nearly over. I decided it was my turn for generosity and I placed my shoebox of divinity on the table. A few hours later, craving that sweetest of treats, I found the box was empty. I had underestimated the power that the taste of American homemade candy would have on the staff.

My other surprise was a large bag filled with several dozen letters from the United States. They were written by the students of my friend Al, who was in his first year of teaching at Notre Dame High School in Sherman Oaks, California. Getting all of those letters did my heart good. I spent that evening writing to his class, describing the conditions in India and my own students:

Loyola School
Jamshedpur, India
February 20, 1965

Dear freshman Knights / Sons of Notre Dame:

You guessed right when many of you wrote that I might be somewhat surprised to receive more than one hundred letters at a single mail call. It's a great feeling, something like hitting the three-bar jackpot on a slot machine. It was great to hear from all of you.

I'll try to answer some of the questions that the majority of you asked about my school, my students, and about general life in India. Loyola School is fairly new. It's large enough for approximately one thousand students. It is different from other schools here, because it has some of the modern conveniences such as electric lights, telephones, and even typewriters. It is run by the Missionary Jesuit Fathers. They are the same order of priests that run your old arch-rival, Loyola High School. This Loyola is the best school in Jamshedpur. Jamshedpur is an industrial city.

My students are about your same age. They realize and appreciate the value of their education. They know that education for them is the only way they can ever amount to anything, or help their country overcome its tremendous problems. There is really not much to laugh about when you live in a country with a population of nearly five hundred million people. A third of them are starving, and many are still living in the New Stone Age. There is very little science or technology.

The boys who live here at school get two meals per day consisting mostly of rice, curry, and dahl, a spicy lentil dish. They sleep on bunks in a classroom. After breakfast, they go to study hall, which lasts two hours in the morning before school starts. After school, they play either rugby or soccer. How they have the guts to kick that hard ball with their bare feet, I'll never know. Also, many of them play cricket (you know, British-style baseball). Afterward comes shower time, study hall, dinner, library reading, and lights out. There is no luxury here like television. But then, maybe that's not the worst thing in the world. It forces them to read for their entertainment, sometimes good classic literature. This helps them with their English, which many speak pretty darn well for a second language. In their native language they speak Hindi, Bengali, Mindari, Gujarati, Marathi, Ho, Tamil, Nepali, Punjabi, or another of the two hundred and fifty-six known languages and eight hundred dialects in India. Still, they are pretty much the same type of guys as you. Whenever they get to hear a radio they go wild over the Beatles or the current rock 'n' roll sensation. Owning a car is pretty much out of the question here. The wealthier students do own bicycles.

They say that in another month the temperature gets pretty brutal. Sometimes, it reaches one hundred fifteen degrees. I recently learned that an unwelcome cobra has decided to make its nest under my classroom porch. In the meantime, until it is captured and taken away, my students and I are being very cautious. We were told to stomp our feet when we leave, to warn it to run back into hiding if it's out sunning itself.

When the monsoon season comes, everything turns to mud and water. They call those the "sick months," when the various types of snakes, bugs, and mosquitoes make the scene.

In closing, I would suggest that if you can spare a few minutes, you should thank God for the countless blessings He has given you every day of your life, which are easy to take for granted. Also, thank God for giving you a life in our beautiful country.

Thanks again for writing and good luck in school.

Sincerely,

Jim Maechling

Meeting Mother Teresa

One day, while touring Calcutta with an outdated guidebook in hand, I noticed an old temple dedicated to the Hindu goddess

Kali. I was intrigued and walked up the broken concrete steps leading to the entrance. As I pulled open the door, a diminutive nun greeted me. She had a Yugoslavian accent and spoke in broken English. She was wearing a simple white sari, veil, and leather sandals. She told me her name was Mother Teresa and this was her hospice home for the dying. I immediately sensed she deserved the same level of respect I had for the caring nuns I had met earlier at a leper colony outside Jamshedpur. There was nothing significant about her that one might expect in a saintly person. I sensed a strong resilience and dedication of purpose. She was managing a hospital and her manner was direct and practical.

Our conversation was interrupted by a shouting incident. A very old, fragile Hindu man was arguing with two of the nuns. They were attempting to clean him and he was angrily resisting their efforts. Mother Teresa explained the argument: "He is a Hindu. We are Christians. We want to comfort him. He only wants to die. He is saying 'Do not bother me. Let me go. I will come back again in another life.'"

Her simple explanation ultimately shaped the direction of my future studies and teaching. I couldn't believe that human religious systems could diverge so sharply on something as basic as death. The enormous differences that were so simply explained by Mother Teresa prompted many questions in my mind. I realized that I was fulfilling one of the objectives of my trip. I had needed to look outside the confines of my happy yet narrow American Catholic view of the world. What I learned in Calcutta would lead me to study and teach comparative religion.

It was 1964. The world had not yet heard much about Mother Teresa. Few knew that she would become an international symbol of charity, champion of the downtrodden, and savior of the poor. And no one could guess that she would win the Nobel Peace Prize in 1979 for her humanitarian work and be canonized by Pope Francis in 2016 as Saint Teresa of Calcutta.

The Riot

Republic Day is a national holiday in India. It is a day to cel-ebrate India's constitution coming into effect in January 1950, completing the country's transition into an independent repub-lic. The national flag fluttered from government buildings and homes. It was customary for Loyola staff and students to partici-pate in the holiday parade. Our boys were proudly each carrying a tricolored native flag of saffron, white, and green.

Waving crowds lined the streets. A marching band was play-ing the Indian national anthem. Suddenly, I heard the sounds of people yelling and screaming behind us and I smelled the pun-gent odor of gasoline. When I turned around, I saw black smoke coming from a burning bus.

Our faculty leader quickly ordered us to run back to cam-pus for safety. Students and teachers scattered and swiftly dis-appeared. I found myself alone on a side street struggling to remember the correct route back to school. I could hear loud screaming and shouting coming from the prosperous Muslim residential area nearby.

Our campus appeared to be empty when I finally reached it. The students and faculty were hunkered down inside class-rooms and basements for safety. The main gate was locked. I ran around to the side where I scaled a low narrow wall and climbed up an outside staircase to the school roof where I some-times slept at night during the hottest months. The acrid odor of burning rubber and kerosene pervaded the air. From the roof, I could see another bus burning near campus. The frenzied Hindu mob went from house to house. If the residents came out, they were severely beaten or murdered with clubs and metal rods. The homes of those who remained inside were doused with kerosene and set aflame. This went on for a very long time before I heard the sound of sirens from police cars and fire trucks. I was shaking from the horror of what was taking place.

Eventually the mobs dispersed. I learned later that the riot had begun at the Jamshedpur train station where earlier that day some Hindu refugees returning from Pakistan had been beaten and maimed by an angry Muslim mob. Hindus then joined forces to take out their revenge on the Muslims.

Sadly, over India's long history, there have been many instances of similar violence. In 1948, when India gained its independence from Britain, even with Gandhi's pacifism and unifying speeches and hunger strikes, the violence never ended completely. When East Pakistan became the new country of Bangladesh, the tribalism took on new forms. This was true again throughout the second half of the twentieth century in western India, and to the north in Kashmir, where the threat of nuclear war still exists.

Dysentery

In the spring, I became very ill. I had been losing energy due to weeklong diarrhea. I became so weak from dehydration that I wasn't able to teach and stayed in my hut. One of the priests came to see me one evening. He woke me, saying he was very concerned and was taking me by jeep to a hospital on the outskirts of the city. When I awoke a couple of days later, Father Norman was standing at my bedside, anointing me with holy oil while administering the last rites of the Catholic Church. When I asked, "Am I dying, Father?" he replied with a smile, "I don't think so, Jim. This is just in case."

The small rural hospital was unlike any you would see today in a major urban city in India. There were no commodes or urinals, just a small open room with a hole in the center of the concrete floor. I remember being barefoot and disgusted to be stepping in feces.

My illness was the result of being careless about eating food and drinking water from the outdoor market vendors. As a result, I had contracted both amoebic and bacillary dysentery. After nearly a week, I improved and returned to school to continue my teaching duties and begin planning my return trip home to the States.

My Last Day in Jamshedpur

The brave men I had come to know in India had become my true-life heroes and friends. They gave me my first teaching experience and supported me every day. They cared for me when I was seriously ill, encouraged me to explore India, and counseled me wisely on the important decisions in my life.

On that last day in Jamshedpur, I knelt before Fathers Curry, Hunt, and Norman on the dusty tarmac at the airport. My eyes filled with tears as I received their priestly blessings. I knew I was going back to my comfortable home while they would be sacrificing affluence and comfort to live much more difficult, dangerous, and possibly shorter lives. They were the embodiment of the two familiar slogans I had learned in high school and college: AMDG ("for the greater glory of God") and "Men for Others."

India is an anomaly. Comparative Religion scholar Huston Smith expressed it well in his first television documentary filmed there. The two great Eastern religions, Hinduism and Buddhism, originated in India. Both teach reincarnation and the principle of karma. In the opening scene, as his train rumbles across the Indo-Gangetic plain, Smith says: "I can't escape the feeling that I know this place and that I've been here before!" That line resonated with me. Like a lingering case of déjà vu, I had that same feeling when I experienced India.

New Delhi

My plan was to return to the States by the end of the summer. I told Ratan that I would be heading for Europe later in the month, but would travel through India, first heading west to visit the Taj Mahal in the city of Agra. My last stop would be in Bombay. She excitedly told me that she too would be traveling to Bombay that summer to visit her aunt and uncle who lived there. She would be staying at their estate.

I still felt tired and weak after my bout with dysentery, but in the limited time I had left I wanted to experience as much as I could of the country I had grown to love. It was an extremely hot day when I arrived in Agra. After touring the spellbinding Taj Mahal, I became faint and collapsed on the tile steps outside. I was disoriented when I awoke and alarmed to find myself in a hotel room bed with two men wearing turbans standing on either side of me.

My fears began to dissipate when I noticed my clothing had been cleaned, folded, and neatly placed on the dresser next to my suitcase, wallet, and passport. These two noble Sikhs had picked me up and rescued me from danger. They had taken me to a nearby hotel to recuperate. This memory still saddens me when I realize that today, in the United States, good people of the same religion are mistakenly branded as Islamic terrorists.

Bombay

The stage was set for my first private rendezvous with Ratan, far away from her parents and the school community. We would be thousands of miles from Jamshedpur, on the other side of India. This was our opportunity to finally be alone together.

The Jesuits had paid for my travel across India, as well as my return airline fare to Rome. They had put me on the "Jesuit credit card." This was in the form of a brief letter addressed to all the Jesuits I would meet on my way home to the US:

4th May, 1965

If Mr. Jim Maechling needs any money, would you give it to him, and bill Loyola Jamshedpur. Thank you very much for your cooperation.

In Corda Jesu,
Reverend J.M. Kennedy, SJ
Rector

This was particularly useful for lodging. I arrived in Bombay late in the morning. I booked a hotel room downtown and as luck would have it, I found a charming theater that was featuring the film *My Fair Lady,* our favorite play. I bought two tickets and went back to my hotel to rest and get ready for my first date alone with Ratan.

A taxi took me from the hotel to a beautiful secluded area of Bombay situated along the Indian Ocean, popularly known as "the Necklace" for the string of lights from the beautiful homes and hotels that stretch for several miles along the shoreline. We came to a roundabout with a bowl-shaped fountain in the middle. My cab driver deftly drove through one of intersections and stopped in front of a large mansion with imposing Victorian gates. I asked him to wait.

I was wearing my newly tailored suit and custom-made shoes. The gate was slightly open. The S-shaped brick walkway was lined with jasmine trees and the air was heady with their perfume. There was a peacock strutting across the lawn, proudly displaying its tail spread out like a fan. I felt as if I were in a dream. I forced myself back to reality and "squeaked" my way up to the main entrance. There was a brass lion knocker on the huge oak door. I gently rapped it twice. Just as the door opened, a pigeon on the ledge high above me relieved itself. Its missile landed on my shoulder. A butler greeted me and laughed when he saw my plight. He assured me that what had happened was a sign of "good fortune." He asked me to remove my jacket and said he would clean it for me.

Ratan came down the sweeping staircase and hugged me. She looked beautiful and radiant. We were anxious to be alone together, although at first it seemed slightly awkward. We sat in the back of the taxi and I took her hand. Soon we were laughing and talking as usual.

The theater was a short walking distance from where we dined. There was a wonderful safe feeling of anonymity that I had never experienced when I occasionally walked alone with her back in Jamshedpur. I took her hand for the first time in public. After several blocks, we turned a corner and saw the marquee at the front of the theater. We entered the elegant old Victorian Playhouse which had been modernized and converted into a motion picture theater. There were bars on several levels and we sat at a small table and were served tea while watching the film.

Our evening was packed with emotion. It would have been easy to miss the moment and think ahead. Instead, we focused on the wonderful Broadway play we both loved from the recording, but had never seen on screen. Afterward, I hailed a cab to take Ratan back to her uncle's villa. Our time together in India was coming to an end. We held each other closely, sharing passionate kisses mixed with tears. As we drove by what looked like a small park, I asked our driver to stop and let us out so we could linger a while.

We sat on a bench looking at each other. We were both facing the realization that we might never see each other again. I was leaving for Europe the next day. Each of us was processing strong feelings for the other and considering how they had grown over the past year. At first, my words came out slowly. After a few false starts, I finally got to the point. "Ratan, if we stayed together and were married, where do you think we would make our home? Would you want to live in India or America?" She quickly replied, "My family is here. My teaching profession is here. I've lived in India my whole life."

She then asked me, "If I went to the United States, with our cultural differences, how would your family receive me?" I took a moment to consider her important and sincere question and responded as honestly as I could. "If you got off the plane in Los Angeles as either my fiancée or wife, I believe my parents and entire family would greet you warmly with smiles and open arms. I also think that as they got to know you, they would grow to love you. However, deep down inside, they would be hurt. They would feel sadness because they would fear for the many struggles and disappointments facing both of us in the years ahead." She looked as though she already knew my answer to her question. She responded: "My parents would be very disappointed, too."

I realized I could never consider having a family and raising my children in India. I was embarrassed that our problem existed because of our different races and cultural taboos. I was ashamed of the racist xenophobia of my own country. Although it was a nation that I was proud of in many ways, I was ashamed of its history: slavery, Jim Crow, segregation, the need for the civil rights movement, and Martin Luther King's unfulfilled dream.

I understood why Ratan's instinctive response was about her parents' concerns if we were to marry. Their culture maintained an ancient caste system that was initially based on skin color, too. We returned to the waiting taxi with sad hearts and held each other's hands in silence on the ride back to her uncle's home. There, at the front door, we said our tearful goodbye.

Beirut, Rome, Paris, and London

The flight from Bombay landed in Beirut at noon for refueling. Passengers were not allowed to leave the plane but as I looked out the window, I could see hundreds of Islamic faithful kneeling and worshipping on the tarmac as they were called for their midday prayers. It was an inspiring sight to see boarding passengers, pilots, and flight attendants in uniform prostrating themselves next to grease-stained airplane mechanics. All were facing the direction of Mecca. They were praying in Arabic to their one God, Allah.

The women were huddled together in prayer directly behind the men. Years later, a Muslim cleric told me this was not a custom implying that men were superior to women in God's eyes, as I had surmised. Rather, it was a more practical, commonsense tradition based on modesty. He explained that males were more likely to be distracted having a full-view vantage point behind females.

The last leg of the flight was a short hop across the eastern Mediterranean. I was excited because waiting for me was "The Eternal City"! After landing in Rome that afternoon, I found a room at a youth hostel. With guidebook in hand, I became a full-time tourist for over a week. I discovered that if I hung out near the back of a tour group and eavesdropped without paying, the guides didn't seem to mind. It was thrilling to walk inside the Roman Coliseum, where two thousand years earlier gladiators fought to the death and Christian martyrs were devoured by ravenous lions. St. Peter's Basilica, the largest Catholic church in the world, captivated me with its enormity and grandeur.

Seeing Michelangelo's *Pietà* at close range left me in awe of the masterpiece. Its beauty brought a hush to the crowd and tears to some who were overwhelmed with wonder at its perfection.

Paris, the City of Light, was made for sightseers. I visited every attraction I could, but found myself returning to the Louvre every day for another look at the *Mona Lisa,* the ancient Egyptian statues and sculptures, Greco-Roman classics, and legendary artworks from every period. I had a tiny room on the fourth floor of a small hotel. Most of the restaurants were too expensive on my budget. After touring all day, I would dine on bread, cheese, wine, and fruit from the open market.

I didn't speak French or Italian, and I missed the social interaction and connection of casual conversation with native residents. The remedy was waiting just across the English Channel in London. There, I lived for over three weeks in an area of the city called Earl's Court. It was a party zone for young adults, with a vibe that reminded me of Greenwich Village. On my first evening, I waited in a long line at a fish and chips stand. When it was finally my turn to order, I was embarrassed to admit to the cashier that I didn't understand British pre-Euro colloquial terms for currency—thruppence, ha'penny, bob, two and six, crown, nicker, tanner, guinea, and so on. I heard a guy in the back of the line say: "Sounds like a Yank to me!" Suddenly, a pretty redheaded girl about my age stepped up and said: "Don't worry. I'll help you?" I gave her a handful of coins and she paid for my fish and chips, which were wrapped in an ordinary newspaper. I thanked her and asked: "Would you care to dine with me?" She nodded and we sat down on a brick wall nearby. Making conversation with Beatrice was easy. When I told her where I was staying, she told me we were neighbors; she lived in the same complex. She invited me to a block party the following weekend. Beatrice was in her early twenties and worked as a secretary at a printing business. After a week, she invited me to move in with her. The rationale was that we could both save money sharing the rent. This turned out to be a sexual affair—my first, although I doubted it was for her.

Over the next few weeks, while Beatrice worked, I spent my days exploring the fabulous British Museum. Like the French, the British had been prolific culture thieves. I inspected every fascinating exhibit: the Rosetta Stone, the key to the translation of Egyptian hieroglyphics; the Elgin Marbles, sculptures that had once adorned the Parthenon in Athens; and loot from the tombs of ancient Egyptian pharaohs. I read the original signed order from Queen Elizabeth I to have her cousin and girlhood playmate, Mary, Queen of Scots, beheaded for high treason. I was glad to have been a history major as I studied the exhibit of Admiral Horatio Nelson's handwritten plan, sketched quickly on scratch paper, just before the Battle of Trafalgar against the French and Spanish fleets. Next to that was a tragic painting of shipmates mourning his death as he lay on deck after being shot by a French sharpshooter.

Earlier that year, on my trip to Darjeeling in the Himalayas, I met a British teacher who was recovering from pneumonia in the Jesuit's small infirmary. His name was Robin Mitchell. Robin was in his late twenties and was teaching English literature at the local college. He had a keen wit and we immediately became friends. I told him my plan to visit London for a few weeks on my way home to the States, and he suggested I contact his family, who lived in a suburb of London. I gave them a call and they invited me to visit and stay overnight with them. I left Beatrice a note explaining my absence and that I would return the next day, and took a double-decker bus to the Mitchell's modest home in Hertfordshire.

Robin's parents greeted me warmly and invited me to join them at a family party that evening to celebrate their younger son's birthday. That night, I learned firsthand about England's pub culture. Pubs, or public houses, were first introduced by Roman invaders, and were havens for the new class of dislocated urban workers created by the Industrial Revolution. Most communities became socially organized around their pubs, unlike in America, where communities often formed around local churches. Pubs were also where organized labor had its roots. I found the local pub to be a warm and friendly environment and a place for family fun.

At this party, the family held a contest and every guest was to wear some kind of costume based on a popular or famous song. One contestant had a cardboard mockup of London's Big Ben clock pinned to his derriere. It didn't take the merry ale-drinking group long to guess "London Derry Air," a song by Phil Coulter that was popular at the time. I pinned a small American flag on my shirt and the group quickly guessed my song, "America the Beautiful," which they insisted I sing. I was rewarded with a lukewarm pint of ale.

The next afternoon I returned to Earl's Court and was met with a very cold shoulder from an unsmiling Beatrice. She had packed my bags and placed them next to the door. When I tried to make conversation, she wouldn't respond or make eye contact. I finally picked up my bags and said: "I'm sorry. I didn't mean to hurt your feelings, if I did." Again, there was no response from her. I left her flat confused, not really understanding the source of her anger.

Berlin

From London, I made my way north by train to the city of West Berlin. By 1965, Berlin had been a divided city for almost three years after Soviet Premier Nikita Khrushchev completed the construction of his infamous wall. I stayed at a new and accommodating youth hostel called the Wilhelm Westcam Haus that was owned and run by the Jesuits. After I showed them the letter from Father Roberts, I was admitted and given a room. The other boarders there were a fun-loving group. I found them to be well-educated, many with refined tastes in classical music and art. They were quite fluent in English, while I was embarrassed because I spoke very little German.

After a week or so of touring, I was called into the head manager's office by the administrator. He told me that I could not reside there indefinitely and would need to pay for my room going forward. As a possible alternative, I could earn my room and board by doing some "good works," but I would need to promise to keep our conversation confidential before he explained the job. I was rapidly running out of money and agreed. He then informed me that as an American with a passport, I was allowed to cross over into Communist East Berlin. My job would be to make several trips a week across the border and clandestinely drop off packages of personal items from relatives in West Berlin who were forbidden to cross. The packages to be smuggled contained innocuous items such as family photos, keepsakes, toothpaste, and medicines for elderly relatives. I was given a shoulder bag and the address of a camera shop that would be my drop-off point. The assignment was exciting and made me feel "cool."

I easily traveled through Checkpoint Charlie without incident. When I entered the camera store, I told the person behind the counter that I wanted to buy some film, as I had been directed to say. Just then, another customer came in and I told the clerk I wanted to look around before I paid. When we were alone again, I opened my bag, took out the contraband, and laid it on the counter. I continued to fiddle inside my bag as if I were having a hard time finding my money. I then left, as if I had absentmindedly forgotten the package.

After playing "spy" a few more times over the next two weeks, I was shocked to learn how naive I had been. This realization came while talking with a couple I had met at the dorm. They told me about two American students from Pasadena, California, who were arrested for trying to smuggle two East Berlin girls over the border by hiding them on the floor of their Volkswagen. These guys were held in prison for several months until their parents paid the two hundred thousand dollars for their bail.

I immediately notified the hostel manager that I was resigning and wired Dad to say I was returning home soon. I asked him to wire the money from the sale of my old Ford to the Western Union, so I could buy my plane ticket. I was heading home.

Lower East Side Manhattan, 1900s

Grandparents Minnie and Hermann Knoebber

Mattie Knoebber

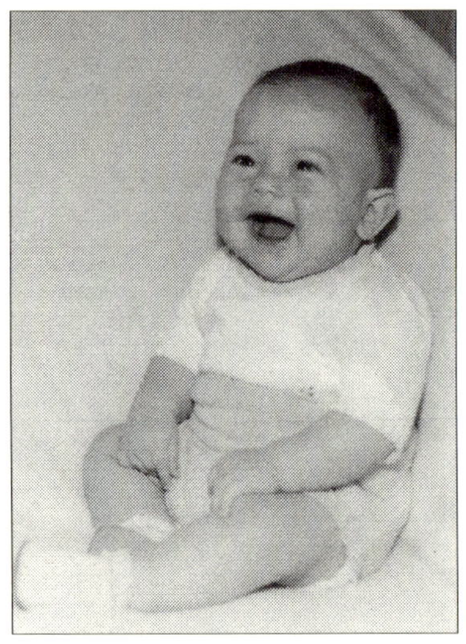

Jim, 6 months old

Dad, Mary, Phil, Jim, John, Mom at Loyola High School

Fr. John's workshop

Bosco's newsstand, 1949

Fr. McFadden making rounds,
Loyola High School, 1959

Football Captain Jim Maechling,
Loyola High School, 1959

Loyola University Lion,
Class of 1964 graduation gift

Jim with his students, Loyola School,
Jamshedpur, India, 1964

Ratan, Loyola School,
Jamshedpur, India, 1965

Shiva, one of the principal
Hindu deities

Mt. Kangchenjunga, Himalayas,
Darjeeling, India, 1964

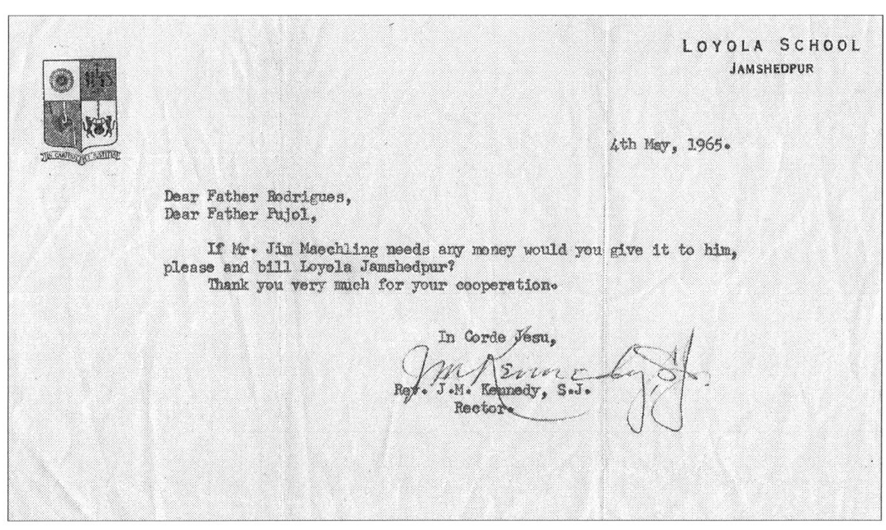

LOYOLA SCHOOL
JAMSHEDPUR

4th May, 1965.

Dear Father Rodrigues,
Dear Father Pujol,

If Mr. Jim Maechling needs any money would you give it to him,
please and bill Loyola Jamshedpur?
Thank you very much for your cooperation.

In Corde Jesu,

Rev. J.M. Kennedy, S.J.
Rector.

"Jesuit Credit Card"

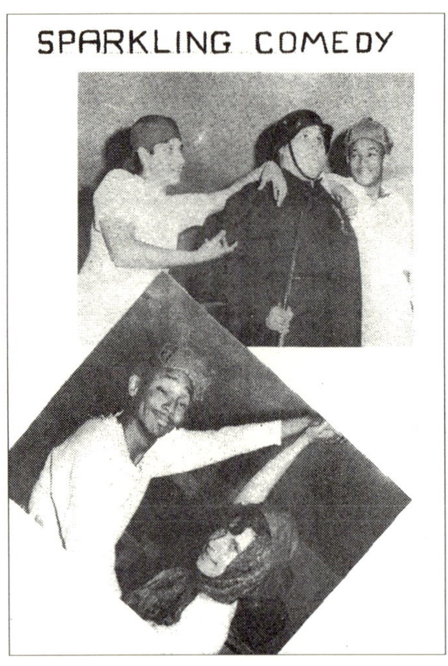

"Animal" and Harry Shapiro in *Stalag 17*,
Pater Noster High School, 1966

Flex Olympics,
Miraleste High School, 1973

Jeanne at the farmer's market in LA

April 4th, 1993

Teaching meditation, *Christian Science Monitor,* 1999

Hare Krishnas visit Jim's class, Palos Verdes Peninsula High School, 2015

Loyola High School circa 1960

Class of 1960 55th Class Reunion

5

BEARING FRUIT

*We will be judged according to the love
we have put into our work.*

—MOTHER TERESA

Returning Home

I flew from Luxembourg to the East Coast where I boarded a flight to California. When I landed at the Los Angeles airport. I was euphoric with excitement and anticipation of seeing my family. I had been gone an entire school year and two summers. I hurried down the concourse to the baggage claim area and spotted my battered old suitcase on the conveyor. A tall man in his late twenties, already with a streak of gray in his hair, walked up to me, smiling, and gave me a hug. It was my brother John. He was wearing slacks, a sports jacket, and a tie. "You look like a bum or one of those hippies!" he exclaimed. I thought he was cracking one of his typical jokes until I noticed the look of concern on his face. "My God, how much weight have you lost?" I had no idea. Our home in Inglewood was not far from the airport but before arriving, John made a sharp turn off Tamarack Avenue onto a side street and into the parking lot of the Sears department store. He said authoritatively, "Come on. Let's get you some clothes that fit. You can't see Mom and Dad looking like this." I didn't argue with him.

Our Tenant and the Watts Riots

Soon after returning home, I noticed Mom and Dad seemed reluctant to leave our house. I learned that the barber who rented one of our apartments was an alcoholic. He had been on a drinking binge for two weeks and my parents were afraid to go near him. As soon as I learned this, I walked outside and peeked through his half-open apartment window. Richard was lying on the floor asleep with an empty liquor bottle next to him. Broken furniture and dirty clothes and dishes littered the floor. I immediately felt empathy for my parents' plight and knew it was my duty to help them.

I drove to the Inglewood Police Department to ask for advice. When I arrived, I could see some kind of serious turmoil was taking place. Military vehicles were parked in front of the station and National Guard troops carrying weapons were arriving. I asked a bystander what was happening. He answered me with an astonished look on his face. "Where have you been, man? Haven't you heard about the Watts riots? This is the second day and they're burning up the place. Now it's spilling into Inglewood!" It was August 12, 1965. I was shocked. I knew this was not a good time to voice a minor complaint with the police so I returned to my car.

As I drove home, I vividly recalled the horror of the riot in Jamshedpur. I couldn't wrap my mind around the fact that violence was happening in our tranquil little town of Inglewood. As I neared Hillcrest Boulevard, I could see military guns being positioned on the upstairs balcony of the Sears department store.

When I arrived home, there was a police car parked at the curb near our house. Two officers were talking in the front seat.

I approached the car. One policeman rolled down the window and said: "What can we do for you, son?" I felt somewhat embarrassed. My problem seemed trivial compared to the major riot taking place. "Hello, officers. My parents live over there. My dad owns the apartments in the back. One of the tenants has been on a drinking binge for a couple of weeks. My parents are elderly and afraid to leave the house. Is there anything you could do to help them?" They explained: "We can't enter his place, but if you could get him to come outside, then we could arrest him." I turned and walked quickly to Richard's apartment while trying to think of a fabrication to lure him out.

Through the half-open window, I could see Richard sitting on his sofa. I called his name and he turned toward me. I said a friend of his was outside; he'd come over to talk to Richard and give him some money. Richard came staggering out his door and followed me down our driveway. I could see my parents peering out of the window. As soon as we reached the sidewalk, both police officers jumped out of their patrol car: "Sir, you're being arrested for public drunkenness." Richard was handcuffed and driven away. Meanwhile, fifteen miles away, Watts was in flames.

While Richard remained in the "drunk tank," I hired a cleaning service, changed the locks to his apartment, and sent his dirty clothes to be cleaned. Three days later, Richard returned to find his belongings packed neatly in boxes outside his door. I said, "I'm sorry, Richard, but you'll have to find a new place. My parents are afraid to leave our home when you're drunk." He didn't argue or apologize. He just picked up his boxes and left.

"You Goin' to the Moon"

In 1965, a few months after returning from India, I moved into a shared apartment not far from USC, where I was taking a graduate course. Around 1:00 a.m. on Thanksgiving morning, I returned home after a party. I opened the kitchen door and flicked on the light switch. Suddenly I felt the cold metal of a gun on the back of my head. The intruder pushed me forward. I said, "Hey, where we going, man?" He replied "Don't know about me, man, but *you* be goin' to the moon!" I put my hands up as he continued to push me forward into the living room. Our drapes were drawn shut. He shoved the barrel of the pistol harder into the back of my head. "Get down on the floor and don't move!"

I heard him mumbling to an accomplice. The thought that I might be killed brought a sickening feeling in the pit of my stomach. I began silently praying. While lying face down on the floor, I could hear them lifting up my stereo and hauling it to the door. The burglar came up behind me, shoved the gun to my head again, and picked the wallet out of my back pocket. I felt cold and clammy. My heart was pounding in my ears. I waited for the end.

Then he warned: "I'm gonna open up this front curtain. We can see you in here. If you get up, we'll blow your eff'n head off." He gave one more shove with the gun and a final warning: "Got it?" I heard our drapes being opened and then the kitchen door close. The tension began draining from my body. I realized that I had been holding my breath. I sucked in a big gulp of air. Not moving for what seemed to be an eternity, I finally crawled on my stomach into the hallway to my roommate's door. Still shaking, I stood up and opened it. My roommate was in bed. He had slept through the whole thing. The next day we moved to an apartment in a safer neighborhood in South Pasadena.

Part-Time Teaching Jobs

Over the next couple of years, while I worked on my graduate degree and teaching credentials, I had various part-time jobs.

I taught in private high schools, tutored students whose parents were celebrities, and taught at a school for students with psychological disorders. I didn't realize at the time that these diverse teaching experiences would ultimately pay dividends throughout my career.

Teaching teenagers with special needs was a challenge. The other teachers and I would often confer with their psychiatrists. Our classes were small, and some of the students were very bright. Their personality disorders made them unsuitable for a regular school environment. Interacting with them was sometimes unnerving and often humorous. During the first week of school, after I parked my car and got out, a student would rev the motor on his scooter and make a beeline for me. It scared the hell out of me! Another student, after learning my name was Maechling and that I was Catholic, called me "Mr. Mackerel" to needle me.

I learned from the start that I couldn't let these kids get the upper hand. Whatever witty or sarcastic retort they made, I had to come up with one better and turn their disrespect into an advantage for myself. I knew I mustn't do this by belittling them or exceeding my authority, so I tried to check their behavior with a style of humor they could relate to. The only way to get them to listen was to tease them back.

The most exciting job I had was teaching English and Drama at an all-boys Catholic high school in a lower-middle-class area of Los Angeles. An order of Catholic brothers from Ireland administrated the school. My interview with Brother Patrick O'Malley, the principal, was critical for landing the job, which required directing the school's first-ever play. I had been in school plays before but had never directed one. I felt I had to convince O'Malley that I had experience. I told him that I had directed Shakespearean scenes and *A Man for All Seasons* at a Jesuit high school in India. This was partially accurate, but definitely an exaggeration. He looked worried, but his concern wasn't my experience. "Jim, I can see you'd be the man for the job, but there is one problem. I'm sorry to tell ya that we don't have a theater or even an auditorium here or money to build or rent one. Do ya think you could put on a play in the school cafeteria?" I smiled confidently, looked around his small, shoddy office, and replied: "Sure! I could put on a play anywhere, even right here in this room! I haven't seen the cafeteria yet, but I'm sure I can convert it into a theater by putting in a stage!"

His next question was anticipated. "What kind of play do ya think you'd want to put on?" I replied quickly: "Well, since this is the first play at an all-boys school, I'd go with a comedy with a lot of parts for boys. I'd choose *Stalag 17,* a play that was made into a popular movie several years ago. It's about American fliers in a German POW camp during World War II." Father O'Malley smiled, shook my hand, and led me to their dumpy cafeteria. It was about to be transformed into the school theater.

Most of the cast members were students I recruited from my English classes. After auditions, we began rehearsals after school. After two weeks, I realized we had a major problem. This was supposed to be a comedy but it wasn't funny. I couldn't figure out why. Finally, it hit me. The kid with the comic lead was trying too hard to be funny. I repeatedly told him to just play the character: a slow-witted, grimy, Polish American whose nickname was "Animal." The student nodded but continued to play his part in the same stilted, inauthentic way. He was about to kill the play so I had to find a replacement. It was a daunting challenge with only a few weeks before opening night. I asked my students: "Who do you think is the most naturally funny guy in our school?" They were unanimous: an African American kid by the name of Dexter Beasley. Dexter was not in any of my classes. I tracked him down and quickly realized he wouldn't need convincing that he could entertain an audience. He wasn't worried about playing a Polish American nicknamed "Animal." He also knew that a black actor playing someone Polish was funny in itself. Dexter's main worry was memorizing his lines in the limited time we had left. I made him a promise: "Dexter, I'll work on your lines with you every day. I'll pick you up for school every morning and we'll rehearse on the way to school. We'll rehearse while you eat your lunch in my classroom, and we'll run lines while I drive you home after rehearsals."

Dexter accepted the challenge, remembered his lines, and turned out to be a natural talent on the stage. In fact, the whole cast received standing ovations every night. *Stalag 17,* the first play in Pater Noster High School's history, was a huge hit. I had learned firsthand that the old saying attributed to Shakespearian actor Sir Edmund Kean on his deathbed was indeed true: "Dying is easy. Comedy is hard."

As an undergraduate, I had taken education courses whenever I had room on my schedule. That paid off for me the year I did my student teaching at Venice High School. At first, I had to observe and write critiques of history teachers as assignments for Dr. Shuman, my director in the Loyola University Education Department. The next step was teaching history lessons in the classroom of a certificated teacher. Because of my year of teaching in India, the profession came quite naturally to me. The regular teacher and I developed a friendship. He invited me to join his private tutoring business in Beverly Hills, which supplemented my income over the next few years. Dr. Shuman came to observe me several times. I was flattered to read his final evaluation of my teaching: "Jim has the most outstanding natural rapport with his students of any teacher I have ever observed!" One day while I was student teaching, my brother John phoned me. "Jim, I just hung up with Mrs. Whitaker, the lady in charge of job placement at Loyola University. I've been looking for a talented person to join our company in sales and management. When

I described the perfect person, I realized I was describing you. Think about coming in with us over here." I was flattered but hesitated. What I really needed was Dad's advice. The next day I told our aging, now retired father. A long silence fell between us.

Finally, he said: "I always thought you were the 'ideas guy' . . . books, history, philosophy. Remember the day I went to your class and watched you teaching? Your students love you. They know you're a terrific teacher. Doesn't that mean anything?" "Okay. Okay, Dad. You made your point. I got it!" Dad knew his sons.

It was easy to find a teaching position back in the sixties. My Loyola education certainly helped. I received job offers from out-standing schools all over the city: Venice High, Culver City, Bev-erly Hills, Santa Monica, and a late offer from Rolling Hills High School in Palos Verdes, which was located in a beautiful area of the South Bay near the beach. I liked the fact that the school was close to the beach because I loved playing volleyball. Ferguson was a good administrator. When I entered his office, he was hold-ing a recommendation from Father Hunt in India. There was a smile on his face when he asked me: "Did you actually have your Indian students build scale models of the pyramids, the Parthe-non, the Coliseum, and the Taj Mahal?" I nodded. "Yes, I did. It helped get them interested in ancient history." He hired me on the spot. It seemed as if the job had been waiting for me.

Rolling Hills and Miraleste

When I began teaching in 1967, Rolling Hills High School was a three-year-old school in Palos Verdes, California. It had an enroll-ment of nearly three thousand students. Two separate lunchtimes were scheduled because the campus was so crowded. I taught Western Civilization with a slightly newer version of the same textbook I used in India. At the time, the ethnic composition of the school was primarily WASP (white Anglo-Saxon Protestant). There were very few students of color. However, the ingredients for change were in the making because the Johnson administration had pushed the Civil Rights Act of 1964 through Congress, restricting segregation in schools, employment, and public accommodations, among other sweeping changes.

Today, Palos Verdes is ethnically diverse. Dozens of foreign languages are spoken on our campus. As a teacher of world history and cultures for over half a century there, I witnessed this transition and regard it as a major advancement in the community's acceptance of cultural diversity. It also enriched the quality of my classes.

While teaching in India, I had noticed that the Jesuits openly discussed their students' development. They also exchanged teaching ideas with one another at the dining table. This was a natural and spontaneous method of "team teaching." At Rolling Hills High, this kind of collegial cooperation was lacking, so I began quietly planning to change that.

Team-teaching collaborations often begin with friendships. I had made friends with another history teacher who taught the same subjects I did. His name was Willy and he was disabled. A childhood illness had left him with a severe limp and pain. He wore a large orthopedic boot. Willy sported a full black beard and wore his long hair tied in a ponytail, like others in the emerging 1967 counterculture. In contrast to the hippies, however, he always dressed neatly. His soft brown corduroy sports jacket with suede elbow patches and Ivy League knit ties were impeccable. He was fond of motor scooters and had traveled around Europe on his Vespa. Willy would circumvent the teachers' parking lot and ride his scooter up to his classroom door, where he parked it. It was the way Willy transcended his daily pain that made him remarkable. As a child, he had spent many difficult hours in hospital operating and recovery rooms. Often absent and behind at school, he spent his time at home learning on his own. Willy was a few years older than I and a fervent Catholic.

There was something about his enthusiasm and sense of humor that reminded me of Father Conneally at Loyola High. Whether it was ancient or medieval architecture, Renaissance or modern art, or history-making battles, Willy was completely engaged in his material. When he was explaining something at the blackboard and ran out of space, with chalk in hand he would continue writing on the brick wall next to the board. Students loved him for these eccentricities.

Every day Willy transformed his classroom into an exciting journey. He brought to life the moment legendary archeologist Howard Carter discovered Pharoah Tutankhamun's tomb. If the subject of study was World War I, you could almost hear the shells exploding and feel the numbing cold rain as you crouched in the muddy trenches. He painted remarkably vivid images with his energy, eloquence, and passion. Willy and I became close friends and frequently exchanged ideas about history, art, classical music, and the teaching profession.

In the spring of my first year, we learned that a newly built high school in Palos Verdes was looking for teachers to develop an innovative team-teaching, flexible-scheduling program. The new school would feature a fused history-English curriculum taught in a two-hour block in a modern multipurpose room capable of accommodating four classes at once. The creative possibilities were exhilarating. Willy and I quickly applied, were accepted, and transferred the following year.

I already knew that four strong cooperating teachers could achieve more than any single teacher working alone. I liked the idea of a fused curriculum. While the students were studying a specific historical period, they could also read the literature and analyze the art of that time.

At the new Miraleste High School, Willy and I taught along with English teachers Jerry, Susan, and later Olivia, in what was called the first Flex team. The Flex program became a team-teaching legend. Today, this setup still prevails at Peninsula High School. It is now named "The Block."

During that first year and for several years to follow, as a team of four, we were inspired by the creative freedom that this new method of teaching offered. If any team teacher came up with a new lesson idea, we would brainstorm it until it became a course of action. The first unit was the study of primitive cultures. We organized archaeological excavations in the hills behind our classrooms. Students formed into groups of primitive Paleolithic tribes and modern anthropologists. The tribes invented their culture and built, encased, and buried artifacts. The next day the anthropologists would dig up these artifacts, analyze them, and present their findings about this primitive, newly discovered culture. Tribes depicted their own unique cultural history and survival stories in drawing cave paintings, such as those in Lascaux, France. On the last day of the unit, the anthropologists would present their analyses and findings, and the primitive tribes would reveal their true identity and origin, and explain the meanings of their symbols.

The ancient Greece unit was always the most popular with students. Each of the four competing classes would organize their own ancient Greek city-state or *polis*. They would select their particular form of government. Then they would compete in various categories, i.e., art, architecture (scale-model building of temples), music, poetry, drama, and oratory. There were athletic competitions replicating the original Greek Olympics. These were held in the school football stadium and featured opening and closing ritualized ceremonies honoring the particular gods of each city-state. One year, a student brought his family's horses and a chariot he had built to school and raced around the school's track. The Flex Olympics became a school tradition, although chariot racing was deemed too risky.

In the Flex program, our classical music unit held a competition similar to the television show *Name That Tune*. In preparation, students would listen to our recommended list of classics by famous composers. We avoided obvious pieces like Beethoven's Fifth Symphony. Instead, we might list Haydn's Symphony no. 94 ("Surprise"), Brahms' Piano Quartet no. 1, Chopin's Nocturne in B-flat Minor, Rachmaninoff's Piano Concerto no. 2 in C Minor, or Aaron Copland's *Appalachian Spring*. Students competed in teams of two or three. When the music started playing, the teams would have a quick consultation. The first team to ring a bell and correctly "name that tune" would win. It made for a fun and exciting learning experience.

Other competitive programs went on throughout the year. Students seemed to be fully engaged by this method of teaching. Unfortunately, this kind of exciting creative learning would be difficult to implement in a high-ranking public school now, with the heavy emphasis on standardized testing and Advanced Placement courses. I'm happy to see there are still creative teachers in Palos Verdes, keeping up the "fun tradition." For example, Mark and Mike, two physics teachers at Peninsula High, are brilliant and innovative. Their students build cardboard boats for a contest and race the length of the huge swimming pool. This activity requires applying Archimedes' principle of buoyancy and calculating the weight of the object being placed in the water; it must be less than the weight of the water displaced in order for the boat to stay afloat.

Teaching Meditation

The first time I introduced meditation was in the early days at Miraleste in my Comparative Religion class. As a learn-by-doing experience, practicing Hindu or Buddhist meditation would be a great way for students to understand the basic concepts. The problem was to find a suitable quiet environment. Classrooms were often interrupted by phone calls, messengers, or announcements over the PA system. One day, I visited the newly built Miraleste Public Library, right next to campus. It had a large carpeted reading room that was perfect for meditation.

A few days later, I led my class of mostly seniors over to the new library. The students settled down on the thick carpet, many in the lotus position, which I had previously demonstrated in class. I dimmed the lights and instructed them to close their eyes and begin a process of Raja Yoga, later referred to as "self-realization."

Suddenly, the door opened and a school administrator asked, "Is this Mr. Mac's class?" School had been over for almost half an hour. My students had missed their buses, rides home, appointments, and sports practice. For the rest of the year we were known at Miraleste as "the class that disappeared." Like the Mayans, we simply vanished without a trace!

I had been reading about guided imagery. It was a type of self-hypnosis that had become popular in the early eighties. Gymnast Mary Lou Retton revealed that it helped her achieve a perfect 10 score in the 1984 Olympics. In her "mind's eye," she imagined performing her routine perfectly every day for months before the Olympics. Then, when it counted, she was able to slip effortlessly into a winning state of mind and perform flawlessly.

I decided to explore this concept and tacked on five minutes for a guided imagery exercise at the end of the regular meditation. About twenty students sat with me in a circle in the semi-darkness. I asked them to go inside their minds and find a very beautiful and quiet place, such as a deserted beach or forest. I asked them to imagine sitting alone for a few minutes, mindfully soaking in their surroundings. I said: "Now, think of a person who loves you, who wants to be with you, and imagine them joining you."

For the next fifteen or twenty seconds, I closed my eyes and prayerfully sent my love to each one of my students individually. When the bell rang, several students came running up to me, exclaiming: "Hey Mr. Mac, it was you. You came into my mind!"

Conflict with My New Principal

During my second and third year at Miraleste High, the Flex program remained popular and our "collective creativity" continued. Willy and I were making slideshows on the life of Beethoven and the themes of the French Revolution. This was during the late sixties and early seventies, when daily protests against the Vietnam War and later Watergate dominated the headlines. We pointed out similarities between earlier revolutions and the ongoing struggle between "haves" and "have-nots" in our own time. Our slideshows were also presented at other schools and churches in the community. Sometimes the liberal nature of these presentations would raise eyebrows and upset conservatives in the audience.

This soon reached the attention of our principal, Dr. Phillips. He looked, dressed, and spoke as someone who opposed any ideas that might be considered liberal. He had served in the Air Force during World War II, had a slight southern twang, and wore his blond hair in a military flattop.

On one occasion, I invited a young college student who was visiting from Yugoslavia to speak. His country had a Communist economy and was led by a dictator, Marshal Tito. The fact that we were having an actual "Commie" guest speaker while still engaged in the Cold War was exciting to our students. It made our principal nervous.

The guest speaker's name was simply "Barney." Several classes and their respective teachers joined mine in the school's multimedia room. After I introduced Barney, I sat down at a table facing the audience. I noticed Dr. Phillips had entered the room and taken a seat. He was furiously making notes on a large yellow legal pad.

Barney was a friendly and charismatic college kid. He answered a few of our students' innocuous questions like how American food compared to that in Yugoslavia. Then Dr. Phillips raised his hand and nervously introduced himself. "Good morning, Mr. Barney. I am the principal of this school. I had the honor and privilege of liberating your country from the Nazis during World War II. My question for you is this: If your Communist country is so wonderful, then why was your government forced to build a wall around it?" He pronounced "Communist" like "Comma-nist," as Senator Joseph McCarthy pronounced it in the 1950s.

Barney looked confused at first and then replied: "I'm sorry, sir, but there is no wall around our country. Perhaps you are thinking of the Soviet Union who rules over East Germany and built the Berlin Wall?" Our principal's ignorance was an embarrassment to himself, our students, and the faculty members in attendance. I could see the eyes of the students widen and the teachers shaking their heads in disbelief.

Kama Sutra Project

One day in my new Comparative Religion elective course at Miraleste, a couple of wacky, charismatic football stars came close to endangering my teaching career. They'd been assigned to make a slideshow presentation on a topic related to one or more of the world religions. They both had sheepish looks on their faces when they approached me to ask if they could do their presentation on the *Kama Sutra,* a Sanskrit text written thousands of years ago. It was the world's first erotic sex manual showing the various ways and positions in which the glorious gods of India made love. When I told them that I had read it, they seemed a bit disappointed. I cautioned them: "You do know Hindu culture views *kama* as one of the essential components of life. In other words, could you make Hindu gods and culture your primary focus, not sex?" They nodded and said they understood my point and would comply.

On the morning of their presentation there was a note in my mailbox from Dr. Phillips informing faculty members that he would be escorting members of the Western Association of Schools and Colleges (WASC) evaluation team for a preliminary look at our campus that day. I suddenly remembered that I had not yet completed my third year of teaching and did not have tenure. I began to panic. I needed to know just how graphic those slides on the Kama Sutra actually would be. Before class began, as they were setting up the slide projector, I demanded: "Look, tell me right now, do you have any slides that show graphic sex?" Simultaneously, one said "some" and the other said "most." I hatched a plan on the spot. "Listen, you can't show the sexy ones! During this period, Phillips is coming into our classroom with some people here to evaluate the school and me. Here's what you have to do: while I'm taking roll, get the other slide projector out, set it up, and load the slides with no sex. Be prepared to talk about those slides for as long as is needed, while Phillips and his visitors are here!" Wide-eyed, they nodded and went right to work. Although I knew them to be clever, I was still nervous. I had a vision of my boss walking into my classroom with the school evaluators while students were laughing and drooling over an ancient Indian "porn show."

They began their presentation. The principal and the evaluation team walked in halfway through the period. As I rose to greet them, the boys immediately turned off both projectors. One of the boys was from a Greek family and knew quite a bit about Greek mythology. As the visitors took their seats, he said:

"In conclusion, I think you can see now that the gods of India that we were just observing in the Hindu paintings were much like the gods of ancient Greece: Zeus, Hera, Athena, and even Aphrodite. They were one big, not always happy family, from generation to generation."

After the visitors left, I sat down at my desk, breathed a sigh of relief, and called the two students over. "Pretty good job, guys! Good 'clutch save' at the end. I especially liked your comparison of India's gods to the gods of the Greeks."

After high school, one of those same students played football at the University of Southern California, as did his brother. Several years later, the brothers opened a popular Greek restaurant in San Pedro. Over the years I taught most of their children and visited their tavern every so often. Occasionally I would tell one of their kids how their father and uncle almost cost me my teaching career. Later, Petros, one of their sons, was also my student. He too played football at USC. Today he is a well-known radio and television sports personality.

Meditation at Peninsula High

By 1990, the student population in Palos Verdes had decreased. The school district decided to consolidate all three area high schools into one mega-school named Peninsula. Its location was on the site of Rolling Hills High where I first taught in Palos Verdes. These seismic reductions in personnel predictably created territorial battles among teachers, department chairs, and administrators.

The school board wisely chose Kelly Johnson as the first principal of this new high school. We'd been friends since he started out working as a custodian at Rolling Hills High. When he finished his education and earned his teaching credentials, he became a history teacher in my department at Miraleste.

Kelly was a charismatic person with outstanding people skills and good common sense.

I was the chair of the social sciences department at Miraleste and interviewed for the same position at Peninsula. The other two department chairs were my competitors for the position. I was the last of the three interviewed by Kelly and the other administrators. He began by saying: "Now Jim, I've known you for a long time and I know you to be a 'gentle man.' Do you think if you were the department chair, you could fire a teacher?" After a short pause, I answered: "No, I couldn't. My pay grade isn't high enough to compensate me for staying awake all night worrying about it. Kelly, isn't that why your salary is substantially more than mine? On the other hand, I would support the decision that you had to make. I would give you valid, reliable information on the teacher's curriculum and performance." He looked at the other staff members that were seated around our large table. With a wide smile, he said: "Well, I think we just found our new social studies department chair for Peninsula High School." They applauded me.

Kelly was an exceptional administrator who made wise personnel decisions. One of his best choices was Mitzi Cress. He appointed her as head of the counseling department. A few years later she became associate principal at Peninsula and then principal after Kelly retired. As a teenager, Mitzi had been my student in the original Flex program at Miraleste. Now, at Peninsula High, she would be my last principal and lifelong friend. Like Kelly, Mitzi had excellent leadership skills. During her seven-year tenure, our school's state testing scores were always among the top in the state and, according to *U.S. News and World Report,* the nation's top one hundred.

At Peninsula, I taught World History, Advanced Placement European History, and Comparative Religion. I continued to use the meditation lesson when we studied Hinduism, the Yogas of India, and Buddhism.

One day Principal Kelly walked toward me at lunch with a concerned look on his face. "Jimmy, your kids' parents really lit up my switchboard this morning. They were worried about your meditation lesson." I paused, cleared my throat, and in my best Indian accent, replied: "Vell, oh let me see, perhaps ve could go inside my ashram, light a few candles, and then do a little meditating together. That vould calm us down before ve talk, no?" Kelly began to laugh. Besides having a sense of humor, he always went with his solid instincts on what was best for the students. Meditation remained a part of the school tradition. Today it is what is called the school's "mindfulness program." Students practice meditation to relieve their stress, especially during final exams week.

Jeff and Healing Power

A new freshman transfer student from Texas enrolled in my history class. It was obvious that he was a burn victim. His entire body was a mass of scar tissue. Portions of his face were bright red and purple. He wore black netting over his neck and arms down to his hands. His condition was so severe that it was difficult to look at him. It saddened me to see his classmates avert their eyes in shock. Jeff didn't participate in class discussions for the first month or so until one morning when I was lecturing on the ancient Greek Battle of Marathon. I was theatrically brandishing an antique sword that a student had gifted me, describing flying spears and burning arrows raining down on warriors. "We're talking pain here, suffering, death!" Suddenly from the back of the room, I heard Jeff say: "I can relate to that!" The entire class was startled to hear him speak, including me.

When we studied India, I taught a class on meditation. To add to the experience, I incorporated Indian sitar music by Ravi Shankar that I played on a cassette tape. The students sat in a semicircle on the carpet in the library. The school bell rang just as we finished. All the students left, except Jeff. I noticed he was crying, and I sat near him and asked him if he was okay. He wiped his tears and said: "Sure, Mr. Mac. It's because I'm happy. This is the first time since my accident that I forgot my pain. I didn't feel it for almost the whole time we were meditating. Can I borrow your tape?" "Yes, of course," I said. "Keep it. I'll get another one."

Several weeks later, I held a class discussion about current events in the news. This is what teachers sometimes call a "sponge activity," meaning a way to use remaining class time productively. Students would bring in an article from a newspaper or magazine, along with several discussion questions regarding the content. They would receive extra credit points if they contributed their own opinions during the discussion.

Just before the class began, Jeff came up to my desk and asked to do a current event talk about his accident. I was surprised but gave him permission. He came up to the front of the room and said: "You guys don't really know me. My name is Jeff. I moved here last summer from Texas to live with my dad. It was right after I had an accident at my mom's house. I was playing in the yard with some matches and a can of gasoline. It blew up in my face. Mom ran out when she heard me screaming. She thought I was going to die. The pain was so bad sometimes I wished I had. The reason I look so weird now and wear these black nets all over my body is that most of my skin has been grafted. My doctors say this will help my skin to grow back the right way."

Humanity, curiosity, and innate compassion emerged naturally from Jeff's teenage classmates. They began asking him the questions they had wondered about but been afraid to ask: "Were your parents mad at you?" "What was it like to almost die?" "How long were you in the hospital?" I was proud of their openness.

After that, Jeff was accepted and seemed comfortable with his classmates. He no longer hid behind his scarred face and the netting that covered his body. He participated in discussions and became a valuable addition to the class. I've never forgotten the phenomenal courage it must have taken Jeff to tell his story to his peers that day. It was my privilege to have been his teacher.

Scars of War

Schools sometimes get caught up in the educational "flavor of the year." For a couple of years, our flavor was the Pacific Rim Program. I joined the program because I liked the opportunity to team teach with some excellent colleagues. There were guest speakers, field trips to various parts of the city, and perks like free night classes at UCLA on Asian history and culture. Teachers like me who volunteered for the program were quite naïve at the beginning. Before a field trip with our students to Chinatown in Los Angeles, we invited a teacher to come to our classes and instruct us for several weeks in basic Mandarin. On the day our bus arrived in Chinatown, we found out our Mandarin lessons were useless because the main language spoken there is Cantonese.

On one occasion, we toured the downtown Los Angeles area known as Little Tokyo. The tour included a visit to a Zen Buddhist temple. Our tour guide was a Japanese monk. As he was explaining features of his temple, I suddenly heard the sound of rock music coming from the headphones of one of my students, who was carrying a small portable cassette player. I glared at him and motioned for him to take his headphones off and follow me outside.

I taught my students to show the utmost respect for people of other cultures and particularly their religion. What surprised me was that my rude student was Asian of Korean descent. Once outside, I got in this kid's face. "What's the matter with you?" His attitude was contentious and he responded in anger. "I hate the effin' Japanese, their monks, and their Buddhist temples!" "Then you picked the wrong tour," I said sternly. "This was voluntary! You should have stayed home." Then I paused. What was behind his attitude? I asked him why he hated the Japanese. "Because my grandparents told me about what they did in the war when they invaded Korea!" he replied angrily. "They raped and made prostitutes of the Korean women and killed most of the men."

I couldn't resist pursuing his remarks. "So you think that this Buddhist monk was a soldier in the Japanese army?" The kid was upset and emotional. "I don't know, Mr. Mac. Leave me alone!" My reply was firm. "You can be alone while you have after-school campus cleanup duty every day next week!" I confiscated his cassette and headphones and escorted him back inside. For the rest of the tour he remained sullen but silent. For a minute, I wished I were Clyde back in my days at Loyola High. I would have assigned him a five-hundred-word essay on "How Prejudice Is Learned."

Another Traumatic Experience

Once during the eighties when school was on summer break, I decided to fulfill one of my New Year's resolutions. I wanted to learn more about meditation and practice it. I preferred a nonreligious setting. Since I was already teaching Comparative Religion, I didn't want so much to learn more religious practices as go more in depth into the experience of meditation itself. After researching different local meditation groups, I found that the dry-docked *Queen Mary* had been retrofitted into a hotel in Long Beach Harbor. It was offering free group meditation every Sunday evening. The leader of the meditation group was the ship's retired captain. He was an elderly man with a British accent, a kind face, an affable personality, and a full white beard. He reminded me of the actor Edmund Gwenn who played Santa Claus in the movie classic *Miracle on 34th Street*.

Every Sunday evening from 7:30 to 8:30 p.m., the captain would host silent nondenominational meditation services in his large cabin. Usually about eight to ten people would attend. Without much socializing beforehand, we would sit silently on comfortable couches for an hour. The session began when the captain dimmed the lights about halfway down.

I went to the first two Sunday sessions in June and then stopped going. It had been twenty years since the robbery at gunpoint on Thanksgiving morning shortly after returning from India. Now I had another extremely traumatic, life-threatening experience.

I'd paid a visit one evening to a friend in Culver City. Afterward, I left his condo and walked out onto the street. In the semidarkness, I saw two men approaching me. I had an instinctive sickening feeling of danger. I could see that the one closest to me was wielding a knife with a long blade. The other guy was clenching what looked like a club hammer in one fist. His other was opening and closing rhythmically.

I yelled out to them: "Look, you guys can have whatever I've got, just don't hurt me!" My hands shook as I emptied my pockets and placed my wallet and wristwatch on the ground. One of them snarled: "No, man, we want *you!*" The man with the hammer was rapidly approaching. Guttural growls were coming from his throat. I thought he might have been high on angel dust, a potent and popular street drug at the time. Pure hatred and rage contorted his face.

Suddenly and miraculously, a car turned the corner. Its headlights pointed directly at us. That was the break I needed. My heart was pounding furiously as I sprinted across the street and around the side of an apartment building. I cautiously looked back and saw them slowly pick up my belongings. They didn't bother to come after me. I found my way back to my friend's condo and he drove me home. I was worried because the assailants had my driver's license with my address, as well as the keys to my house, so I requested a Redondo Beach police watch for the next several weeks.

I was traumatized and unable to concentrate, study, or sleep. I had vivid and violent dreams and would wake up sweating, my bedsheets in knots. When I left my apartment, my brain functioned like radar, searching all around me for any sign of potential danger. This continued for almost three weeks. Any and all creative projects and social relationships were on hold.

Finally, one Sunday evening, I decided to drive to Long Beach and rejoin the meditation group on the *Queen Mary*. Arriving slightly early, I told the captain about nearly being murdered in Culver City and how the shock of that experience was severe and persistent, leaving me unable to function. Soon the lights were dimmed and the meditation session began, as usual. But this time, at the end of the hour, the captain turned the dimmed lights up slightly and softly said to the group: "Our friend Jim has recently had an extremely traumatic experience. Could you now turn toward him and quietly send him the loving energy you have just received from this meditation experience?"

Over the next few minutes, an amazing thing happened. The fear and mistrust that had taken over me began evaporating from my chest, almost like steam rising from hot asphalt. It was replaced by a feeling of peace. The session was life-changing. Afterward, a couple of people came over and hugged me as they were leaving. Few, if any, words were spoken. I felt energized and drove home without the cloud of depressive negative feelings that had plagued me and rendered me unproductive. I slept peacefully that night for the first time in weeks and I was finally able to put the terrible experience behind me.

My Fifteen Minutes

Over years of teaching Comparative Religion, I've introduced different types of meditation, particularly those originating from the Eastern tradition, to my students. Initially, teaching about Hindu yoga and Zen meditation was controversial in the public high school setting. There was a suspicion that meditation was a religious practice, perhaps even religious indoctrination, instead of a technique for relaxation.

In May 2001, the need for global understanding and religious tolerance became more of a priority in Social Studies. The nuclear tension between India and Pakistan and the Palestinean/Israeli conflict was increasingly concerning around the world. On October 18, 2000, two suicide bombers on a small boat near the USS *Cole* detonated several hundred pounds of explosives. The blast tore a hole in the ship, killing seventeen sailors and injuring thirty-nine others. Al-Qaeda claimed responsibility for the attack against the United States.

As a result of this increased awareness from the media, there was a growing debate on whether religion could or should be taught in the public schools. The PBS show *NewsHour with Jim Lehrer* decided to feature this subject in a segment that would coincide with the release of a document called *A Teacher's Guide to Religion in the Public Schools.*

Consequently, the show's producers searched to find teachers who were teaching religion in public schools. They found only two of us: an intermediate school teacher in Concord, California, and me. The *NewsHour* reporting team came to our school for an entire day to videotape my Comparative Religion class and to personally interview my students and me, as well as my guest speaker, Reverend Kusala, a Los Angeles-based Buddhist monk in the Vietnamese tradition, who was giving a demonstration to my students about how he meditates.

At lunchtime, students in our school's Muslim Club, which I sponsored, were televised lying on the classroom floor, prostrate in prayer facing toward Mecca. A non-Muslim girl said because of the class, she now understood the reason why many Muslim girls choose to wear a veil and what it means to them. Another student revealed that the class helped him to better comprehend the mentality of Christian fundamentalists, even though he was not one himself. The PBS TV crew culminated their fifteen-minute documentary by going to the home of a Catholic student's parents and interviewing them about their views of the class. Their comments were favorable.

I was criticized on national television by Charles Haynes, Senior Scholar at The First Amendment Center at Vanderbuilt University in Nashville, Tennessee. Along with others, he had contributed to *A Teacher's Guide to Religion in the Public Schools*. He suggested that despite my experience, I needed guidance on how to properly teach religion. Also, he felt that my meditation class was "inappropriate." He added: "Just because a Buddhist monk says it's okay doesn't mean it is. You wouldn't want students to role-play the Catholic Mass and Communion, would you?"

His comparison of meditation to the Catholic Mass was ridiculous to me. This disagreement led to an online debate between the two of us on the PBS site. My position was that meditation can always be a secular activity. As I said in the television interview: "This is a school, not a church. I'm here to teach, not preach. My job is to help the students think. I don't advocate any one particular religion, but I do try to broaden their understanding of all the major religions of the world." That year I was honored with the "Educator of the Year" award in Palos Verdes. I was proud to have pioneered a program at Peninsula High that promoted religious tolerance and understanding among our students of diverse ethnicities and religious backgrounds.

A few years later, some of the magic dust still lingered. We learned that our school was to be visited by the Secretary of Education of Venezuela. His advisors chose Peninsula High out of all the other high schools in the United States because they had seen me on PBS. They wanted to learn how we were able to integrate so many students of different faiths into the same school successfully.

The Education Minister arrived on our campus in a limousine driven by a State Department official who would serve as his interpreter. They were given a tour of the campus. Photographers from the local newspapers covered the event. The centerpiece of the visit was to observe my Comparative Religion class. My lesson plan was to hold an open discussion among the students regarding the existence of God and the pros and cons of religion. The fact that they were being videotaped for national television didn't intimidate them. From time to time, the interpreter would translate for the Minister.

During the middle of the program, Principal Kelly came in and walked up to the front of the class. He pointed to me and in a loud voice said to the entire group: "This man is a Communist!" My students and I burst out laughing. I noticed the interpreter speaking rapidly in the ear of the Minister.

At that time, Venezuela was controlled by a Communist dictator, Hugo Chávez, who had very recently proclaimed to the United Nations General Assembly in New York about President George Bush, who had spoken there the previous day: "Yesterday, the devil came here . . . and it smells of sulfur still today!"

Principal Kelly posed for photos and then left. I could see that the Minister was very eager to speak to me. He had a broad smile on his face. I thought it was because he liked Kelly's bold characterization of my political views. The translator asked: "Are you really a Communist?" I replied: "No. However, I have often favored socialist governments that help the poor and unfortunate. I favor some social welfare programs that helped my father survive the Great Depression here in the 1930s, programs like our President Franklin Roosevelt initiated during those years, or ones like Scandinavia, Canada, and Australia currently have."

The Minister huddled again with his interpreter. "Why did your principal, Señor Kelly, state that you were a Communist?" I said: "Mr. Johnson enjoys humor. When he was a young teacher, he knew I was liberal and enjoyed teasing me by calling me a 'Commie bastard.' I would respond by calling him a 'Fascist pig.'" They began laughing. I continued: "Another important reason is that Mr. Johnson is also a history teacher. He knows that 'Communist' is a controversial word in our society. So if he labels me a 'Communist,' it will make our students wonder, 'what is a Communist?' It's an excellent teaching technique." They nodded their heads in approval and said "Bueno!"

Family Secret Revealed

One evening in the late 1980s, I enjoyed delicious barbecue ribs at the Montgomery Inn in Cincinnati. I dined with my brother Phil and his wife Joan. Over coffee, Phil suddenly became serious. "Jim, over the years, you have asked me so many questions about our family background, I think I should tell you something you don't know. The reason I don't look much like you, John, and Mary is because I had a different father. Mom is my real mother, but Dad is not my biological father. We were told that story to protect Mom's reputation because she gave birth to me out of wedlock. She placed me in an orphanage in Arizona that was run by nuns. That's where I was adopted by Dad and his first wife, Mercedes. When Mercedes died, Dad returned to the orphanage where I was adopted because he wasn't sure he was able to care for me. The nuns got in touch with Mom in Kansas. She came out to see me and during that time, she met Dad . . . and within a year they were married."

I asked Phil when and how he found out this information. He explained: "I learned this from Father John when I was a teenager. He felt obligated to tell me because I had a crush on Mom's niece Edna. Because of what I had previously been told, I didn't know that Edna actually was my first cousin. Father John asked me to promise before God that I would never speak of this while Mom was alive." Phil's eyes welled up with tears. This was a major catharsis for him. Sitting next to me was Joan, his wife of twenty-five years. We were both shocked to hear this truth for the first time. Phil was actually my half-brother.

Mary, Father Tom, and Notre Dame

My sister Mary married Ed during the spring semester of her senior year in college. He was an officer in the United States Air Force. Ed was a brilliant man with a degree in economics from Loyola University. They settled in Santa Barbara when their kids were young. A few years later, Ed was hired by General Electric to represent their interests in the Middle East and they moved to London. Meanwhile, their eldest son attended the University of Notre Dame in South Bend, Indiana. Their older two daughters attended St. Mary's, a nearby Catholic women's college.

The day before Thanksgiving, tragedy struck their family. As Mary and Ed were driving in the outskirts of Cambridge, Ed felt extreme pain in his head. He pulled over to the side of the road where he suffered a cerebral hemorrhage. Mary was able to flag down a couple who drove her to a nearby restaurant where she phoned for help. The paramedics arrived and took them to the hospital. Ed was pronounced dead a day later.

Mary showed tremendous strength during that time of crisis and sorrow. She knew she had to function wisely and still deal with her own shock and grief as well as the grief of her children. She was surprised to find that Ed had made complicated business deals all over the world. She had to determine whom she could trust to help make important decisions regarding her finances at home and those investments Ed had made.

The University of Notre Dame, run by the Congregation of Holy Cross, gently cradled Mary's children during this tragic time. The university's prominent president, Father Ted Hesburgh, CSC. personally notified the children of their father's death. Father Tom Tallarida, the priest in charge of their son's dorm, took it upon himself to play a fatherly role and looked after the entire grief-stricken family. He gave them wise counsel, abiding love, and compassion.

I got to know Father Tom on several visits to South Bend. At first the friendship was pragmatic on my part. Since high school, I had wanted to play football for the "Fighting Irish." I particularly respected the values of the university that were reflected by the athletes on the team. Tickets to a Notre Dame home game were very difficult to obtain. Now, through my sister's connection to the school and my relationship with Father Tom, I had access to tickets. I invited three of my Loyola friends—attorney Ron, LAPD Sgt. Dave, and Fernando—to a Notre Dame home game against Stanford.

It was a crisp fall Saturday as we arrived on the campus. My friends were in a jovial mood and their teasing me bordered on childish. They were aware of the effort Father Tom had put into obtaining our tickets but they were playfully "yanking my chain" by pretending they didn't care that much. We were about to have breakfast with Father Tom and the other priests and afterward he would give us our tickets. I warned them to be on their best behavior. "Look, you guys, you'd better show some respect this morning or I'll kick your asses. I'm not afraid of the LAPD or the California Attorney General's Office!" My sternness caused even more laughter and teasing.

It's been said that there is no sight like the Notre Dame campus on a fall Saturday game day. The campus was ablaze with gold and scarlet from the leaves of maple trees and green-and-gold woolen sweaters. The air was filled with the mouthwatering odor of barbecuing brats on the many grills. My buddies were dragging their heels. They wanted to admire the scenery, visit the famous grotto, and ask pretty coeds for directions. The band music in the distance and the majestic architecture all around us enriched the experience. I barked at them to focus. I knew that Father Tom would be waiting on his porch at Corby Hall with the tickets. My friends finally stepped up their pace. The porch was packed with Father Tom's friends and former students with their wives and children. Not surprisingly, soon after meeting him, my Jesuit-educated Loyola friends became equally in awe of his intelligence and compassion. He was a brilliant, beloved, and humble priest.

I had asked my nephew Mike, who was by then an alumnus, if there were any unique tourist spots we should see in South Bend. He quickly replied: "Let Father Tom take you to dinner at Bruno's. That's where he took me almost every week after my dad died. The food and atmosphere are great!"

I put in my request to Father Tom and after the game, he drove us there to dinner. There was nothing particularly impressive about the outside of this old, slightly rundown, family-owned Italian restaurant, except for the parking lot which was jammed with cars. When we entered, there was standing room only with hungry football fans eagerly waiting for a table. It was obvious there would be an incredibly long wait before we would be seated. Like everyone there, we were tired, hungry, and thirsty from the long day.

I was pleasantly surprised when we were greeted by an enthusiastic waiter who led us to a large reserved table in the back room of the restaurant. A platter of cheeses, olives, and salami was placed in the center of our table, along with a big pitcher of ice-cold beer. Judging from how attentive our waiter was, Father Tom was somewhat of a celebrity. When the tray was passed around the table, I was caught up in the fact that Notre Dame had won the game and the joy of the moment. Without thinking about propriety, I grabbed a handful of salami and wolfed it down with the warm bread they provided. Nothing was said until on the way back to our hotel, the guys ribbed me:

"What happened to the salami?" They chided me about my sins of greed and gluttony. I did a mafioso impression and retorted, "I got ya salami for ya!" The following Christmas, I sent each guy a large salami as a remembrance of our wonderful experience together.

Father Tom had helped inspire the popularity of Bruno's Restaurant decades earlier. One day, two women of Italian descent from the town of South Bend wanted to go to confession and be heard by a priest who spoke Italian. Someone suggested Father Tom, who was of Italian descent and a professor at Notre Dame. The women knocked on the front door of Corby Hall, where he resided. He heard their confessions and a week later they returned with several dishes of delicious Italian cuisine to thank him.

Father Tom encouraged the football team to eat at Bruno's and raved about their outstanding menu. There were not many Italian restaurants then. The restaurant's fame grew over the years as people learned that the Notre Dame football team and its recruits frequently dined there. They were attracted by the possibility they might mingle with the players. Bruno's became a tradition and Notre Dame fans still flock there.

On Sunday morning, before returning to Chicago to fly back to Los Angeles, my irreverent friends became "altar boys." We attended Mass in the Basilica of Our Lady of Notre Dame. Ron indicated he was going to confession. Dave whispered: "Ron, if you start confessing all your sins, we won't make it to O'Hare Airport before the plane leaves."

I wanted to speak to Father Tom privately. I found him in his office. "What's on your mind, Jim?" he asked. "Father, there's something I've always wondered about since I was a kid. It's the Sacred Heart of Jesus. My mother was devoted to Him. I used to hand out leaflets at church for her every week. There was a picture of flames coming out of the heart of Jesus. What was that about?"

Father Tom replied with a simple personal metaphor. "Jim, your sister Mary has told me that you are a tremendous teacher. To be one, you have to have something burning inside you that won't let you stop loving and caring about your students." He continued: "Jesus was like that, except that His love encompassed all the people in the world and everyone who has ever lived and will live in the future. He gave his life for us because of that incredible love." When we said goodbye to Father Tom that day, my Loyola High friends and I knelt at his feet to receive his priestly blessing.

As we were driving through the streets of South Chicago toward the airport, I couldn't help but notice we were in a dangerous-looking area. Rundown liquor stores were on almost every corner. Homeless people were slogging along on uneven slabs of sidewalk, their sockless feet in shoes about to fall off. They were pushing rusty shopping carts filled with empty beer and soda cans along with their life's belongings. Some were crouched, rocking back and forth, holding paper bags containing a bottle of cheap wine to help deaden the hardness of street life. Every building, street sign, and delivery truck was covered with graffiti. I felt uneasy having to stop at a red light. On the corner of the crosswalk, two tough-looking guys with gang tattoos on their shaven heads stared at us with brazen curiosity. We definitely didn't fit in. Dave, our LAPD police officer, was driving. "Dave, are you 'packing heat'?" He smiled. "No need to. We're protected. We just went to confession this morning!"

Holocaust Survivors

A very effective way to make history real for students was to invite guest speakers. These "primary sources" revealed personal testimony of their experiences, leaving far more powerful impressions than reading accounts from textbooks or watching a film.

The most memorable and spellbinding of all were Holocaust survivors. During the decades I was chair of the History Department, the visit of the survivors was an annual event carefully planned to coincide with our study of World War II. Every year I reserved the school auditorium for six hour-long periods throughout the school day. I would invite six Holocaust survivors. Each speaker would have almost a full hour to tell their harrowing story. I made personal contact with these unique individuals through Jewish friends or the Simon Wiesenthal Center in Los Angeles. Although it was painful to relive their horrific memories, every survivor felt it was important. Many believed they owed the retelling of their experiences to future generations on behalf of those who did not survive.

Sometimes they weren't able to detach themselves from the tragic narrative they had recounted earlier to the students that day. As I drove her home, one elderly woman couldn't stop weeping over her memory of watching a Nazi guard grab a crying baby from her mother's arms and smash her head against a brick wall. Another revealed that whenever she saw a dog, particularly one without a leash, she experienced the same terror she felt as a child running to escape attack from the Gestapo's German shepherds.

A Holocaust survivor named Bob escaped from the Warsaw Ghetto by hiding with his younger brother under his mother's long skirt. One afternoon, he witnessed twelve thousand people murdered in a cemetery by a firing squad of Nazi soldiers. He was forced to watch and wait, believing it would soon be his turn to die and be thrown into the same huge ditch as the others. He was fortunate that day because at dusk the soldiers grew tired and let the remaining survivors go home.

Another time, his quick-thinking grandmother saved Bob and his brother from the Gestapo by cleverly hiding the boys in a closet and piling fresh pine logs in front of the door to throw off the dogs' scent. At age six, lonely and frightened, Bob hid for a month in a chicken coop on a remote farm. A benevolent Polish couple gave him bread and water. He ate raw chicken eggs to survive. He told my students that sympathetic non-Jewish people who helped Jews like him to survive were now called "The Righteous."

Bob was put in a boxcar headed for Auschwitz. At some point, while the train was temporarily paused, he jumped out and unlocked the boxcar hitch. When the train pulled away, the boxcar was left behind and dozens of prisoners escaped.

Of all the survivors to give testimony, one stands out to me in particular. His name was Mel. He described the morning of September 1, 1939, when Hitler violated the Munich Agreement by invading Poland. That morning, Mel's father died of a heart attack. A few days later, Mel's little town was overrun by German soldiers. A week later, as young Mel was returning from a friend's birthday party, Nazi soldiers caught him, dragged him to the top of a church tower, and threw him off, simply for their entertainment. He could hear them laughing as he was hurtling down.

Mel was severely injured. Ironically, this act of cruelty saved his life. He was taken to the town hospital. That saved him from the Gestapo, who were going house to house rounding up every Jew, including his mother and teenage sister.

After being released from the hospital, Mel moved to a Polish city, hoping it would be safer. There, he was quickly identified as a Jew. Fortunately, instead of being sent to a camp, he was sent to work in a weapons factory. One day the factory was attacked by Allied bombers. A shard of flying glass hit Mel directly in his right eye. He was taken to Therezienstadt, the Nazi's showpiece camp. There, the Nazis took public relations photos depicting happy Jewish prisoners in recreation facilities, singing, dancing, and playing musical instruments. This propaganda was made to appease the human rights rules of the Geneva Conventions.

While in that hospital, without the benefit of anesthetics, German doctors removed Mel's damaged eye and replaced it with one made of glass.

Mel shocked, charmed, and completely mesmerized the students with his stories. He told us that as the Allies were closing in on their camp to free the prisoners, the sound of approaching gunfire was audible. All the prisoners were gathered together to stand at attention. A speech from the Nazi Commandant gave them further horror. "Listen, you Jews, don't get too happy about being liberated. When our enemies arrive, which will be soon, we are going to blow up this entire camp with all of you in it!" Soon, tons of bombs exploded, killing many. Somehow Mel survived that, too. Three weeks later, he woke up in an Allied hospital, describing it as something akin to an out-of-body experience. He opened his eyes to the brilliant, gleaming white lights of the hospital room and saw a vase of flowers on the nightstand. He thought: "I must have died and now I'm in another world." Then he saw something even more wonderful. His mother was standing by his bedside. She bent down and kissed him. She had survived. Sadly, his teenage sister had perished in this incomprehensible human tragedy.

Mel always showed my students his identification number tattooed on his left arm. He told us the needles that injected the dye into the skin were never cleaned from prisoner to prisoner, often resulting in infections and disease.

Despite Mel's gruesome experiences, he maintained a wonderful sense of humor. One day, as I escorted him around our campus, we walked through an area under construction where the cement sidewalk was severely cracked. I cautioned him. "You have to be really careful here. Keep both eyes peeled by looking down and looking ahead so you don't fall." He laughed. "Should my glass eye look down or ahead?"

The story of how Mel met his American wife takes the concept of kismet to another level. Seeing her at a party, he was immediately attracted to her and they talked at length. At the end of the evening, he asked her for her phone number. When he didn't make a point to write it down, she asked him why. "I don't need to," Mel said. He rolled up his shirt sleeve to reveal that her Beverly Hills phone number was the same (minus the area code) as the tattoo on his arm.

As the years went by, I would always make a point to pick Mel up at his house so I could have a chance to talk with him personally. I felt being with Mel was my special reward for all the work of organizing those six different Holocaust speaker assemblies. Sometimes he would tell me stories that could never be told in his lecture to the students. For example, before leaving for America, Mel lived temporarily in West Berlin, where he had a brief intimate affair with an attractive German woman. One morning after they had spent the night together, not knowing Mel was Jewish, she revealed her intense feelings of anti-Semitism. Mel's closing goodbye line was, "It's too bad about your dislike of Jews. Now you've got a little something Jewish inside you."

World Wars

As I write, today is the one hundredth anniversary of the original Armistice Day on November 11, 1918, marking the end of the Great War, said to be the war to end all wars. However, another even more devastating war followed twenty years later. Now mankind possesses the means of destroying all life and there are those who would probably do it if they could.

As a student of history, I believe World War I was the pivotal downward turn for human civilization in the twentieth century. As Barbara Tuchman pointed out in her book *The Guns of*

August, this was the world's first modern global war and a war that did not have to happen. Fortunately, John F. Kennedy had read that book before he faced the Cuban Missile Crisis of 1962.

When teaching World War I, I used the acronym "MANIA" to analyze the war's primary causes: Militarism, Armaments, Nationalism, Imperialism, and Assassination. The first four were all temporary boons for big business. The last was an isolated incident but effective in starting the war by means of a nationalistic chain reaction. After Franz Ferdinand, the nephew of the Austrian emperor, was assassinated, the alliance system made it virtually impossible for the European powers to escape total war.

The same mercenary incentives remain among the large and small nations of the world today. The emoluments of wealth and status continue to influence the seats of power. Machiavellian principles, such as "the end justifies the means," are still considered wise by modern dictators. In the past, trade wars have often led to real wars. World War II and the Japanese attack on Pearl Harbor come to mind. During the 1930s, economic relations between Japan and the US were on an upward trajectory despite concern over Japan's ambition to become a major global power. Japan was dependent on imported oil and gasoline for its military. The US supplied eighty percent of that need. Japan was facing the problem of insufficient natural resources.

In retaliation for the Japanese occupation of key airfields in Indochina and subsequent agreement with Nazi-occupied Vichy France, Franklin Roosevelt froze all Japanese assets in the US and established an embargo on oil and gasoline exports to Japan. Britain and the Dutch East Indies followed suit. As a result, Japan lost three-fourths of its overseas trade and most of its oil imports. Now Japan's dilemma was to either back off its control in oil-rich Southeast Asia, Korea, and China, hoping the embargo would be lifted, or continue its aggression. Japan went ahead with its ambitious plan and attempted to sink our Pacific fleet in Hawaii to prevent US interference.

Fortunately, all three of the US Pacific fleet's aircraft carriers were away from Pearl Harbor on the day of the attack. There has been speculation over the years, but no solid evidence has been found to support the theory that Roosevelt knew of the impending attack. Whether it was planned or just good luck that our aircraft carriers were out at sea on routine maneuvers on December 7, 1941, we may never know for certain.

My cousin Sammy was at least twenty years my senior. When I was growing up, he was in the Navy and would visit our home when he was stationed in San Diego. He would occasionally tell some interesting stories about his war experiences. He never talked about the gory ones. I think they must have been too painful so he kept those down deep inside. Mom said that when Sammy returned home, he had nightmares about the war.

I remember one of his stories in particular. On December 7th, 1941, Sammy was serving as an ensign in the Navy and stationed at Pearl Harbor. It was the morning the Imperial Japanese Air Force surprised the United States fleet with an all-out attack. After sinking much of our fleet anchored in the harbor, they attacked our airplanes that were grounded on the airfields. Our sailors and soldiers began firing rifles and machine guns at the enemy planes as they strafed our airfield.

A Japanese plane was hit and crashed into a nearby hill. Sammy was the duty officer in charge of the squadron that was ordered to inspect the enemy aircraft. He told us that the plane was burning as they approached it. As soon as they doused the flames with an extinguisher, he walked up to the still-smoldering cockpit. He could see that the pilot was dead. He noticed the plane's radio, reached in, and pulled out a tube. To his surprise, upon close inspection, he could read the words on it: "Made in Camden, New Jersey, USA."

Atomic Bomb

We know that the early Greek philosophers were also the first scientists. Democritus postulated twenty-five hundred years ago that matter is ultimately composed of tiny invisible and indestructible particles that he called "atoms." He reasoned that atoms were in constant motion in a void, and sometimes collided. His ideas were philosophical; at that time there were no scientific tools to test this.

In the early twentieth century, legendary Nobel laureates Albert Einstein and Enrico Fermi advanced our understanding of physics. It was discovered that the atom was much more than a theoretical concept. It could be split, creating a nuclear fission chain reaction, releasing tremendous amounts of energy.

The story of how the atomic bomb came to be has fascinated me throughout my life. Naturally, I had no idea what it was as a four-year-old child in 1945 when the bomb ended World War II. I do remember sensing the enormity of the event because the image of my parents cheering and dancing in our living room still remains. I remember my mother singing over and over, "The boys are coming home, the boys are coming home!" while laughing through tears of joy.

I was reminded of it again in college during the Cuban missile crisis. By 1962, nuclear weapons possessed the power to destroy life on earth. Unfortunately, governments don't have the trust, political will, negotiating skills, or moral courage to figure out a way to end this threat of nuclear war forever. Even more than climate change, this is the greatest threat to the future of humanity.

My history, religion, and philosophy students have debated the morality of sacrificing hundreds of thousands of innocent civilian lives to end World War II. I still ponder the enormity of the decisions made by Roosevelt and Truman and what they meant (and still mean) for the destiny of the human race.

One warm, sunny day several years ago, I drove to visit my brother John in San Marino. He decided to give me a tour of the CalTech campus. From the car, I noticed an old brick building on campus that resembled a typical two-story home. There was a sign over the front door: The Albert Einstein Museum. I asked John if we could stop and take a look inside. The walls of the main floor were covered with framed photos, plaques, awards, and exhibits about Einstein. A placard near the stairway leading to the basement read "Archives." We descended into a very large room. Its four walls were entirely lined with large, black, heavy-duty fireproof filing cabinets. Inside were over five thousand of Einstein's transcribed and translated scientific and popular writings, drafts, lecture notes, and diaries from 1879 to 1923.

The secretary greeted us and asked if there were any documents we wished to see. A question arose in my mind. "Do you think you might be able to find the letter from Albert Einstein to President Franklin D. Roosevelt about the military use of atomic power?" "We'll try," she responded quickly and politely. She asked when I thought it was written. My estimation was sometime in the late 1930s.

She immediately began researching the information I had given her. After a few minutes, she rose from her desk, walked over to one of the filing cabinets, and opened it with a code-key. A moment later, she turned to me with a smile. "This is it. Would you like a copy?" I was flabbergasted. "You bet I would!"

Below is the letter in part from Albert Einstein to President Roosevelt that ultimately led to the top-secret Manhattan Project. The project, under the leadership of University of California physicist J. Robert Oppenheimer, brought numerous scientists and military minds together to construct the first atomic bomb. These were the bombs that were dropped on the Japanese cities of Hiroshima and Nagasaki, killing hundreds of thousands of people. They ultimately led to the surrender of the Japanese Empire and the end of World War II.

Old Grove Road
Peconic, Long Island
August 2nd, 1939

F. D. Roosevelt
President of the United States
White House
Washington, D.C.

Sir:

Some recent work by E. Fermi and L. Szilard, which has been communicated to me . . . leads me to expect that the element uranium may be turned into a new and important source of energy in the immediate future . . .

In the course of the last four months it has been made probable through the work . . . in France, as well as Fermi and Szilard in America that it may be possible to set up a nuclear chain reaction in a large mass of uranium, by which vast amounts of power and large quantities of new radium-like elements would be generated in the immediate future.

This new phenomenon would also lead to the construction of bombs and it is conceivable—though much less certain—that extremely powerful bombs of this type may thus be constructed. A single bomb of this type, carried by boat and exploded in a port, might very well destroy the whole port together with some of the surrounding territory. However, such bombs might very well prove too heavy for transportation by air.

In view of this situation you may think it desirable to have some permanent contact maintained between the Administration and the group of physicists working on chain reaction in America.

Yours very truly,
Albert Einstein

September 11, 2001

It was 7:00 a.m. and just before the Zero Period bell rang. I was at the Xerox machine in the teachers' workroom running off materials for my Advanced Placement European History class. A secretary from the attendance office burst into the room. She had a startled look on her face and was trembling. She blurted out that a disaster had occurred in New York City. An airliner had crashed into one of the World Trade towers. I walked quickly up the stairs to my classroom and turned on the television that was mounted on the front wall. Students were laughing and chattering as usual as they entered and sat down at their desks, but as they saw the images on the screen, a hush came over the room.

It appeared that a plane had accidentally crashed into one of the Twin Towers and the people inside would be ultimately rescued. The idea that this was done deliberately had not yet occurred to us. When another plane slammed into the second tower, it became apparent that a manmade disaster was progressing. Massive plumes of black smoke billowed out of the gaping hole in a broken high-story window. It was horrifying to see a man jumping out and plummeting to his death in desperation to escape the heat and flames. I could hear some students begin to cry, as well as nervous giggles coming from the back of the room.

My students and I were glued to the television where we witnessed multiple planes in the air that were unaccounted for. Our immediate reaction was that they were enemy planes. The shaken newscasters confirmed our trepidation. Shortly, we were relieved to learn that they were our own fighter jets. The concept that our nation was vulnerable was beyond comprehension before those moments.

It was announced over the PA system that there would be trauma counseling available to those who wanted it. On my students' faces, I could see a mixture of confusion, anger, grief, and patriotism. I knew that it would be difficult for them to concentrate on the lecture given the stress of the circumstances. I told them we would have a "free period" to work on homework and I invited them to come up to my desk individually if they had any concerns or questions they needed to express.

One student by the name of Nathan came up to talk. His face was solemn. I had met his siblings and his warm and friendly parents, and knew that he was very proud of his Jewish heritage. He told me that he had relatives working on Wall Street in the heart of New York City. He asked: "What do you think all this means to our country, Mr. Mac?"

I recalled the year before when I had taught him Ancient History. Nathan had done his report on the fall of Rome. Perhaps these tragic events taking place in New York reminded him of Rome; he feared the fall of our own civilization. "I don't know, Nathan, I just hope our leaders have learned from Roman history and can triumph over terrorism without the bloodshed of our people." That was the only historical analogy I could think of that day. After college, Nathan went on to live in New York City and became a speechwriter for the Israeli Ambassador to the United Nations.

Seventeen years later, I received a letter from a former student. It reawakened my memory of that day of national grieving, and also the seemingly endless repetition on television of the Twin Towers being hit by terrorist planes. This is an abridged version of his letter, which was mailed from Maine, sent to Palos Verdes Peninsula High School, and forwarded to me several years after I had retired:

Dear Mr. Maechling,

My name is Evan. I graduated from PVPHS in 2002 and you were my teacher for several classes.

Today is September 11, 2018. I have thought about writing you this letter on the anniversary of that day for at least the past five years. I awoke on September 11 to my mother telling me that a plane had hit the World Trade Center. I stumbled out in time to see the second plane hit and then I went to school. It was the beginning of my senior year. Other than the whole day being surreal, I can only remember one specific thing. As your class was set to begin, students took their places. As was the case in every classroom, the news was playing. My peers and I were young and we didn't know what to think or do. We were all scared and sad and shocked. Some of us tittered nervously. Many were in tears. You looked out over the class and back at the news. You paused and tried to conceive the right thing to do. And, then, you began to weep. It was the most genuine unembarrassed crying I had ever seen a man display.

Suddenly everything about the situation became clear to me. You solidified the complexity of the situation in a way that we were too confused and shocked to express and it helped validate our own feelings. It is truly a profound moment in my life.

I am thirty-four years old, and I have a masters in education. I have worked with young people in many settings. I hope to never be put into the situation you were in that day.

But, if I do find myself in a situation such as it was, I hope that I have the fortitude to dig deep and come up with exactly what my students need. Please know that you had the fortitude to give me exactly what I needed in that moment. For this, you are my September 11 hero.

With gratitude, respect, and love,

Evan

Prayer, Freud, and Paramedics

So many situations in life seem out of our control. Forest fires, hurricanes, tornadoes, earthquakes, and floods terrify us. Then there are traffic accidents and flu epidemics. Last year my wife Jeanne and I were hit hard by pneumonia and were housebound for nearly a month. Aging plays a larger role the closer I get to eighty. I can still meet with friends and take long walks in the hills near my home, but I can no longer play basketball, tennis, or my beloved beach volleyball. The difficult personal news of aging friends' illnesses, back pain, strokes, general deterioration, or move to assisted living facilities feels foreboding. The fear of death has never bothered me. However, suffering before death scares the hell out of me. Even worse would be if Jeanne suffers while I am a helpless bystander!

Just watching the nightly news is disheartening, not only for the sensationalized content of the stories, but also for the endless fearmongering of the pharmaceutical commercials. After the benefits of the drug are briefly and pleasantly portrayed comes a long litany of its painful and dangerous side effects, raising concern over whether the drug is worth taking in the first place!

Praying is a psychological mechanism that mitigates my feeling of total helplessness. Freud, the founder of modern psychology and a prominent atheist of his day, wrote that the belief in God, since the Stone Age, was a protective illusion, compensation for the terrifying void caused by the death of our parents. He postulated that this fantasy of God was central to so many religions because it helped us rein in our destructive impulses.

For me, Blaise Pascal's wager argument regarding God was insightful. Pascal was a brilliant mathematician and logician who used probability to explain why any rational person should believe in God. To paraphrase with an oversimplification: Even if you are not positive that God exists, it's smarter to bet on the side of the "house" because in the "big casino upstairs," the house always wins in the end. Believing in a higher omnipresent being that listens to my worries, petitions, and sorrows actually does give me comfort. A few moments of prayer releases a catharsis and I usually feel somewhat better.

"You are in our thoughts and prayers" has become such a popular cliché that you don't even have to type out all of the words because the computer auto-completes the phrase for you. This fact does not make the phrase disingenuous. Offering a prayer for people in trouble is a habit I learned from the nuns in elementary school. Any time I heard the shrill siren of an ambulance, fire truck, or police car, I would automatically say a prayer. I still do.

One day we had a faculty meeting. Our guest speakers were firemen and paramedics. Their purpose was to teach the faculty CPR in case of an emergency in the classroom or on campus. Afterward, I bribed a small group of them with the promise of pizza if they would come to my Comparative Religion class and answer questions from my students. They accepted. There, I asked them whether or not, during their years on the job, they had ever witnessed any unusual coincidences or seemingly "miraculous" occurrences. Several of them replied almost in unison: "All the time!" Their stories left us pondering. One was about a woman who was walking down a remote dirt path that wound through a wooded area leading to a neighbor's farmhouse about a mile away. The neighbor had just moved in and the woman was carrying a basket of freshly baked rolls as a welcome gift. On the way, she had a heart attack, became unconscious, and fell to the ground. Providence favored her that day. The new neighbor was walking in the opposite direction on the same path at the exact same time. As she was turning a bend in the path, she saw her neighbor fall, ran to her, and called the paramedics. She was a nurse, so she then applied CPR until they arrived, and the woman's life was saved. It was obvious to me in the retelling of that story that these brave paramedics felt they had experienced a real-life miracle.

That story reminds me of a similar "miracle" that a friend recently confided. Vince's daughter had suffered a stroke while alone in her house. She would have died if it hadn't been for a worker who was outside repairing her roof. He climbed down from the roof and was about to knock on her kitchen door to tell her he was taking a break. Through the kitchen window, he saw her lying on the floor and called 911. The paramedics arrived in time to save her life. Many logical people would say this was merely a lucky coincidence. It would be hard to convince Vince that if it weren't for a miracle, his daughter would not be alive today.

My Friend Has a Problem

I usually ate my lunch alone in the classroom with the door propped open unless I had a meeting of the social studies department or wanted to speak privately with a colleague. Sometimes students would drift in to ask my advice, usually about school-related issues. One day a young man entered as I was eating my sandwich. He looked worried. "Mr. Mac, I have this friend who has a drug problem. Last night he got in trouble with his drug dealers. He owes them five hundred dollars. They roughed him up and told him if he doesn't come up with the money by tonight, they'll come back and really hurt him and maybe even kill him. What do you think I should do? Should I try to help him get the money or what?"

I responded by saying, "I think you're asking the wrong guy. I'm the guy to come to with questions about the fall of Rome or the causes of World War I. I don't know anything about the situation you're describing. There is someone I can recommend who could give you advice. That would be our principal, Mr. Johnson." He looked startled. "Are you kidding me? Go to the principal and tell him about my friend who buys drugs?" My suggestion seemed incredible to him. I explained that Mr. Johnson had handled similar situations and would know what his best options were. I told him to think about it while I excused myself to go to the teachers' lounge next door. I knew there was a telephone there and I called Kelly. He said to bring the boy to his office immediately and he would meet with us.

Within five minutes the student and I were sitting across from the principal's desk. Kelly leaned into the boy's face. "What is your friend's name, son? We can't help you unless you tell me his name!" The boy remained quiet. He was extremely uncomfortable. He was biting his lower lip and his hands were fidgeting as he tried to decide if he should break the promise of confidentiality he had made to his friend. It was clear that if he didn't, something very serious was imminent. At this point I began to wonder if the real identity of his "friend" was actually himself. This was more pressure than the boy could handle. Finally, he burst out frantically: "Mr. Mac, what should I do? You got me into this! What do I do?" Speaking slowly and carefully, I responded: "When it comes to human life, safety and protection from bodily harm or psychological injury take priority. Then there is property. Every person's money and material things should be secure." As he was deciding what to reveal, I excused myself, saying, "I don't want to know who it is. My class is waiting."

Kelly told me the next day that the police had arrested the drug dealers that evening and the student was safe. I never knew if the boy and his friend were actually one and the same or not. I could only surmise.

Child Abuse

Sometimes the personal problems of teenagers are overwhelming. They require an immediate response from teachers, counselors, and administrators. Two common issues are suicide and child abuse. Sometimes a school assignment would reveal a "cry for help." These were occasions when a judgment had to be made as to whether the situation called for intervention. When it appeared to be serious, I would ask the school psychologist or crisis counselor to look into the student's mental, emotional, and physical well-being.

One day a girl by the name of Kim Su came to see me at the end of the school day and asked: "Mr. Mac, how would you define child abuse?" I replied that she would have to describe the situation more fully. She was calm and unemotional as she recounted a conflict that had taken place with her father the previous night. He was berating her for having low grades. She retaliated verbally with profanity. This breach of parental respect led her father to open a nearby closet and begin hurling her mother's shoes one by one directly at the girl's face. She was not allowed to leave the room until she knelt down and kissed his feet.

She explained that her mother was visiting relatives in Asia and her brothers were snowboarding in the mountains. Without their protection, she was afraid to be alone with her father that evening.

I immediately walked the girl over to the school's crisis counselor to repeat her story. The next day, I was told that the girl's father, a prominent business executive in the community, was arrested at his office and taken away in handcuffs. The girl did not return to school for several days, after which she remained silent to me about the matter. I wondered whether or not she had reconciled with her father and their damaged relationship had been mended. I knew that an enduring bond, even with an abusive father, was possible. However, it was unlikely that what happened between them would ever be forgotten. Hopefully, the violence did not happen again.

Suicide

One of the greatest rewards of teaching is helping a student to mature intellectually and spiritually. Liam was one of those students who showed an enthusiastic and keen interest in my Comparative Religion class and kept in touch after he graduated from high school. He sent me several emails from his Northern California college dorm and I enjoyed hearing how he was doing his freshman year in college. I knew him to be an eager learner and a "happy-go-lucky" kind of kid. I told all of my students on the last day of class: "Once you are no longer my student, I hope you will consider me a friend."

Liam was on winter break and made a surprise visit to my classroom one afternoon. I immediately detected a sadness in him but didn't understand its cause. His shoulders were slumped and his former gregarious nature had been replaced by melancholy. The subject of our conversation revolved around his classes and what he thought of the "world of higher learning." Suddenly he surprised me by blurting out that he was dropping out of college at the end of the term. I immediately asked, "Liam, how are you? Are you depressed?" He nodded affirmatively. "Do your parents know this?" He hesitated before saying: "I'm not sure." I followed with: "Maybe they can find a therapist who will help you." The bell rang and my next class of students began filing in.

I didn't receive any more visits or emails from him for over a year. This concerned me and I sent him a couple of emails asking how he was doing, to which he never responded. Then, one afternoon, just as the bell rang signaling the end of school,

I noticed him standing outside my door. After the last student left, I motioned for him to come in. He appeared older, thinner, and even more weary. I greeted him cheerfully and shook his hand. "It's great to see you!"

His smile seemed forced and his handshake was limp. We sat on top of desks and made small talk for a while. It was hard to figure out how he was really doing emotionally. I finally asked him if he had been receiving any professional help. He told me he was living at home with his parents and that he was seeing a therapist. He avoided eye contact with me. He got up and started walking around the classroom, inspecting the many religious artifacts displayed on my shelves and hanging on the walls. There were statues of Shiva and Ganesha, several different Buddhas, and a Quran on my desk next to the Bible. Suddenly he put down the Tibetan prayer wheel he had been inspecting and began sobbing. I wanted to help this young man in pain, but I really had no idea what to do. I couldn't hug him. As teachers, two of the most important rules in our code of ethics were to never be alone with a student, and if you happened to be, don't have any physical contact, not even a hug to comfort them if they were distraught.

An idea suddenly came to me. I walked to a wall where I had mounted a crucifix. It was a gold replica of Jesus nailed on a brown walnut cross. It had been made in the 1940s in the orphans' workshop in Missouri that was run by my priest uncle, Father John. I pulled it off the wall and handed it to him. "I don't know what to say. Why don't you take this with you? Maybe you'll get a sign." After a moment, he managed to control himself, and rubbed his swollen, tearful face on his shirtsleeve. I walked to the door. "I gotta go. If you ever need to talk, I'll be here for you." I patted him on the shoulder as he left.

About two weeks later, I was at my desk grading papers when the phone rang. I recognized Liam's voice immediately.

His voice radiated energy and positivity. "Hi, Mr. Mac! Hey, can we talk? Yesterday, I think I got one of those signs you were talking about!" We met after school at the coffee shop across the street from campus. The transformation in him was heartwarming. Instead of seeming disheartened, disconnected, and lost, he showed real signs of optimism. He began: "Okay, it happened yesterday, a little after eleven in the morning. I was in Westwood where I had an appointment with my shrink. I didn't want to go because we haven't been hitting it off. His office is in a tall building about twenty-five stories high. I got there early and went up to a bar on the top floor. I sat on a barstool. There was nobody around, not even the bartender. The TV behind me on the wall was turned on to some kind of daytime talk show. I didn't watch. Instead, I turned my back to the TV and looked out through the open door to the balcony. I noticed a safety wall about five feet high. It looked easy to climb over. I sat there thinking about ending my life. I began pumping myself up to jump. It would be a quick way out of the pain. Suddenly the voice on the television said: 'Today's program is about suicide and how it affects the families and loved ones of those who have taken their lives.'"

Liam continued: "I sat on the barstool not watching, just listening carefully. Then I began praying. I started crying. I hadn't thought how my suicide would affect my parents, brothers, and sisters. They love me so much. I just couldn't do it to them. Somehow, I realized that my life was not worthless. I got up and walked to the elevator. By the time I got down to Alan's office, I felt better. I told him about what had happened. We had a good session. I've already made an appointment for next week." I sat speechless. He continued: "Oh, but I forgot to ask you. Can I keep the cross?"

"Sure, keep the cross! Do you mind if I ask you a question?" He nodded affirmatively. "How many channels do you think are on that TV?" He replied: "I dunno. Probably hundreds." I asked: "What do you think the odds are that a prerecorded program, maybe weeks, months, or years old, could be playing on the TV right behind you with the exact message that you needed to hear at exactly the moment you needed to hear it?"

He stopped and thought for a minute. "I don't know, maybe a million to one." I continued: "Okay. Now if you took a million tiny pieces of paper the size of postage stamps, wrote your name on just one, and threw all the pieces into an Olympic-size swimming pool, what are the odds of your picking the one with your name on it in one try?"

"I don't know, maybe one in billions?"

"That's why your story is one more example of why I believe that when it comes to matters of life and death, it's possible there aren't any coincidences in the universe."

Liam has kept in touch. He told me he learned his aunt was diagnosed with genetic clinical depression and he had inherited it. He said it had been a long, slow healing recovery for him, with many therapy sessions. It took his physicians a long time to figure out just the right medication to keep his bipolar disorder in check. He has a new zest for life and is doing fine. He reentered college and graduated, married, and is now the father of a little son.

Gay-Straight Alliance

Today the name is archaic, but years ago, a club at Peninsula High School was called "Gay-Straight Alliance." I liked the name for the value it implied: the acceptance of people's differences. These days it seems as if another term to describe another type of sexual orientation comes into vogue every few months—among them lesbian, bisexual, transgender, transsexual, queer, questioning, intersex, asexual, ally, and pansexual. Still, some feel "left out of the club," indicating that as sexual creatures, we humans are incredibly complicated.

For most of my life, I've had gay friends, relatives, and students. Some of them have privately confided their sexual identity to me over the years. I think they felt comfortable doing so because they knew I would accept them as they are and never betray their confidentiality and trust. They know I'm not a religious fundamentalist and prefer to follow the admonition of Jesus to "judge not, lest ye be judged."

I was the faculty advisor for the Model United Nations Club. This meant traveling to other cities and supervising our students at the hotels where we stayed. During the day, there was some free time for me and the other faculty advisors while the students debated their assigned topics in committees. On one occasion, I ran into an old friend who was the MUN faculty advisor at a Catholic high school. He was also attending the same convention with his students.

We had a long talk by the fireplace in the hotel lobby. Over the course of our conversation, he confided that he was gay. At that time, there was a debate in California over a controversial ballot proposition to decide whether homosexual teachers should be allowed to teach in the public schools. I asked him about his situation teaching in a Catholic school. His answer was: "Jim, the administrators at my school know that I am gay. They've known it for years because I told them before I was hired. They also know that I would never hurt or take advantage of any student. So, it's never been an issue for me."

Many years later while teaching at Peninsula, I had a student whose name was Brennan. He was tall and handsome with a chiseled face slightly pockmarked by teenage acne. His shoulder-length dark hair half covered his face. He approached me just before class one morning and told me he was gay and wanted to "come out" in my Comparative Religion class when he gave his final class presentation: "How Homosexuality Is Regarded by Different Religious Perspectives in Different Areas of the World." I thanked him for his consideration in telling me this beforehand and said I would get back to him. I wanted to consult with Kelly, our principal.

As it happened, there was a Theravada Buddhist monk visiting my class that day. When he finished his lecture, he asked if there were any questions. I asked him about Buddhist attitudes toward homosexuality. The monk's response was interesting. He told us that the Buddha never mentioned it in any of his teachings. However, Buddha did emphasize compassion over all other values. This monk expressed his own opinion derived from nature: "When humans, plants, and animals are born, there is always a certain amount of suffering in that process. When a plant breaks through the soil of the earth, it must feel a certain amount of stress to become something new and unique. Therefore, when a human is in the process of transitioning in something as basic as sexuality, we should be extraordinarily kind and compassionate toward that person because what they're experiencing involves much suffering."

I approached Kelly to discuss my student's request to come out during his final presentation. Kelly wanted to know my opinion of the sensitivity and maturity level of the rest of the students in the class. I told him they were genuinely good kids and I thought they would be understanding and not dehumanizing. So, he gave me a thumbs up. The presentation went well and the students showed respect for their classmate's openness. In the years that followed, other gay students in my classes and at the school felt secure enough to come out. Eventually, the Gay-Straight Alliance Club was created.

Very Special

Over the course of a career, a teacher can be blessed with many memorable students. One of these for me over twenty years ago was a teenager by the name of Jason. He was a special education student, but the adjective "special" falls far short in describing how exceptional he was. Born with Duchenne muscular dystrophy, a genetic disorder, Jason was severely handicapped. I learned that he had actually been a poster child to raise public awareness for the victims of this tragic disease. I remember welcoming Jason on the first day of Comparative Religion in his senior year. His tiny body seemed to be held together by an intricate assembly of metal braces. At first his speech was difficult to understand. When I became accustomed to it, I realized the amazing ideas emanating from his beautiful mind.

Jason had a devoted special education growth professional assigned to assist him. Whenever he wanted to ask a question or make a comment, Kathy would raise her hand for him. From the first day, Jason was enthusiastic about learning and wanted to share his ideas and opinions in class. I initially worried that some students might lack patience or show disrespect because it was so difficult for Jason to speak and it would often take a considerable amount of time and effort for him to make his point. To my relief the students were patient listeners.

One day I was lecturing on Hinduism and explaining the general concept of reincarnation. After I related it to the concept of karma, the universal principle of "cause and effect," I closed with a simple generalization. "Suppose, just for example, you were born into a very wealthy family but lived your life selfishly. Perhaps in your next life you might reincarnate into a very different set of circumstances. You might have to learn what it is like to be really poor."

As soon as the words came out of my mouth, I regretted saying them. I was concerned that Jason might deduce from his present circumstances that he had said or done something terrible in his previous life to deserve his current body. I looked over at him to see how my example had affected him. To cover my error, I quickly came up with another example: "There are many different theories about reincarnation and karma. For example, I read one that suggests that after death, your soul searches for however long it takes to find a new body. This body will help you learn and fulfill your cosmic destiny. In other words, I'm implying that you may have chosen your own parents."

Jason became animated. Kathy raised her hand, signaling that he had a comment. The class turned toward him and I swallowed nervously, wondering what to expect. "You know, Mr. Mac, I've thought about this for a long time. I think your point is right that we picked our own parents. I've always thought that I probably had it too easy in my last life or lives. I believe I needed to learn how to live a much harder life. I think I really needed a major challenge and well . . . I got one!"

After class I often walked with Jason and Kathy to his next class, just to chat. On one occasion, the sky that day was exceptionally clear. Jason tilted his head back and said: "Check out the contrail!" We stopped to watch. Climbing fast at a very high altitude was a military aircraft. I said: "Jason, what do you think people in a remote tribe somewhere on earth would say if they saw that?" He quickly replied: "The gods must be crazy today!" It was a reference to a South African film we had discussed.

Jason passed away a few years later while he was attending college. The last time I saw him was at his high school graduation. He gave me a gift, a copy of *The Cambridge Dictionary of Philosophy*. Inside the cover was this inscription:

Mr. Mac,

Like all my memorable teachers, you have taught me much on your respective subject, but you did one exceptional thing in addition. You taught me to think. If there is any person or movement in philosophy you don't know about (are there any?), then I am sure this book will have it!

Jason, June 1999

In the end, Jason gave me the best gift of all, the gift of knowing him.

First Days of Comparative Religion

The first day of class was friendly, casual, and humorous. The students, usually juniors or seniors, were often a bit uptight and nervous, so I would try to put them at ease and let them know that the class should be a social as well as an intellectual learning experience. "I want you to enjoy your time here and get to know each other. Now please, get up from your desk and sit down next to somebody you don't know. Introduce yourselves, and ask each other your reason for taking Comparative Religion and what you hope to get out of it. If you aren't sure of your answers, that's okay."

Then I would propose this hypothetical ethical dilemma: "You are a passenger on an airliner flying alone to New York City. You plan to spend the night in a hotel before boarding a plane to Europe where you will meet up with friends on a tour. Sitting next to you on the plane is a polite, slightly older, attractive stranger. After a long, pleasant talk, he or she propositions you with an offer to spend the night together having consensual sex in exchange for twenty thousand dollars. What would be your answer? Yes or no? Why or why not?" I would divide the students into groups of four or five to discuss the issue.

The next day would be a discussion of the pros and cons of wealth, fame, and power. I would bring up examples of celebrities whose lives ended in tragedy: Marilyn Monroe, Elvis Presley, Jimi Hendrix, Janis Joplin, Jim Morrison, etc. Many students shared keen insights, such as: "Some felt isolated because their so-called friends only befriended them because they were wealthy and famous." This ultimately led students to another topic: What do people really need in order to achieve long-term happiness?

Religious Autobiographies

The first assignment for my students in Comparative Religion was an autobiographical essay. It consisted of fifteen questions, including: (1) Are you a practicing member of any religion? (2) Do you consider yourself theist, atheist, or agnostic? Why? (3) Have you ever had what might be called a religious or spiritual experience? Explain. (4) Why did you take Comparative Religion and what do you hope to gain from it?

Students were required to submit a photo of themselves along with their essay. That was an idea I retained from Doc Sullivan's English Literature class in college. Occasionally, some would include a photo of themselves practicing their religion, perhaps at a bat mitzvah, confirmation, or other celebration. I especially remember a humorous one. A student attached a photo of herself with her hands up in the air and her eyes looking upward, searching the heavens. Next to it she wrote "CONFUSED AGNOSTIC!" in capital letters to answer the question of her religious affiliation.

The assignment was effective because it got students to begin thinking about the religious content of the course right away. Also, it was a "jump start" in my efforts to get to know them at the beginning of the school year. Sometimes their experiences were so interesting, I would ask them to read their paper out loud to the whole class. I'm going to share some of their fascinating stories here.

In one, a girl wrote about a harrowing summer break experience. She and her young friend, both thirteen, visited her grandmother who lived near the beach in Santa Cruz. It was a warm and sunny day as the two girls carried their beach towels down a steep embankment to the ocean. They were looking forward to sunbathing and relaxing in the quiet, secluded cove. Except for a man not far away, they were the only ones on the beach. That didn't concern them at first, but when he moved closer, it seemed a little creepy, so they moved further down the beach. Again, he followed them. They became even more uneasy and decided to leave. As they walked up the steep path, they noticed a mobile food concession stand and decided to buy lunch. The large, burly proprietor greeted them through an open window. As they were inspecting the menu painted on the side of the trailer, the door burst open and he grabbed both girls by their arms and pulled them inside. He pulled down the metal service shade while he blocked the doorway with his large frame. Terrified, they began screaming for help. Suddenly, the door was jerked open from outside. "I'm a police officer!" The startled perpetrator turned rapidly to see a man holding a badge. It turned out that the man the girls thought was stalking them on the beach was a plain-clothes policeman. He overpowered and subdued the surprised attacker, handcuffed him, and calmly took the girls' names and addresses. He then told them to run home and he would get in touch with them later.

An athletic-looking boy using crutches and wearing a back brace wrote a surprising autobiography about his near-death experience the previous summer. Although he was not a Mormon himself, he had gone on a river-rafting trip with a Mormon youth group. Late one afternoon, they stopped to eat in a remote area along the Colorado River. After finishing his meal, he went rock climbing with some of his friends. While navigating a steep boulder, he slipped and fell into the canyon below. He was severely injured with a broken back. The paramedics were immediately called, but because the group couldn't give clear instructions about their remote location, it took the paramedics all night to reach them. While they waited, the teens formed a close circle near the edge of the canyon and began to pray as the injured boy down below shivered and cried in pain. He wrote: "I believed I was close to dying. Sometimes my mind would fade to black. I thought, this is it, I'm going to die. Then I would wake up again and I could hear them still praying for me. This went on virtually all night. I couldn't speak to thank them, but I wanted to. In spite of the pain and the cold, the most overpowering emotion I could feel was their love. The helicopter finally arrived in the early morning and flew me to the hospital. My Mormon friends stayed through it all and I truly believe their love and prayers saved my life that night."

Another student wrote that when she was a small child, there was a ghost residing in her home. "It wasn't an apparition. I just accepted this 'playful energy' as being real and my friend." This "friend" seemed to hang out on the second-floor landing near the door to her bedroom. "Once, Dad peeked into my room and noticed I was engaged in an enthusiastic conversation." He chuckled and said to her mother, "Sophia has an invisible friend! Isn't that cute?" She had no idea that her parents or older brothers were aware of their "house ghost" until a few years later. The student described them as being realistic people. Her father was the principal of a local high school and her brothers were college students studying science and math. When she was six years old, her parents decided to sell their house. Her mother was pregnant and the house would be too small for their needs once the baby arrived. The home was listed with a real estate agent. While researching the property, they learned that the previous owners had a teenage daughter who had committed suicide in the same bedroom where the little girl slept and played. "Buyers seemed interested but then something unexplainable would happen that would 'weird' them out and ruin the deal. Plates would rattle in our cupboard for no reason, doors wouldn't open, or light switches wouldn't work properly.

Weeks went by without any offers. One day, another couple left after viewing our home. It did not go well. I could see my mom was upset and clearly frustrated. Suddenly, she yelled up at the landing of our stairs: 'Okay, enough is enough! Stop it! We really need to sell this house. Leave us alone!' I lost touch with my friend and playmate that afternoon and we sold our house the following week. At first, I expected my 'ghost' would show up in our new house, but she never did."

Chris, a personable, enthusiastic student, wrote a moving tribute to his grandfather in his religious autobiography. He described him as a spiritual man who loved nature. "Once we were out in his rowboat in the middle of a lake when it began to rain. Grandpa said: 'Listen to the sound of God.' Grandpa had a special love for butterflies. He regarded them as beautiful expressions of God." The grandfather was a powerful role model for his grandson. When the old man's heart finally gave out, the family decided to hold the memorial service in a park that he had loved. The service began with a silent prayer, during which a single beautiful monarch butterfly landed on the grandson's wrist and remained there until the prayer ended. He wrote: "I believe it was my grandfather's way of showing that his spirit was still with me even though he no longer had an earthly presence."

Another autobiographical essay was written by a student who stood out for her intelligence and maturity. The previous year, she had excelled in my Advanced Placement European History course. Here, she openly expressed her anger over the limitations of religion: "My dad is a Jew, though not a practicing one. He has loved Buddhism ever since he traveled to India. We have statues of Buddha on our porch. He became interested in Hinduism and we have a Ganesha wooden mask on our wall. Ganesha is the Hindu god of creativity and wisdom. My mom was raised as a Christian Scientist, but she is now an atheist. I, too, am an atheist. If God is real, how cruel is He/She/It?

I look at events like the Holocaust or the 9/11 attacks and ask myself what kind of a God would end millions of lives like that? I can see how it might be comforting to some to have someone to talk to. But a psychologist never inspired ISIS like 'God' did! A sports team never started an inquisition. Humans have done atrocious things in the name of God: the Crusades, the Armenian genocide, the Thirty Years' War . . . the list goes on and on. A few beautiful churches and artworks do not make up for the catastrophic loss of life that religion has caused throughout history. I also do not believe in the afterlife, which of course means no heaven or hell. I believe that when we die, we die. I believe that we have one life to live and it is up to us to live it to the fullest. I am a ballet dancer. I started taking ballet classes when I was about five. I love everything about it. What was it inside me that made me choose ballet? That part cannot be explained by science. How do composers create symphonies? Why do certain people have an incredible affinity for animals? What is that undeniable passion that each one of us has? In Hinduism, it can be explained through our Atman which came from Brahman. In Christianity, it can be explained by the soul. I want to learn how all the religions explain the soul. In addition, I want to have a better understanding of the mechanics of each religion. If I am going to live in a world where eighty-four percent of the population is religious, I want to understand all I can about them." At the end of her essay, I penned: "Rebecca, thank you for the candid honesty of your essay. Something to think about: If God exists, His or Her only limitation is not impinging on our own free will."

Grieving can take many forms and often those of a spiritual nature. A young Asian girl wrote that when she was in the fifth grade, her mother died of cancer. In her autobiography, she said: "The night my mother died, I had the most vivid dream of my life. In the past, my dreams were always in black and white, but in this dream my mother appeared to me in color. She looked beautiful, radiant, and completely different from the way she had looked during her sick months. In the dream, she told me: 'Don't ever let yourself become sad because you miss me. Whenever you think of me, know that I am always with you and you will feel my love.'"

Teaching Christianity

Teaching Comparative Religion in public schools was one of my greatest challenges. Usually well over half of my students were followers of non-Christian religions, i.e., Hinduism, Buddhism, Taoism, Judaism, and Islam. The limits of human understanding, religious tolerance, and my powers of expression were well tested over those years. It was always of primary importance to treat all faiths fairly and with respect.

The course lasted a semester. During the first quarter, the Eastern religious and philosophical traditions were featured. The second quarter was given to the Western tradition and the study of the world's great monotheistic belief systems: Judaism, Christianity, and Islam. As I did with every religion, I described Christianity in a positive light and emphasized its importance in history.

In teaching Christianity, I would explain the essentials of what Christians believe about their faith, and the dual nature of Jesus. My lectures would focus on some of the core events of the Christian story: the Incarnation, the Redemption, the Resurrection, and the healings and miracles in the Bible. Of all of them, the Virgin Birth was the most intriguing and difficult to explain. Moreover, both Jews and Muslims have difficulty with the idea that any mortal human could possibly *be* God. Their understanding is that God is a completely different entity from humans and that a transformation of that order would be impossible. On the other hand, Hindus seemed to have no difficulty comprehending the concept of a divine power in a human form. This coincides well with their cherished conception of an avatar.

Once the students learned the basics, I would show an interesting motion picture about the life of Jesus Christ. In the early days, it was difficult to find films about Christ that did not insult the intelligence of a bright teenage audience. For example, Jesus was usually portrayed as a handsome blue-eyed Scandinavian, bearing no resemblance to a Semitic Jew. Finally, I found a film called *Jesus* starring Jeremy Sisto that maintained most students' attention. Unlike most of the film characterizations at that time that depicted a slightly zombie-like Jesus virtually hypnotizing his followers, this film showed a more realistic, charismatic Jesus who captivated his believers by his ideas, humor, and forceful, loving personality.

Knowing as a teacher that nothing can kill a student's interest faster than reciting all the details of a religious leader's life, I frequently hosted guest representatives of different Christian traditions to explain the details of their faith and then answer questions afterward. It was fascinating to realize that the students of other faiths, particularly Hindus, Buddhists, and Muslims (who regard Jesus as a great prophet), seemed to be the most respectful and receptive toward Christianity. Unlike Christian students who had dropped out of parochial or Sunday schools, they found the Christian story new and fascinating.

Hinduism

Since my year of teaching in India after college, I retained a fascination with the Vedic religions. In our Hinduism unit, I would explain the basic terms and concepts, such as karma, dharma, Maya, and reincarnation; the major Hindu deities, such as Brahma, Vishnu, and Shiva; and the mind-boggling concept of the multiple forms of Brahman (God). I would lead class discussions on all of these concepts and then invite Hindu guest speakers to particularize these abstract concepts by explaining their own religious practice.

Among those invited were devotees of Sri Aurobindo, a spiritual teacher in India in the nineteenth century. The experimental city of Auroville is named after him. In 1966, UNESCO passed unanimously a resolution commending it as a unique project of importance to the future of humanity. There have been numerous self-proclaimed avatars to come out of India over the millennia. A more recent one was Krishnamurti, a philosopher who lived from 1895 to 1986. He is regarded as one of the greatest philosophical and spiritual figures of the twentieth century.

As part of our studies into Hinduism, I would invite the Hare Krishnas to speak to the class. I first invited them to Miraleste High School in 1969, three years after their original guru and spiritual master, A.C. Bhaktivedanta Swami Prabhupada, arrived in the United States to preach his version of Hinduism. In twelve short years, he converted millions and made the chanting of the "Hare Krishna" mantra known throughout the world.

You would see Krishnas on downtown sidewalks and at outdoor events, public beaches, and especially airports. Their unconventional appearance alone brought notoriety. The men dressed like Hindu Brahmans in bright orange robes. Their heads were shaved, except for a long braid that hung down their backs. On their faces, they painted a *tilaka,* a double line made from cream-colored clay that ran from the hairline down to the tip of their noses. The women marked their noses as well, and always wore colorful saris. In the center of their foreheads would be a *bindi,* the traditional Hindu red dot. Hindu tradition holds that people have a third inner eye; the two physical eyes are used for seeing the external world, while the third focuses inward toward God and is a constant reminder to keep God at the center of one's thoughts.

I would contact the Hare Krishnas through the International Society for Krishna Consciousness. A few days later, six or more visitors would arrive carrying boxes of books, vegan cookies, musical instruments, and a large banner featuring their sixteen-word mantra. They would begin chanting and dancing, playing along with finger cymbals and drums. Halfway through their ritual, they would invite my students to join in with them:

> *Hare Krishna, Hare Krishna, Krishna Krishna, Hare Hare*
>
> *Hare Rama, Hare Rama, Rama Rama, Hare Hare*

A kind of festive atmosphere would ensue. While the devotees passed out freshly baked cookies, they would advertise their vegetarian restaurant, Govinda's Kitchen in Culver City.

The day before their arrival, I would point out to my students that the repetition of the words Hare, Krishna, and Rama, different Sanskrit names for the universal Brahman, is actually a Hindu practice called *japa,* the meditative repetition of the names of God. The Krishnas believe that the sound vibrations created by repeating God's name actually bring forth God's existence as well as "God consciousness" into their minds.

Students are incredulous when they learn that every Hare Krishna devotee has a rosary with one hundred and eight beads. Each day, he or she is required to make sixteen rounds of their sixteen-word chant on that long string of prayer beads. They repeat God's name over twenty-seven thousand times in the course of a day. I remember the boredom I experienced as a kid while kneeling with my family in front of our May altar in my parents' bedroom, saying a separate prayer for each of the fifty-two beads of the Catholic Rosary.

After the music, chanting, and cookie-eating, the Hare Krishna visitors answered students' questions about their core beliefs: reincarnation and abstinence from wrongful behaviors. These wrongful behaviors included using alcohol or drugs, eating meat, sexual promiscuity, and gambling. Because of the party-like atmosphere, the students would leave my class in a happy and joyous mood.

Some of the older Hare Krishnas had been practicing their faith since the nineteen sixties. They freely admitted that the strict rules of their faith helped them to overcome serious drug addictions, including heroin. One girl told us that as a hippie, she arrived in San Francisco with little else than dirty clothes and "flowers in her hair." The Hare Krishnas gave her food, shelter, and a new commitment to lead a healthier life.

I was always intrigued by the lengthy Hindu names of the visiting devotees, similar to their founder, His Divine Grace A.C. Bhaktivedanta Swami Prabhupada. Once, a student asked a Hare Krishna devotee by the name of Archita Naratarakumari what his original name was before he joined. He answered with a smile: "Harvey Schwartz."

Cults

After the Hare Krishnas' visit to our class and twenty-four hours of reflection had taken place, the festive atmosphere of the previous day would usually be replaced by cynical realism among many of the students. I would ask the class a loaded question that became a platform for a quality discussion: "Do you think those nice people who were here yesterday could be considered a cult?" Professional educators would call this question an attempt at "cognitive dissonance."

My intent was to get them to formulate their own definition of the word "cult." To most of my students, the word at first conjured up extremist figures like Jim Jones and David Koresh. I would volunteer a simple definition: a cult is "an organization in which your leaders do your thinking for you." Many students realized that by my definition, the levels of cultism can be subtle and apply to many religions, both major political parties in the United States, and totalitarian governments around the world. Some students agreed that the Hare Krishnas were a cult, but not necessarily a bad one. Others pointed out that some people might consider any non-Christian belief system a cult, while opposing religions might believe that Christianity was a cult, too. Many first-century Romans considered early Christians to be members of a cult made up of cannibals who ate the body and drank the blood of their deity, Jesus. Until the fourth century, Christianity was illegal. Christians were hunted down and fed to lions in the Coliseum. Their persecution continued for centuries. In a tragic turnaround a few centuries later, after the Roman Emperor Constantine converted to Christianity, newly empowered Christians took out their righteous wrath on the people who lived outside the city walls. These were the "pagans" who worshiped the earlier Greco-Roman gods of nature, like Bacchus, god of wine; Ceres, goddess of agriculture and fertility; and Diana, the goddess of the hunt. This pagan tradition included believers in witchcraft and they were hunted and murdered by Christians for many centuries.

Over the years, I've had representatives of other Hindu belief systems speak to my students. Among them were members of the Vedanta Society, a scholarly Hindu organization. They seemed sophisticated, with somewhat liberal views. Unlike the Hare Krishnas, they allow the drinking of alcohol in moderation.

India has produced many gurus, or spiritual masters, and some have visited the United States. One was Meher Baba. He coined a phrase, "don't worry, be happy," which became the slogan of his followers as well as a popular song written and sung by Bobby McFerrin. Many of his devotees were connected to the entertainment business. On one occasion, five disciples of

Meher Baba came to my class as guests. They all spoke about the film business except for one, an awkward-looking young man who sat facing the class without saying a word for forty-five minutes. Finally, I asked him: "Sir, you haven't said anything yet. Are you in the motion picture industry as well?" He nodded affirmatively and explained how he made a living: "One day I was sitting on the set of the film. The director pointed to me and said: 'You look like a jerk. If you could design a stupid-looking car, what would it be?' I told him it would be like a dog . . . it would be a dog-car." From his unique idea, the dog-shaped dog-grooming van was constructed and used in the hit movie *Dumb and Dumber,* starring actors Jim Carrey and Jeff Daniels. That is how he became a prop designer.

Sathya Sai Baba

One of my most memorable students was a devout Hindu girl of Indian heritage. She surpassed the highest academic standards in high school and upon graduating went to Harvard on a scholarship. During the year that I taught her, she suffered from a life-threatening case of anorexia nervosa. She and her parents made several pilgrimages to India. They were devoted followers of Sathya Sai Baba, a famous guru and holy man from a rural village in southern India. When Sai Baba was fourteen years old, he announced to his stunned family that he was the reincarnation of a previous Indian holy man with the same name. Sai Baba, whose name means "father," developed a global following of over six million people and amassed a fortune of almost nine billion dollars, which was used to establish a network of free hospitals, schools, and drinking water projects. Even though a BBC documentary aired accusations that he had sexually abused young boys, he was never prosecuted. Sai Baba dismissed these accusations as "the mere cawing of crows."

Sai Baba was famous for materializations, considered tricks by some and evidence of divinity by others. He would conjure up objects, such as exotic fruits, religious relics, and even Swiss watches. His "calling card" was *vibhuti,* believed to be sacred dry ash from burned wood used in Hindu funerals. Sai Baba would mysteriously materialize the ash, seemingly from thin air, and pass it generously among his crowds of followers. Cynics reported that he literally had a bag of it up the sleeve of his long robe.

At least twice during that school year, my student returned from India and appeared to be looking healthier and happier. She told me that she had been healed by Sai Baba. At the end of the year, when students signed up to present their final projects, she asked me if she could select Sai Baba as her topic. I consented. As usual, her research was impeccable from an academic standpoint. She talked openly about her anorexia and how Sai Baba had healed her through prayer and *vibhuti.* She had brought along tiny postage stamp-sized bags of the healing sacred ashes. She held them up to the class and explained their healing power.

The bell rang and as most of the students were leaving, I noticed that she opened one of the tiny packages, bowed, said a prayer, and placed the ashes on her tongue. Then she packed the materials from her project into her backpack and left for her next class.

Buddhism

Buddhism was the second great world religion to originate in ancient India. Five hundred years before Christ, a Hindu prince was born in a Nepalese mountain kingdom in the Himalayas between China and India. He was named Siddhartha, which means "He who brings good." Just as Christianity emerged from Judaism, Buddhism shares many similar values with the ancient traditions of Hinduism. In other ways, however, it is very different.

As a prince, Siddhartha's privileged life shielded him from witnessing the ordinary sufferings of life, such as sickness, old age, and death. According to tradition, the young prince was protected and pampered by his father and was forbidden to go outside their royal palace. Eventually, however, he escaped from the confines of his privileged life and became a wandering witness to the real world of tragedy and misery.

Under an ancient fig tree, the Bodhi, he meditated deeply, trying to gain an understanding of the essential causes of human suffering. As legend has it, after forty-nine days of meditation, Siddhartha attained enlightenment and hence became Buddha, which means "the man who woke up." Then he gave his first teaching on the Four Noble Truths. These represent his insights on the causes of all human suffering and how to end it. I'll try to summarize them here:

- Life is *dukkha,* or suffering. To live is to have pain and there is no way to avoid it. However, this pain can be reduced.

- The primary cause of all our suffering is *tanha,* which has been translated as "ego craving."

- Suffering can end if we overcome the need to feed our own ego cravings.

- We do this by following the Eightfold Path. This is the "prescription" that "Doctor Buddha" suggested to cure the suffering caused by our ego. Most Buddhists believe that following the Eightfold Path leads to a form of liberation called *nirvana,* a place of perfect peace and happiness.

1. Right views
2. Right speech
3. Right action
4. Right livelihood
5. Right effort
6. Right mindfulness
7. Right concentration
8. Right resolve

Some scholars of religion consider Buddhism to be the world's original "self-help" movement. It teaches that genuine inner happiness can be obtained by those who have learned to control their own ego's constant cravings by placing others first. Some people believe that because Buddhism doesn't mention God, it is an atheistic or agnostic philosophy, not a religion. In a sense this is true. This would depend upon one's definition of religion.

One summer during his college years, my son Greg had the experience of living and practicing Buddhism in a Zen monastery for an entire week. At the time he called it "Buddha Camp." I believe that during that week he gained an experiential understanding of Buddhism that I never could by studying it. Reading and considering the "mindfulness messages" of Buddhist Thich Nhat Hanh, for example, is a good thing. However, engaging in a daily disciplined meditation and interaction with a Zen master is quite another. It is about calming the ego's noisy constant craving for attention and finding peace.

After finding enlightenment, Buddha lived another fifty years, walking and teaching all over India. A century later, the Hindu Emperor Ashoka converted to Buddhism and the Buddha's teaching surpassed Hinduism's hold on India. When the Buddha died, the partial remains of his body were buried, along with precious jewels, in nine ancient shrines, from the mountains of Nepal in the north to the island of Sri Lanka in the south. In 2013, National Geographic produced a fascinating documentary about the discovery of those grave sites in Nepal, India, and Sri Lanka.

There are many Laughing Buddha statues all over the world. They usually depict a stout bald man with a largely exposed pot belly, smiling or laughing. This image graces many temples, restaurants, and homes. Buddha's laughter suggests he was a man who had achieved self-mastery, which in turn brought an abundance of happiness, contentment, and wealth.

Reverend Kusala

For over two decades, Reverend Kusala was a guest speaker in my Comparative Religion class. Originally named Karl, he is a tall Caucasian, born in Wisconsin, and baptized as a Lutheran. In his twenties, he became a Buddhist after reading the chapter on Buddhism in Huston Smith's *The World's Religions*. Upon ordination as a monk, he was given the name "Kusala," which means "skillful." He said he was already skillful but the name reminds him to continue to develop skills in the teaching of Buddhist doctrine, the dharma.

He is soft-spoken, articulate, and a gifted, down-to-earth person with a brilliant mind. He can summarize and explain complex concepts in everyday terms to students and those unfamiliar with Buddhism. He lives in Koreatown near downtown Los Angeles. He used to ride his motorcycle on the freeways to our school in Palos Verdes. Before entering my classroom, he would don his Buddhist robe over his jeans in the hallway.

I met Reverend Kusala after seeing his photo and reading about him in the *Los Angeles Times*. The photo was taken at the Los Angeles County Central Juvenile Hall, a detention center for boys. He was wearing the typical robes of a Buddhist monk and playing his harmonica. What caught my attention in the photo was one of the boys who appeared to be in his early teens. By the look in his eyes and the smile of pleasure on his face, he had been momentarily transported from the restriction, fear, and isolation of imprisonment into a new, happier realm of consciousness. Reverend Kusula taught these young boys (some of whom had committed murder in their teens) how to play blues harmonica and how to meditate so they could relax and get to sleep at night. Many were tortured by what they had done in a moment of angry passion and lack of self-control. Also, they were terrified to be in prison. Clearly, the boy in the photo was experiencing a realization of a path to peace and forgiveness for himself by understanding new concepts of acceptance.

When Reverend Kusala was my guest, I would invite him to lunch at a nearby restaurant. On one occasion, I asked him what he was going to do later that afternoon. He said that he would be visiting a boy in his jail cell. A few years before, the boy had lost his temper at the dinner table and stabbed his older brother with a fork, killing him. I asked Reverend Kusala if he thought the boy was a sinner or an evil person. He responded: "No, we don't believe in anything like that. The boy did not have an understanding of how to control his pent-up anger. In order to 'kill the dragon' of his pain, he used violence. He needed to learn a more skillful means of controlling his anger."

Reverend Kusala would sometimes begin my class by conducting the same meditation he taught to the juvenile prison inmates. He would then explain basic Buddhist principles and answer questions. He told us that the Buddha is not regarded as a "god" in his sect of Buddhism and is not necessarily prayed to. "He is respected as a wise teacher in the same way we respect Abraham Lincoln as a great president. There is also nothing in the teachings of the Buddha that suggests how to find or worship God. The Buddha was more concerned with the human condition: birth, sickness, old age, and death. The Buddhist path is about coming to a place of acceptance regarding the reality of life's impermanence, i.e., everything changes in life and our understanding and acceptance of this reality can reduce our suffering."

Sinbad

When I was in my mid-fifties, I made a Friday visit one evening to Loyola High to attend a championship football game. Although I rarely attended games, I still followed the football team in the paper because it was such a huge part of my life as a teenager. The son of my old classmate Dave was playing on the team that year. As was the custom, once the team bus returned to campus, the players went into the chapel to pray, while their families, friends, and fans waited outside. As I was waiting in the crowd, I recognized the large muscular African American man next to me. He was the popular late-night comedian, Sinbad. I had watched his show for the first time only a few weeks before. I had videotaped it because Sinbad's guest that night was the Buddhist monk who came to my class, Reverend Kusala.

Sinbad was waiting for his friend's son who played on the Loyola team. I extended my hand. "Pardon me. Are you Sinbad?" He nodded affirmatively, smiled, and shook my hand. "I think we have a mutual friend," I continued. "His name is Reverend Kusala. I saw him on your show a couple of weeks ago." Sinbad smiled in recognition. "He's a very, very cool dude! Are you a Buddhist?" "No, I'm a Comparative Religion teacher and Reverend Kusala has been a regular guest speaker in my classes for the last few years." I told him I thought Kusala had good things to teach kids, especially regarding nonviolence. Sinbad replied: "Amen, brother."

I then asked him if he would mind if I asked him a question related to his race. He looked a bit puzzled but told me to go ahead. I told him that when I was a kid, before I attended Loyola

High, I lived in Inglewood. One day I was walking in Centinela Park. He nodded affirmatively. "Yep. Know the place well." I described how a group of older African American kids had come up behind me and pushed me around. "Let's say they had fun with me," I said. "Later, when I came here to Loyola, the Jesuits taught us to see every student here was our brother regardless of color or creed. Kids of color became some of my friends and teammates. After that experience in the park years before, I could have become a racist, but I couldn't make the direct connection between those guys that beat me up in the park and my friends and teammates here. How would you explain something like that?" He said thoughtfully: "Well, just look around at this place. It's the education, man. That's so huge! It's the guy who can see the big picture instead of the little one. It's the values taught here."

New Age

Sometimes I would invite guest speakers who weren't proponents of any particular religion. Students always seemed curious about New Age practices, whether they were miraculous healings, clairvoyance, astrology, palm reading, or magic.

I invited a middle-aged woman named Linda as a guest speaker to the class. She lived in Palos Verdes and claimed to be a psychic medium. Her primary approach was called "channeling." She would begin with a prayer, which she would end with the words "Amen, Awomen, Alife." With her eyes closed, she would chant a Hindu mantra by "oming" several times before she went into what appeared to be a psychic trance. A few moments later, she would quickly assume a different persona and speak in a high-pitched voice with a British accent. "Hello, my name is Lindra. I am simply a vibrational entity. I come from another part of the universe. I once lived on your planet thousands of years ago in Egypt. Then my name was Lindari. Do you have any questions for me?" Sometimes the answers to questions posed to Lindra by my students were completely wrong. She was clearly fallible and could be fooled by students who would make up stories. One student asked: "Can you reach my Uncle Louis in Cincinnati?" Linda took the request seriously and concocted something in the form of a message.

The next day, there would be a class discussion and I would ask the students what they thought of Linda's validity. "Is she actually psychic or do you think she merely relies on intuition?" The student who asked Lindra about his Uncle Louis said he thought she was a total fake. He admitted he had lied; he did not have an uncle in Cincinnati.

On other occasions she would truly amaze us. One year there was a slender teenage girl in my class who lived in the foster care of her grandparents. Several weeks before Linda's visit, this girl began to bring in boxes of donuts and other sweet treats to share with her classmates, almost daily. It was obvious that my student had a serious sweet tooth. I was usually lenient about letting students eat in class as long as they paid attention and cleaned up afterward. They also knew food was not allowed when we had guest speakers. So on the day Linda spoke to the class, the girl did not bring any treats.

After Linda went into her channeling trance, students' hands went up for questions. The girl who brought the treats raised her hand. "Can you put me in touch with my mother?" Linda closed her eyes and paused for an unusually long time. Suddenly she spoke, but not in the voice of Lindra with the British accent; she continued as if she were actually this teenage girl's deceased mother, who had come back from the other side. "Honey, I'm so sorry I had to leave you the way I did. I made some bad decisions in my life and got in with the wrong people. That's really what happened and why it happened. I'm so sorry, so very sorry!"

If this was an acting performance, it was worthy of an Oscar. The girl was overwhelmed. Her voice was breaking when she asked: "Mommy, do you have any advice for me?" Then came: "Yes, honey. Please stay away from all the bad sugars you keep putting into your body. They are not healthy for you or your friends. They give you a sugar rush, but will ultimately make you very sick." The girl began to sob and asked if she could leave class to see her counselor. I gave her permission to go along with her friend who I knew to be responsible. I immediately phoned the counselor so she would be ready for my distraught student. The girl never brought sweets to class again or discussed the incident.

Linda also claimed to have healing powers. One day she put me in a very embarrassing situation. Usually I would walk my guest speakers to their car after class, when the lunch break began. As we were walking, Linda noticed I was limping. When I told her that I was scheduled to have hip replacement surgery in a week due to all my old sports injuries, she confidently said: "I can heal you!" We were standing outside the school cafeteria. She began repeatedly passing her hands over my hip, while students walked by in groups for lunch. Linda had her head bowed and was completely unaware that dozens of students were beginning to gather around us, whispering and giggling while studying what must have looked very strange!

My teenage students loved my Comparative Religion and Philosophy classes. These classes provided an environment where they could contemplate their lives and express ideas about subjects important to them. They must have taken their enthusiasm home because a group of parents called me to ask if I would teach a Comparative Religion class at night for them. I agreed to do it the next semester and my classroom was packed. The parents were so enthusiastic about learning, talking about religions, relating ideas, and asking me questions that I would barely have time for a bathroom break. I gave these parents no tests or grades. Instead of a final exam at the end of the semester, I invited them to my house the final evening for dinner. I knew the adults would find it entertaining, so I also invited "Linda the Psychic" to attend.

At the time, my wife Jeanne worked in an office and invited a colleague who regularly went to a fortune-teller for advice. Cheryl was an unmarried single woman in her late thirties. When Linda went into her channeling trance and turned into Lindra, Cheryl asked her if she could put her in touch with someone in her past who was deceased. Lindra responded without hesitation. "You had a stillbirth. It was a baby boy."

Cheryl's eyes grew wide and she put her hand up to her mouth, as if in disbelief. When she recovered, in a trembling voice she confessed that she had had a child long ago out of wedlock. After moving from her Minnesota home to California, she had never confided this information to her new friends.

My own theory to describe psychics is that they function like hitters in a batting cage. In seconds, they will carefully study the ball before it whizzes over the plate. I've seen Linda doing this frequently before my class begins. While I'm taking roll, she is carefully looking over my students, analyzing them, noticing any quirks or "tells," and formulating her own quick profile.

One day while Lindra was channeling, there was a lull with no questions from students, so I asked: "Can you put me in touch with William Hall?" About a decade before, my first team-teaching partner and dear friend Willy had died of cancer. It had reached his throat and impeded his speaking ability. I visited him at his bedside on the last morning of his life. He tried to say goodbye to me but it was too difficult because of his condition.

After pausing for a while, Lindra suddenly began speaking in a raspy voice, like Willy's on his last day. "Jim, I'd like to talk to you more, but my throat hurts too much. I'll try to answer a brief question." I asked him: "Where are you now, Willy? What are you doing now?" "I'm working inside the minds of environmental scientists, helping them to figure out how to make this a better, safer planet." My response was: "That sounds like you, Willy. We need your help." I doubt Linda actually could have known Willy or his intense interest in the environment. He was a history teacher who had been involved in many liberal causes, one being "Save the planet."

Over the years, the demographics of Palos Verdes changed. As the Asian population increased, I noticed Lindra's British accent began to change, too. It evolved into more of a mixture of Korean, Chinese, Japanese, and English. I assumed she did this because it helped her to appeal to her new clientele. Maybe it was good for business.

Judaism

The comparison of different religious traditions was what I taught daily. Visitors of all faiths were welcomed to my classes. One was Rabbi Shulman, an articulate representative from a conservative Jewish synagogue in Palos Verdes. Since Jewish students were a minority, their rabbi appreciated being invited to my class to explain Judaism from his perspective. I have always been fascinated by Jewish history, especially the survival stories in the Old Testament. Since the word "rabbi" means teacher, I thought it would be valuable to explore this Jewish scholar's interpretation of some of the same miraculous events in the Torah, the Old Testament of the Christian Bible.

One day in class I asked: "Rabbi Shulman, do you think some of the amazing stories in the Torah are actually true? For example, in Exodus, do you really believe that God, through Moses, actually parted the waters of the Red Sea so that Moses and the Hebrews could escape from the army of the Egyptian pharaoh and cross over to the 'promised land'?" Rabbi Shulman answered: "Yes, I do believe that something like that happened. However, over thousands of years, like the Greek myths, the narrative may have changed considerably with the many repetitions in different circumstances told over time. Let me give you a modern-day analogy. About forty years ago, in 1984 and 1985, Ethiopia underwent a terrible famine. Millions of people were displaced. Famous recording artists performed 'We Are the World' to raise global consciousness and raise funds for the plight of those unfortunate refugees. Over eight thousand Ethiopian Jews lived there, their ancestors going back for centuries. The Knesset, the Israeli parliament, voted to send airplanes to rescue these stranded Jewish people. Huge Israeli military cargo planes landed in the desert. Within hours, thousands of suffering human beings were rescued. They were quickly transported to the safety of a modern city with automobiles, televisions, skyscrapers, and electric lights. This was a 'modern miracle' that actually happened about thirty years ago. Now imagine centuries from now, after this modern miracle has been retold thousands of times. If the narrative is 'We were starving in the desert and praying for relief. God sent giant, shiny birds that landed and opened their huge beaks. We walked inside, and they lifted us up into the sky and flew us to the Promised Land,' would that be technically accurate? No. But was it essentially true? Is that analogy worth considering?"

Another possibility the rabbi raised regarding Exodus was the theory that certain areas of the Red Sea were shallow and swampy and were actually called the "Reed Sea." He suggested that it might be possible that these ancient survivors crossed out of Egyptian bondage at a geographically beneficial location.

The incredible story of the survival of this small wandering band of people living with little else but their own cunning and their faith in Yahweh, the ancient god of Abraham, and his promise to protect them is nothing short of awesome and inspiring. It also reminds us that the three great Abrahamic religions of Judaism, Christianity, and Islam are spiritual cousins, all related by common histories and centered in Jerusalem.

The Axial Age

The Axial Age refers to a shift in human thinking that occurred in the Middle and Far East from about 600 BC to 300 BC. This was a time of spiritual teachers and sages such as the ancient Greek philosophers, the Jewish prophets, Zoroaster in Persia, Buddha in India, and Confucius and Lao Tzu in China and Tibet. This "original enlightenment" was first identified early in the twentieth century by the German philosopher and historian Karl Jaspers. He was able to perceive the parallel between religion and ethical philosophy. The prevalent concept of karma was able to link human destiny with morality.

Ultimately, in China, Tibet, Japan and Southeast Asia, these Hindu and Buddhist concepts mingled with the teachings of Lao Tzu and Confucius, leaving lasting impressions. In the West, following the death and the widely believed Resurrection of Jesus, the nascent religion of Christianity expanded as the Roman Empire began its gradual decline. In another six centuries, Islam, the world's fastest growing new religion, would be born in Arabia.

Teaching these ancient concepts clearly was a challenge for me and certainly they were a challenge for my students to understand. Sometimes I reverted to oversimplification to help them grasp the key points. For example, there was the core concept of good and evil. This eternal struggle forms the basis of Judaism, Christianity, and Islamic thought. To get my point across, I would go to the board and write "Good vs. Evil," then I would cross out an "o" in Good and add a "D" to Evil. The result would be "God vs. Devil." The collective similarity of many of the world's religions is clear. For example, a more recent religion, arising in Iran over the past few centuries, is the Bahai faith whose founder, the Bahá'u'lláh, considered the world's religions to be like beads on a string, each with a specific purpose, but all of them influencing one another over centuries.

Confucius

In ancient times, China had the world's largest governmental bureaucracy. Confucius was a civil administrator in the Chinese government. This meant he was literate. During the dynasty of his day, there were major internal dissensions against the government, causing riots and rebellions. Devastating natural disasters, including floods, fires, and earthquakes, were blamed on the emperor. People believed that he had lost the "Mandate of Heaven." This meant he had lost the blessing of the gods and the respect of the people. At this critical point in Chinese history, Confucius developed his philosophy. It was founded on basic human relationships and imparted simple wisdom that promoted social harmony from generation to generation. His teachings were collected into a book of wisdom, *The Analects*. It became revered over millennia and continues to play a prominent role in Chinese thought. The Communist leader Chairman Mao Tse-Tung included quotations from Confucius and Lao Tzu in his *Little Red Book.*

It was Confucius who first amplified the value of a moral order in a balanced society. He encouraged the "middle way" of living: "Nothing in excess, everything in proportion." Astonishingly, five centuries before Jesus, Confucius taught the Chinese people the Golden Rule, which was expressed in negative terms: "What you do not wish for yourself, do not do to others."

Confucius sought to create lasting social harmony by focusing on the bonds that held society together: family, home, government, and friendship. He identified the mutual obligations of people toward each other, each with different levels of power, in "The Five Relationships," which he considered the key to holding society together. They were:

1. Ruler: to Subject
2. Husband: to Wife
3. Parent: to Child
4. Elder Sibling: to Younger Sibling
5. Elder Friend: to Younger Friend

In class, I would write these five relationships on the board and then ask the students if they could see a common denominator among all five. It was easy for them to detect that the common denominator was "power." The person on the left side of the list had more of it than the one on the right. I would ask students: "What is owed from one to the other?" Some very insightful values would be suggested: loyalty, obedience, respect, protection, information, honesty, wisdom, and love.

Then it would be storytelling time to reinforce the point of my lesson. My stories were sometimes cautionary tales that hopefully illustrated the wisdom of Confucius in a way that the students could relate to. One story involved an incident that had occurred a decade earlier in the same classroom. It was right after lunch. As I was taking roll, a girl suddenly fell out of her desk onto the floor. It looked as if she had fainted. I immediately told the teacher's assistant to call the school nurse. The student appeared unconscious. I could see the whites of her eyes. Suddenly she began to vomit and I could immediately detect the odor of alcohol. Soon, the paramedics arrived and transported her to the hospital.

After school, I drove to the hospital to see how my student was doing. She was sleeping. The doctor informed me that there was another sophomore girl from our school who had also passed out that day and was sleeping in the next room. They were both in very bad shape and remained in the hospital for the rest of the week. I learned that there had been a lunchtime "cocktail party" at a student's house near school. The parents were out of town. Their two boyfriends were seniors who had broken into the liquor cabinet. My student had consumed nine shots of vodka in half an hour. She was fortunate to have made it back to campus before passing out.

I emphasized this true story as a moral tale. I explained that a caring older friend, brother, or sister should take the wise parental or guardian role, which is about "protection." They would never offer alcohol or drugs to their younger siblings or friends.

Lao Tzu

His name meant "Old Fellow" or "Grand Old Master." Lao Tzu is believed to have been a contemporary of Confucius in ancient China around 500 BC. Scholars consider this era a time of intellectual and spiritual progress and enlightenment throughout the Middle East and the Orient. Many famous sages emerged during this period. There are legends of precocious children, such as the Buddha and later Jesus, who were destined to become great spiritual teachers. There are so many of these myths and stories it is difficult to separate fact from venerable fiction. For example, it has been said that in ancient Persia, Zoroaster (sometimes called Zarathustra) came into the world laughing, as opposed to crying.

It has been suggested that Confucius and Lao Tzu once met in China and admired each other's teachings. An ancient Chinese painting shows them laughing together. Of course, we cannot be positive this ever happened. Legend tells us that Lao Tzu did not preach his messages in China for very long. He sought peace and quiet in his later years so he decided to ride his water buffalo northwest out of China into Tibet. When he reached the border, the Chinese gatekeeper recognized him as the famous "Grand Old Master," and asked him to stay three days in order for a scribe to write down his words of wisdom. This writing became at least part of the legendary Chinese book of wisdom, *The Tao Te Ching (The Way and Its Power)*. It became the basic text of Taoist thought.

In class we would talk about how the naturalistic principles of Taoism have influenced nearly every aspect of Chinese culture and thought, including medicine, diet, the martial arts, architecture, and military strategy. In fact, Taoism has even reached California real estate. As a result of the enormous Asian influence in Southern California over recent decades, consultants advise perspective homebuyers on whether a specific property on a hill, canyon, cul-de-sac, or other location has a natural flow of Chi energy. The term for this is "feng shui." Wind and water are associated with good health in the Chinese culture, so good feng shui indicates good fortune, and conversely, bad feng shui has the opposite effect. Feng shui principles explain that placing a Laughing Buddha statue in the southeast sector of the main hall, dining room, or bedroom of a home will bring residents good luck and increased income.

The general translation of Tao is "the Way." Taoism teaches us to observe nature and follow it as a guide. Also, the objects we see and create should try to blend with nature. Referencing Asian architecture, I would ask students, "What does a pagoda remind you of?" "A tree" was usually their correct answer. The naturalistic architecture of ancient China, which influenced Japan, Korea, and Southeast Asia, is very different from the Egyptian pyramids, European cathedrals, or skyscrapers of modern cities.

As with Zoroastrianism, Taoism is dualistic, manifested in the opposing yet united forces of yin and yang. Yin represents the receptive, that which is female, cold, dark, and passive. In contrast, yang represents the active, that which is male, hot, and light. It is important to note that during the ancient Period of Enlightenment across the Middle East and Far East, male patriarchal society was dominant and women at every level occupied a lower position. The subservience of women to men was considered natural and proper. At the same time, men did accord women a measure of honor and power as mothers and mothers-in-law within the family.

Similar to the western practice of wearing tight-laced corsets to achieve a "wasp waist," foot binding in China was associated with higher class status and sexual attractiveness. Chinese girls as young as five years old were forced to submit to this painful practice, which rendered them unable to run, play, or walk naturally. For families with marriageable daughters, a three-inch foot size translated into a most desirable bride, which could help her family achieve upward mobility. If a woman's foot was any longer, her marriage prospects dimmed. Foot binding lasted well into the early twentieth century.

Taoist principles were reflected in the war strategy of General Sun Tzu, who was famous for the advice to "keep your friends close, but your enemies closer." His military strategy was to "let your enemy advance into your territory, and then surround and entrap them." This principle worked effectively when utilized by Japan in the Battle of Tsushima, the decisive naval battle of the Russo-Japanese War in 1905. This was the first time in modern history that a great western nation was defeated by an Asian power. Another Sun Tzu principle is to take advantage of the enemy's unreadiness. This worked well for the North Vietnamese and the Viet Cong against American troops during the Tet Offensive of 1968. The Viet Cong secretly invaded South Vietnam. During Tet, the Vietnamese New Year, they attacked its stronghold capitol of Saigon and fired on US troops at the US embassy. Up until that point, the American public believed South Vietnam was winning the war. The Tet Offensive came as a psychological blow and caused a major change in the American public's opinion of the war.

Good Luck, Bad Luck. Who Knows?

There is an ancient Chinese story of a poor farmer who depended on his only horse to till his fields. One day the horse escaped into the hills. When the neighbors sympathized with the old man about his bad luck, he replied: "Bad luck, good luck? Who knows?" A week later, the horse returned home along with twelve new horses. This time the neighbors congratulated the farmer on his good luck. He replied: "Good luck, bad luck. Who knows?" Later, when the farmer's only son was attempting to tame one of the wild horses, he fell off its back and broke his leg. Everyone thought this was bad luck. The farmer's only reaction was: "Bad luck, good luck. Who knows?" Some weeks later, the emperor's army marched into the village and conscripted every able-bodied young man they found. When they saw the farmer's son with his broken leg, they bypassed him and went on their way.

When good or bad events invade our lives, sometimes we take them as a sign that fate has either smiled on us or dealt us a hard blow. Some react with strong feelings of anger while others "praise the Lord." Could these events ultimately be mere coincidences that signify nothing? Who knows? A rational conclusion might be the juxtaposition of outside forces, individual effort, and simply fate.

Advanced Philosophy

After more than a decade of teaching Comparative Religion, I received a request by the students and administrators to combine two Comparative Religion and Philosophy classes and develop the curriculum to upgrade them to Advanced Placement status. That idea was popular with students and parents (even though the Advanced Placement classes are more difficult) because students would receive weighted credit on their transcripts, raising their grade point average (GPA). I opposed this idea, however. I had already been teaching Advanced Placement European History for decades. My view was that the same material would be available to students in college. The downside of AP classes was that students were forced to memorize great amounts of material in a short period of time. The constant pressure all too often can kill the joy of learning, and cause students to consider intellectual material superficially.

I enjoyed the fact that my Comparative Religion and advanced Philosophy electives, both non-AP, had no time pressures to complete each chapter. We could choose those themes and ideas that we felt were the most interesting and important. This approach fostered the students' interest, intellectual development, and discussion skills. Both courses were filled with many bright and articulate students. There was time to enjoy class discussions, debates, and guest speakers, and to form friendships.

On the first day of Philosophy class, I would write on the whiteboard in capital letters: "We are all philosophers!" I would tell my new students that *philos* means lover and *sophos* means wisdom. "We are all lovers of wisdom. I hope!"

I then explained that the original Greek philosophers on the Ionian coast of Asia Minor were the first humans we know of to consider the major scientific and philosophical questions, such as: What composes matter? Different philosophers had their pet theories, but they ultimately came up with the big four classical elements: air, earth, fire, and water. Aristotle added a fifth element, ether.

In ancient Greece, two important pre-Socratic philosophers arrived at different conclusions about the nature of reality: Does reality change or is it permanent? Heraclitus, born in 544 BC, believed that matter changes and is constantly in a state of flux. He said: "No man can ever step in the same river twice, because it's not the same river and he's not the same man." Heraclitus was directly opposed by Parmenides, who believed that permanence is the fundamental nature of reality and change is mere appearance. "All things and beings essentially remain the same."

I would divide students into pairs and ask them to discuss the following questions:

1. Which is more real, the chair you are sitting on, the molecules that make up the chair, or the sensations and images you have of the chair as you sit on it?

2. Have you ever made a decision that is entirely your own responsibility and no one else's but yours—that is, it was not because of the way your parents raised you, or the influence of your friends, or the influence of television, books, or movies, or any outside force? Explain.

3. "Life is but a dream," says an old popular song. Is it possible, or at least conceivable, that you are dreaming at this very moment, that you are still asleep in bed and only dreaming about being in philosophy class? How can you prove to yourself that you are indeed awake?

The title of "philosopher" freed many students from the confines of beliefs they had been taught previously and the words of sages they had read in books. This empowered many students to come up with fresh and sometimes very creative ideas of their own. Students were able to give voice to their unique understanding of truth in an open forum without fear of contradiction or judgment. This bonded them. Differences of opinion were not only acceptable, but actually welcomed, because they could freely discuss them.

Plato's Cave

Imagine a group of prisoners living in an underground cave. These prisoners are chained so tightly by their necks and legs that they can barely move. In fact, they have never seen the light of day or even the sun that shines brightly outside the cave entrance. They face the cave wall in front of them and cannot turn around. Behind them is a burning fire. As people move behind the prisoners, the objects they carry cast shadows on the cave wall. Those distorted images are the prisoners' reality.

What would happen if these prisoners were suddenly freed and they were able to see true reality? Would they seek more freedom or would they become disillusioned and want to return to the only reality they knew, which is their shadow world? What if one prisoner became free and found his way outside of the cave and saw the sun? If he came back inside to tell the prisoners, would they believe him or even understand him?

The allegory of the cave appears in Plato's *Republic.* The theme of how we can know reality appears frequently in literature and motion pictures, including classics such as *Moby Dick, Alice in Wonderland, Gulliver's Travels,* and *Huck Finn,* as well as modern and futuristic works such as *Brave New World, 1984, Fahrenheit 451, The Matrix,* and *The Giver.*

In philosophy class, after we discussed the meaning of the allegory, I would ask: "So, what is our cave today? What cave are we, the prisoners, living in today?" After a few seconds of silence, dozens of hands would go up simultaneously. The more reflective students quickly pointed out powerful criticisms of the superficialities in our everyday lives. If you don't wear certain clothes, drive a particular car, or have the latest mobile device, you are not very "cool."

In the early sixties, I was ignorant of the severe conditions in Harlem and even areas of my own city of Los Angeles. My view of reality was limited. Los Angeles was about to explode with the Watts riots. Store employees were beaten to death while mobs invaded supermarkets to pilfer essential items like toilet paper, milk, bread, and baby food. When I read *The Seven Storey Mountain* by Thomas Merton, he revealed a rare depth of insight into human conditions that I had never considered before. This was his description of the horrible conditions of the people living in Harlem during the nineteen thirties:

> Here in this huge, dark, steaming slum, hundreds of thousands of Negroes are herded together like cattle, most of them with nothing to eat and nothing to do. All the senses and imaginations and sensibilities and emotions and sorrows and desires and hopes and ideas of a race with vivid feelings and deep emotional reactions are forced in upon themselves, bound inward by an iron ring of frustration: the prejudice that hems them in with its four insurmountable walls. In this huge cauldron, inestimable natural gifts, wisdom, love, music, science, and poetry are stamped down and left to boil with the dregs of an elementally corrupted nature, and thousands upon thousands of souls are destroyed by vice and misery and degradation, obliterated, wiped out, washed from the register of the living, dehumanized.

In an ethics discussion in class one day, I asked students: "If you were poor, do you think you would steal food to keep your child from starving? If you were living in a country controlled by criminals and a ruthless dictator, would you try to escape and find a better place to live?" The majority of them replied affirmatively to both questions. These are all too relevant existential issues in our own country and around the world today.

It's the Question That Drives You

Twenty years ago when the motion picture *The Matrix* was released, I had mixed feelings because I deplored the film's depiction of never-ending violence. Less than a month later, the horrific real-life killings took place at Columbine High School by two students who attended there. The mass murderers imitated Neo, the hero of the film. They wore the same black, ankle-length coats and military boots, and armed themselves with knives, semiautomatic firearms, and explosives. I did, however, appreciate the film's philosophical implications and clever dialogue. The analogy to Plato's Cave was not lost on my students. My favorite line came near the beginning: "It's the question, Neo; it's the question that drives you . . . It's that splinter in your mind!" The question posed to Neo was left to the viewer to figure out as the film developed. This seminal question was: "What is the Matrix?" The film was about a futuristic high-tech dystopia run by robots. One scene depicted thousands of humans, including children and babies, being used as "batteries" for the robots' source of energy. I thought the genius part of the film was that it raised a metaphysical question introduced by the French philosopher René Descartes centuries earlier. Descartes distrusted perception as a means of understanding reality. He felt we must use our minds rather than rely on our senses. Descartes most likely took his idea from Plato's Cave because the famous allegory frames the essential metaphysical question "What is reality?" If you were one of those brains being kept alive in a pod in *The Matrix,* how would you know whether or not you were experiencing actual reality or just being fed sensory input?

According to his illustrious student Plato, Socrates represented the apotheosis of the true educator. He realized that it was "the questions" that drove his students and fellow citizens to think more deeply and critically. In that spirit, every year when it came time to organize my World History course, I would sit down and ask myself two questions: "If Socrates were teaching today, what would he say are the most basic questions one can ask? Also, how would he devise a course of study that would inspire his students to delve into our human origins, nature, and destiny?"

Over the years, I realized that the typical "teach and test" method was limited and mind-numbing for far too many students. For example, very few ninth and tenth graders could easily transition from World History to US History. They couldn't see that Reverend Martin Luther King's inspiration for a nonviolent civil rights movement was influenced by the passive resistance of Mahatma Gandhi. King closely studied the methods Gandhi used during India's drive for independence from the British earlier in the twentieth century.

I searched for new strategies that would fire up my students on their own paths of discovery. I asked myself, "Why are most of the things I've learned in life still inherently interesting to me? How am I still able to remember so many stories from the past?" Why do students remember the Greek myths more than actual ancient Greek history? Why do Hindus recall the many legends of their gods of India? Most of these poetic, intriguing, and sometimes gory stories, like those in Homer's *Odyssey,* originated in pre-literate societies. Bards, priests, poets, and shamans repeatedly retold these tales many thousands of times to people gathered before them around the campfires. Ultimately these stories reached a level of perfection and were eventually written down by scribes for posterity. It is believed by scholars of Sanskrit that this was how the original Vedic scriptures were initially created. Perhaps in different times and ways, this process may have been similar in the creation of the Judeo-Christian Bible and the Holy Quran of the Muslims.

I returned to the classical Greek tradition, looking to the original master teacher, Socrates. He believed in *educere,* one of the original definitions of education. It means "to lead out that which lies latent within the student's mind." In my classes, I adopted a Socratic style of teaching by asking students questions and listening carefully to their answers before asking deeper questions.

Playing Socrates

I found that the Socratic method of teaching by asking questions was a winning technique. I taught my students this concept during the first week of philosophy class. Since we have no direct evidence of anything that Socrates ever wrote, we can only rely on his iconic student Plato to inform us. I developed my own technique from Plato's descriptions of how Socrates taught. However, there were some necessary modifications.

Socrates taught in the streets of Athens or at symposiums held in Athenian homes. The discussions would always begin with a question from Socrates directed toward a particular student. In my class, I would first ask students to volunteer to be on a panel. A group of four to six students would sit in the front of the room in a semicircle facing the class. I would move from my desk to a lower chair in the center of the group and begin my imitation of Socrates by asking the students a chain of questions relating to one idea. There was one major difference between my classroom style and that of Socrates. Socrates would often dialogue with one individual for perhaps twenty to thirty minutes or longer. I could never do that in a classroom setting without losing the interest of the rest of the students. The following is a recollected version of me playing Socrates with my students:

MR. MAC *(speaking as Socrates): "What is courage? Tell me, Robert."*

ROBERT: *"Courage is being cool under pressure."*

OTHER STUDENTS: *"Standing tough," "Not letting someone push you around," "Standing up to a bully," "Facing your fears, "Risking your life to save others."*

MR. MAC: *"Are those examples actually courage itself, or are they descriptions of the behavior of one who possesses the virtue of courage?"*

STUDENTS: *"They are only examples."*

MR. MAC: *"Where is that element of courage to be found within the body of the courageous person?"*

STUDENTS: *"It is in his heart."*

MR. MAC: *"Why is it in his heart? Because the heart pumps the blood? What about his mind? Doesn't the mind fire the heart to make courageous actions?"*

STUDENTS: *"Yes, it does. It's in the mind, too."*

MR. MAC: *"So now we have changed our definition of courage to be more of a thought in the mind rather than a part of the body. Is that true?"*

STUDENTS: *"Yes, it's true."*

MR. MAC: *"Now what is your definition of courage?"*

STUDENTS: *"It's a combination of thoughts in the mind and feelings in the heart that energizes the body. This creates the courage to do brave things, such as saving a life. It's both in a person's mind and in his heart to want to risk danger to save another and be able to do something brave and courageous."*

I continued this method thoroughly and systematically, trying to imitate Socrates, who used his questions like a surgeon's scalpel. I would try to dig away at falsehoods and logical inconsistencies. We would pursue all the questions until human reason had brought the students to an acceptable level of agreement on the definition of courage. Then we would begin all over again. I would choose other students and pose another question. The questions were always universal. They covered a wide range of ideas, values, and perceptions. Some examples include: What is love? What is happiness? What is beauty? What is wisdom? What is truth? What is justice? What is reality? What is the good life?

One of my greatest satisfactions as a teacher was to walk across the campus at recess or at lunch and observe some of my students sitting around a table or on the lawn under a tree, participating in a Socratic-style discussion of their own. As I walked by, I would pause, bow, and say to them, "Ah, the philosophers' table!" They had learned that discussing ideas and values was highly enjoyable and a worthwhile activity in itself. They no longer needed the class, or me. I was proud of them.

It was disappointing that there were so many ideas to explore and so little time in class. One year, the students, mostly seniors, created their own philosophy website so they could continue with their discussions. After graduation, many went on to attend outstanding universities. In recent years, the students at school formed a Philosophy Club that met at lunch. I was given the honor of being their first guest speaker.

Comparing Socrates and Jesus

The executions of Socrates and Jesus come to mind as among the most prominent deaths in the ancient world. Much has been written about the wisdom and integrity of both individuals. Each seemed to have dedicated his life to the fulfillment of noble principles and to have paid the ultimate price for speaking the truth.

As we know, five centuries before Christ, the life and death of Socrates was thoroughly documented by his brilliant and faithful student, Plato. Plato had been a witness to the teachings and ultimately the trial and death of his beloved and controversial mentor.

In the case of Jesus, the writings of the four evangelists—Matthew, Mark, Luke, and John, the authors of the Gospels of the New Testament—along with some other writings, contain the bulk of Christian beliefs and teachings. Although these accounts of the life, teachings, death, and Resurrection of Jesus were written at different times and places, and from different individual perspectives, it is noteworthy that there appear to be no inherent contradictions among them. This in itself speaks volumes about their integrity. In fairness to Christian critics, it is possible that over the centuries, some of these texts were "doctored" to conform to each other. To me, this has never been convincingly proven. However, in the cases of both Socrates and Jesus, and for the sake of historicity, it is fair to note that these accounts were written by their followers, as opposed to their detractors.

At first glance, it is not difficult to find similarities between these two outstanding teachers. Socrates engaged the mind through a progression of penetrating questions. Jesus captured the imagination and the hearts of His audiences by telling unforgettable, compelling parables. Both teachers' value systems seemed to have been roughly comparable regarding wealth and poverty. Each spoke of the primary importance of the truth. Socrates preached: "Are you not ashamed of caring so much for the making of money and for fame and prestige, when you neither think nor care about wisdom and truth and the improvement of your soul?" Jesus reminded us: "Again, I tell you: It is easier for a camel to go through the eye of a needle than for a rich man to enter the kingdom of heaven." Both opposed greed and the violent bloodshed of war. Socrates publicly denounced the Athenian leaders to his young followers during the Peloponnesian War against Sparta. When Athens ultimately lost the war, Socrates was charged with corrupting the Athenian youth and with impiety toward the Athenian gods, who obviously supported the war effort.

Although their situations were quite different, both individuals opposed the existing immorality and sometimes publicly expressed their anger about it. Not long before the time of his death, we have the incongruent scene of the wise, loving, peaceful, mild-mannered Jesus storming into the Temple, berating the merchants and money changers as he angrily overturned their tables and freed the captive sacrificial doves.

Socrates was usually at odds (almost on a daily basis) with the majority of his fellow Athenians. He railed against the war, as well as the overly crowded conditions caused by the walls that kept out the invading Spartans. The Athenians were forced to live behind these city walls and between the long walls that led down from the Acropolis to their port at Piraeus. Ultimately, the walls of the Athenians could not keep out the plague and Socrates' admonishments must have seemed like a curse on them.

Socrates described himself and his role as "a large horsefly, stinging the sluggish body politic of state." Socrates had an arrogant attitude toward his citizen accusers. During his trial before a jury of five hundred Athenian citizens, Socrates asserted: "The unexamined life is not worth living." He then severely admonished them for not being grateful for his wisdom and service to Athens. He stated that he did not deserve to be penalized, but rather should be rewarded with free meals for life for teaching the citizens.

This was far different from the silent Jesus who willingly accepted his sentence of an excruciating crucifixion, asking his Father in Heaven to forgive his executioners and those who mocked Him because "They know not what they do." He was oppressed and He was afflicted, "yet He did not open His mouth; Like a lamb that is led to slaughter, And like a sheep that is silent before its shearers, So He did not open His mouth."

When it finally came to their executions, both Jesus and Socrates seemed resigned to their fate. Although Socrates self-righteously admonished his accusers at his trial, he showed another side to him when he willingly drank the cup of poison hemlock. Beforehand, he even bathed himself to show consideration for the women who would have to clean his body before burial.

The fundamental difference between these two stories is that in Christian belief, Jesus resurrected three days after his burial.

His empty tomb that contained only his death shroud confirmed to his followers that He had risen, as He predicted, and would later return to them for a short period of time. There is also the testimony by many of Jesus's followers who claimed to have seen and conversed with him after his resurrection and before his ascent into heaven. This miracle has been a matter of faith for Christians for the last two thousand years.

Lawyers, Sophists, and Teachers

Throughout our lives, Jocko and I have frequently enjoyed teasing and verbally sparring with each other. This goes back to our high school and college days. When the popular motion picture *To Kill a Mockingbird* was released, I had a field day imitating the characters. One was Bob Ewell, the racist villain who molested his own daughter and blamed it on an innocent black man. His nemesis was attorney Atticus Finch, portrayed by Gregory Peck. When it was clear that Jocko was destined for law school, I had fun teasing him with Ewell's lines from the movie: "What kinda man are ya?" and "Ya gotta watch out fer them tricky lawyers!"

One summer day over a decade later, Jocko paid me a visit at my house near the beach. By then, I had been teaching for almost fifteen years. I still cherished our bonds of friendship and the humor we shared. We walked on the sand and simply talked, laughed, reminisced, and caught up on what was happening in our lives. He described a few of his latest courtroom experiences for me. As usual, his tales were funny, clever, and entertaining. By then, his success didn't surprise me. Over the years, I became aware of how multifaceted Jocko was. He could successfully plead a case during the day and then perform as a stand-up comedian at a local comedy club the same night.

Yet, there was another, very different side to him. Underneath, he had a burning ambition. I felt certain that with his intellect, burgeoning professional skills, and steel resolve, he would quickly climb the ladder of success, which he definitely did. He was hired by one of the top-ranking law firms in Los Angeles. As a leading trial lawyer, he represented almost all of the commercial and civil aircraft manufacturers in the US, as well as other Fortune 500 corporations. He became the youngest attorney in the firm's history to become partner, and later served as chairman of the board.

At one point, our discussion turned to my teaching career. Jocko hesitated a few seconds before speaking: "Ya know, Jimmy, if there ever was a guy I thought was gonna be emperor of the universe, it was you, but . . . a teacher?" He wasn't being derisive. He just wanted to understand why, with so many options that our Loyola education gave us, I chose the profession I did. I thought for a moment before replying: "How do you know I'm not emperor of my own universe?" Even though I never pursued wealth, power, or status, I respected those who did for the hard-earned fulfillment of their ambitions. I felt that way about both of my brothers and in a way, Jocko seemed like another brother to me. Yet I wasn't sure that the achievement of one's personal ambitions is actually what makes people happy. I had learned long before in India that the secret to my career happiness was teaching. I also knew the price tag that came with it was that I would never be rich in terms of material wealth.

In the classic motion picture *A Man for All Seasons*, written and directed by the brilliant Robert Bolt, King Henry VIII's Chancellor, Sir Thomas More, is begged by an ambitious young man for a position at court. When More refuses him with the words "Be a teacher, Richard," the disappointed man urgently implores: "And if I were a good teacher, who would even know it?" Thomas More replies: "You, your pupils, your friends, God. Not a bad public, that!"

In fifth century B.C. Athens, the Sophists became popular and powerful as the anti-Socrates element. Sophists blended in extremely well with the flourishing development of Athenian democracy and its growing material wealth. These were bright men who had traveled among cosmopolitan cultures and understood different languages and many points of view. Ultimately, they adopted the philosophical position of skepticism, sometimes called relativism. The Sophists believed that since there is no way of determining the truth about reality, reality is in the eye of the beholder and must be said to have whatever characteristics are claimed for it. From the Sophists, we derived our word "sophisticated." The Sophists were very effective and often popular politicians whose points of view were quite nuanced. Well-developed in the art of argument, they were very different from the real truth seekers of the day, i.e., Socrates, Plato, and Aristotle. Socrates admonished his fellow Athenians, particularly the Sophists: "If truth could be proven to be relative, then what would happen to all the other verities and traditional values?" His trial speech to the Athenians was an indictment of the flourishing materialistic values of the Sophists.

In my advanced Philosophy class, students learned how to argue effectively when we studied the great nineteenth-century German philosopher Friedrich Hegel and his concept of the dialectic. The structure of an argument or disagreement creates a necessary ideological conflict between the thesis, and its opposing opinion, called the antithesis. Any solution requiring a compromise results in a synthesis. The synthesis nullifies the conflict by introducing a solution which becomes a "higher truth." Students were taught during many discussions and arguments, particularly on ethical issues, to look for the synthesis that would cancel the argument on both sides, and still retain the element of truth within each. Upon reaching this point, the conflict could ultimately transcend into a higher truth. An example of this was during a highly charged ethical debate on abortion between students who were "pro-life" and students who were "pro-choice." The pro-life students were hard to dissuade from their view that abortion was not acceptable under any circumstances and should not ever be legally allowed. The pro-choice group countered by asking: "What if the mother were a victim of rape, or incest, or would die if her pregnancy were brought to full term?" When these circumstances were made clear, the pro-choice students' staunch views began to soften. They ultimately agreed that abortion could be permissible, but only in certain cases. That was an example (albeit simplified) of a Hegelian synthesis.

In my garage, I found a large, old brass bell. It was initially used in the 1940s to ring at Loyola football games to celebrate touchdowns and victories. Whenever a student in the class made a "Hegelian synthesis," a student temporarily nicknamed "Quasimodo" would ring the bell to signify the celebration of a successful synthesis. The whole class would pause and stand to applaud this intellectual achievement.

The Tripartite State

In his seminal work, *The Republic,* Plato described the unique teaching techniques of Socrates and many of his own values. Plato's classical masterpiece has withstood the test of time for nearly twenty-five hundred years. The modern British philosopher Alfred North Whitehead wrote in 1979: "The safest generalization of the European philosophical tradition is that it consists of a series of footnotes to Plato."

Plato perceived humans as having different levels of intelligence and abilities. He envisioned that the cooperative union of these different classes of citizens would result in an ideal Athenian society. His "tripartite state" comprised three different types of people or "souls." At the bottom of this system were the producers. They were the majority of citizens. They worked in the fields, picked the grapes, and produced the wine. They were also the merchants who worked in commerce and trade, exporting Athenian goods around the Mediterranean. They were the artisans who made functional as well as decorative items, and the architects who designed theaters and magnificent temples, such as the Parthenon and other Greek wonders that adorned the Acropolis.

According to Plato, the producers were necessary for sustaining everyday life, but they were not intellectually well-rounded and usually had little interest in government. They tended to be more concerned with physical needs. Athens was the world's first democracy and because the producers were free male citizens, they had the right as members of the assembly to vote on the day-to-day issues of government.

The next level upward in Plato's tripartite societal scheme were the citizens he called the spirited element. These were the warriors, the men who were fearless in the face of danger. They were ideally suited to be soldiers and sailors. In addition to courage, intelligence, and bravery, they also possessed the virtue of exceptional loyalty to each other, their leaders, and Athens.

At the pinnacle of Plato's ideal tripartite state were those citizens known as the guardians. They became known as "The Philosopher Kings." They included philosophers and teachers such as Socrates himself. They were bred, raised, and trained to lead this idealistic society. The parents of the guardians were to be selected by the Athenian state for the purpose of producing children with the brightest minds and healthiest bodies. Their parents' actual identities were to be kept a secret from them for life. Plato called this deception a "noble lie" to ensure that these quality people would not be distracted or corrupted by petty family rivalries or the lower elements of society.

The producers and the spirited element had access to elementary education, but advanced education was reserved for the guardians, those citizens "of promise." Their lives were sheltered and their education was secluded and protected. At a certain level of maturity, they were allowed to spend a year outside their sheltered environment, working alongside the producers or members of the spirited element, as long as they were carefully protected. The purpose of this exposure to the "real world" was for the future guardians to gain a clearer understanding of human nature and the roles of the other two elements. Later, they could then pass on this knowledge to future guardians.

To better understand this concept of the tripartite state, we need look no further than the Greco-Roman classic statue of the charioteer. He is being pulled by two horses. Think of the chariot race in the classic film *Ben Hur*. The horse on his right is strong, fast, and high-spirited. The horse to the left is just the opposite. Although as big and powerful, it is unmotivated and sluggish. Directing them from behind is the charioteer who uses his whip to either spur the less-spirited horse to speed up or keep the more-spirited horse under control. The charioteer represents the guardian, who with superior intelligence fulfills the role of either motivating or controlling the other two types of citizens.

What led Plato to create this strange, Orwellian view of society? He mistrusted the misguided passions of the masses. He thought the best citizens to hold the body politic together were the rational and intellectually superior people like himself. There was one unique, unexpected feature in Plato's ideal government. Women were considered to be just as capable as men to lead the government and to be selected as members of the guardian class. However, this perception did not last long after Plato's death.

When I look back on some of my closest friends in high school, college, and adult life, I like to consider their personalities in terms of this concept of the tripartite scheme introduced by Plato.

I have purposely left out Jocko because he is an amalgam: part guardian/part spirited element. He has the comprehensive intellect of a guardian with the ability to break down, analyze, and understand the core elements of complicated issues. He does this with the powerful employment of geometric logic. Yet, simultaneously, he possesses a fierce loyalty toward individuals such as his family and friends. When their interest is concerned, he becomes emotionally driven to employ his ample intelligence fighting for their causes and cases. An example of this will be described later.

Sergeant Dave

I think of Dave as the perfect example of Plato's spirited element. Earlier, I described him during our high school years as a provocateur when it came to starting fights. He relished the excitement of conflict. As a teenager, Dave already showed signs of being a "fearless warrior." Of all my old friends mentioned in this book, I've known Dave the longest. We went to St. John's elementary school together before attending Loyola High. After college, he attended the police academy. There, he spent twenty-one grueling weeks learning state laws, criminal investigation techniques, patrol procedures, firearms training, traffic control, defensive driving, self-defense, first aid, and computer skills. Upon graduation, Dave became an officer of the Los Angeles Police Department.

Dave told me that when he joined, there was a great deal of racial bigotry in the police department. An experimental program was implemented at that time called "The Salt-and-Pepper Team." Before 1965, most LAPD departments were all white or all black. The only African American in Dave's department was an officer by the name of Dale.

Due to blatant racism, few officers wanted to partner with him. Dave's commander asked him if he would volunteer to be Dale's partner and he agreed. One of their first assignments was to deal with a family dispute in a tough part of town. One night, three African American women called 911 fearing for their lives and for the life of a neighbor. The husband of one of them was threatening to kill her. As the two partners arrived at the scene, Dave was the first to get out of the police car. He looked up to see a six foot five, three hundred pound African American male swinging a large two-by-four running toward him in a rage. Dave immediately pulled out his weapon, but was spared from shooting the man by his new partner. Dale quickly came up behind the giant and took him down with a powerful karate chop. The salt-and-pepper racial partnership paid off for Dave and earned both men commendations and a lifelong friendship. Unfortunately, it didn't eliminate the racial tension in the department. More than once, Dave saw his locker covered with handwritten graffiti with the words "n . . . lover."

During the Watts Riots in 1965, Dave worked in some of the toughest parts of Los Angeles. Almost three decades later, he witnessed the Rodney King riots in 1992. He has seen unspeakable tragedies in his work that few witness in other careers. Early one morning, Dave phoned me and asked if we could get together for a talk. When we met, I could tell that he was extremely down about something. He remained silent for a long time. I sensed he didn't have the heart to talk about what was bothering him. I asked: "What's this about, Dave? Did you get fired?" I saw a tear in the corner of his eye as he began: "Last night we found the body of a young girl who was raped to death on the beach in Playa del Rey. Nobody deserves to die like that." He shook his head, repeating it softly to himself. I had often thought about the physical danger of being a police officer, but had never considered the psychological stress that came with the job. I knew Dave was tough and resilient, but this particular incident touched him to the very core of his being.

Several years later, Dave was appointed head of the Los Angeles Police Department Airport Security Division. His job was to coordinate with five different agencies—the FBI, FAA, Customs, Border Patrol, and Bureau of Narcotics—and assign different problems to the proper agency. There was also a War Against Crime Unit to survey gangsters arriving from cities such as Chicago or New York, some of whom were involved with organized narcotics dealing and smuggling. It was also Dave's responsibility to allocate the multimillion-dollar budget to these various agencies.

Dave told me fascinating stories that involved all kinds of intriguing topics: smuggling, narcotics, kidnapping, undocumented aliens, organized crime, and the American and Russian mafia. Dave was always interested in human behavior. Over the years, even though we have disagreed with each other, usually over politics, it never got to the point of damaging our friendship.

Over twenty years ago, our friend Fernando began to get into serious debt. As an adult he was having trouble managing his money and making his house payments. Part of the problem was that Fernando was a generous, "drinks on the house" kind of guy. It finally caught up with him. Dave was the first to be aware of this. He stepped up and came to the rescue by letting Fernando rent his pool house. Dave, along with Ron, virtually took responsibility for Fernando's health care, companionship, guidance, and social interaction.

Ron

Among my close friends, Ron would be my first nominee to be a member of Plato's guardian class. Although we live in a very different age from Plato, Ron is intellectually, emotionally, and psychologically well-suited to be a judge and a wise leader in any society.

After college and law school, Ron became an outstanding attorney working directly under the Attorney General of the State of California. He oversaw all types of criminal and civil litigation. He investigated and litigated corrupt practices in all areas of society, from senior citizen homes, trust funds, charities, corporations, and funeral homes to race tracks, gaming casinos, and the state boxing commission.

The reason I always thought Ron would make an excellent judge is that he combined a brilliant intellect, good character, and a strong sense of fairness that extended to religion and politics. Ron has never seemed politically biased to me. You could always talk about politics with him without feeling he was promoting a particular agenda. In the past, he has described himself as a moderate or sometimes even a liberal Republican. Those political species once existed here in California. However, today I fear they are nearly as extinct as the condor.

Ron is also a gifted poet. He understands how to meld beautiful words, images, and ideas together. This is a poem Ron wrote about me for my seventieth birthday.

> *Mister Mac*
> *An involved ever-evolving spirit*
> *Kept young by the young spirits he infuses*
> *   with his wisdom and love*
> *And by the glow reflected upon him from*
> *   those he has so tenderly touched*
> *Throughout his three score and ten*
> *And still counting*
> *And still teaching, still caring*
> *Still touching, still loving*
> *This man, our Jim*
> *This Mister Mac*
>
> *—RR, 12/18/11*

Ron has an innate sense of kindness. On the last trip back to a Notre Dame game, I had scheduled the journey too soon after my hip replacement surgery. I couldn't keep up with my friends while walking around the campus or in the stadium. At first, I tried to conceal my pain, but finally at one point I fell to the ground. Ron was first to notice. He quickly helped me up and then phoned for a cab that got me back to the hotel room. He recognized that I was in trouble and came through for me.

Al

Another candidate for the guardian class has been one of my closest friends throughout my life. Al and I were good friends at Loyola High and became even closer in college, where we were both history majors and earned masters' degrees in history from Loyola University. During our undergraduate years, Al and I often studied with Jocko and John. Al took meticulous and accurate notes during our professors' lectures. The rest of us were beneficiaries of his note-taking skills. They paid off for all of us at exam time.

Al is a genuine scholar of intellectual depth. He became an outstanding professor at the University of South Australia in Adelaide after emigrating in 1969, not long after Neil Armstrong walked on the moon. His reasons for leaving the United States were complicated and personal, but I would just say that America's loss became the Aussies' gain.

Al and I both became teachers because we loved learning and truly valued some of the outstanding professors we had. We continued sharing our developing knowledge with each other throughout our long academic careers. In spite of the miles that separated us, we exchanged countless letters, phone calls, cassette tape recordings, and now emails. We remain like-minded, finding satisfaction in communicating our ideas and life experiences with each other.

Al has done tremendous favors for me that were life-changing in both professional and personal ways. Many teachers burn out after a decade or two of teaching. This began happening to me in the early 1980s. Even though I enjoyed my classroom interaction with students, I began to feel I was going nowhere in my career.

During two summers, Al arranged an opportunity for me to lecture as a visiting professor in religious studies and education at the University of South Australia, where he taught. This interesting job change was therapeutic and renewed my enthusiasm for my teaching career.

On my second trip to Australia, I worked on an educational committee directly involved with reorganizing hiring procedures for new teachers. My recommendation was that before hiring, administrators should observe the prospective candidate teaching and interacting in the classroom. This could be done by videotaping the candidate. Often, a candidate for a teaching position can be convincing in the interview, but turn out to be a disappointing teacher. I learned this lesson by frequently sitting in on hiring interviews as a department chairman. Later, I was proud to learn that my recommendation was accepted as policy in South Australia. Unfortunately, my same recommendation was never approved in the California public schools.

Hegel's Legacy

During the last quarter of my Philosophy course, students learned about some of the most influential philosophers of the nineteenth and twentieth centuries. I had already taught Hegel's concept of the dialectic. His sweeping concept directly influenced his two prominent students, Karl Marx and Friedrich Engels, authors of *The Communist Manifesto*. In fact, these two world-changing intellectuals in their early days were members of a group of radical thinkers called "The Young Hegelians." Hegel's admirers simply called him "The Philosopher."

Hegel believed in the concept of what he called the world-historical individual, someone who manifests the energy of the world spirit as it prepares to move to a new phase in challenge to the existing one. There is no question that certain people—military generals, kings, presidents, giants of science, religious leaders, artists and writers—have directly changed the world. From Hegel's personal experience, he described observing Napoleon Bonaparte from his balcony. Napoleon was on his horse, reconnoitering and about to give the orders to invade and capture Hegel's city of Jenna. Hegel was awestruck.

> I saw the Emperor—this world-soul—riding outside the city on reconnaissance. It is indeed a wonderful sensation to see such an individual, who, concentrated here at a single point, astride a horse, reaches out over the world and masters it.

It was a unique observation for Hegel to make at the time, especially since his own house was about to be sacked by the French army. Professor Hegel would also lose his teaching position at the university as a result of the invasion.

My goal was to help the students understand these heady philosophical concepts and incorporate them into their final projects. I asked them if they had ever seen or met a "world-soul." The first student to raise her hand said: "I saw Aretha Franklin, the Queen of Soul, at a concert once!" Another student mentioned he had seen Michael Jackson performing at a concert. It was interesting how the word "soul" had changed from the nineteenth century. The students' answers were not exactly what I had in mind, but I tried to look at it from their perspective.

When it comes to music, art, movies, books, or philosophy, everyone has their own taste and preferences. Hegel's observation of a world-soul individual reminded me of my own unforgettable experience in 1963, watching Dr. Martin Luther King delivering his "I Have a Dream" speech broadcast live on television. I remember the exhilarating feeling I had witnessing this

exceptional moment in American history. An iconic American
was saying exactly what was needed to be heard by all Americans about race relations and civil rights at that volatile time.
His eloquent, poetic words touched me deeply and brought tears
to my eyes.

> I have a dream that my four little children will one day
> live in a nation where they will not be judged by the color
> of their skin but by the content of their character. I have
> a dream . . . When we allow freedom to ring, when we let it
> ring from every village and every hamlet, from every state
> and every city, we will be able to speed up that day when
> all of God's children, black men and white men, Jews and
> Gentiles, Protestants and Catholics, will be able to join
> hands and sing . . . "Free at last! Free at last! Thank God
> Almighty, we are free at last!"

Zeitgeist

Another interesting concept that Hegel expressed was the zeitgeist. This term, derived from the German word *geist,* meaning "spirit," means the "spirit of the age." As we study history
through the centuries, we see that every era had its own driving
forces and defining characteristics. The Greco-Roman classical
age, for example, including its wars, governments, rulers, and
cultural manifestations from Greek drama to the Roman Coliseum, is quite distinct from the Renaissance with its humanism,
the Enlightenment with its emphasis on reason, or the Romantic era which exalted senses over intellect.

In philosophy class, we took a look at modern American
political and social history and how it reflected the spirit of the
time. Students would study, research, and present how art,
music, dance, and popular culture dictated the unique zeitgeist

of each colorful decade from before World War I up to the present.

For example, we discussed the punk rockers of the mid-seventies. They conveyed their message about socioeconomic inequality by wearing secondhand clothing as an anti-consumerist statement. They expressed their individualism with spiked hair, tattoos, and piercings. Many became squatters, staging punk rock food drives and conveying their anger through loud, aggressive rock music.

I still have nostalgic memories of students dressed as gangsters with fedoras and striped suits borrowed from the drama department wardrobe. They reenacted the story of Al Capone and the St. Valentine's Day Massacre of 1929. Students read dialogue from F. Scott Fitzgerald's *The Great Gatsby* while girls wearing fringed flapper skirts danced the Charleston.

The thirties was a very different scene. Students read scenes from John Steinbeck's *The Grapes of Wrath*. They created posters depicting gaunt men, women, and children lined up outside of soup kitchens and barren and eroded landscapes ravaged by drought and dust storms.

Patriotic World War I tunes, such as George M. Cohan's "Over There," contrasted strongly with the anti-war protest songs of the 1960s, written by Bob Dylan, Joan Baez, John Lennon, and others. The sixties was a wonderful topic for a cultural debate. Was this decade merely an expression of reckless self-indulgence by youth, or was it something deeper? The counterculture was suspicious of the government, rejected consumerism, and generally opposed the Vietnam War. A few were interested in politics; others were concerned more with art, music, painting, poetry, or spiritual and meditative practices. Parents helplessly stood by while their children rebelled against the traditional values they held dear. Going to San Francisco "with flowers in your hair" become the symbol of freedom. Individuality was celebrated. Afros, beads, bellbottom jeans, and tie-dyed shirts became the rage. Vegetarianism became popular among young people and health food stores popped up everywhere selling wheat germ, wheat grass, and granola.

This was the era when Harvard professors Timothy Leary and Richard Alpert, later known as Baba Ram Dass, advocated the psychedelic drug LSD and coined the phrase "turn on, tune in, drop out." Experimentation with marijuana, mushrooms, and pills became common. The term "dropping out" became popular among many high school and college students who would often abandon their education for a summer of "sex, drugs, and rock 'n' roll."

Many older Americans believed Communism was threatening democracies across the globe. They felt that non-intervention in South Vietnam would lead to communist revolutions across Asia. As the war dragged on and the death and suffering of American soldiers and the Vietnamese people increased, more and more people began to reconsider its moral and economic value. The mounting costs of war were taking monies away from social programs such as welfare, housing, and urban renewal.

The draft system was another source of contention. College students argued that if young Americans were old enough to fight and die, they should be permitted to vote and drink alcohol. This criticism eventually led to the Twenty-sixth Amendment, which granted suffrage to eighteen-year-olds.

Steven Stills' classic counterculture song "For What It's Worth," recorded by Buffalo Springfield, was actually written as a protest against a Hollywood curfew imposed by local businessmen and residents, and not as an anti-war song, as is often believed. Late-night traffic congestion caused by young people loitering outside bars and clubs along the Sunset Strip had become disruptive and a local ordinance enforcing a strict curfew was passed. In response, young music fans retaliated against the infringement of their rights, and organized as many as a thousand demonstrators, including the young actors Jack

Nicholson and Peter Fonda. "For What It's Worth" demonstrated the rising tension of the era between the counterculture youth and the establishment.

> *There's something happening here*
> *But what it is ain't exactly clear*
> *There's a man with a gun over there*
> *Telling me I got to beware*
> *I think it's time we stop*
> *Children, what's that sound?*
> *Everybody look—what's going down*
> *There's battle lines being drawn*
> *Nobody's right if everybody's wrong*
> *Young people speaking their minds*
> *Getting so much resistance from behind*
> *It's time we stop*
> *Hey, what's that sound?*
> *Everybody look—what's going down*

In 1962, a young student by the name of Tom Hayden wrote a manifesto for the founding members of the Students for a Democratic Society (SDS). In it he condemned racism, conformity, materialism, and anti-communism. Radicalism increased throughout the decade. Mass demonstrations for peace on streets and campuses turned violent when police arrived to disperse crowds. In 1970, an extreme branch of the SDS splintered off to form the Weathermen, an underground organization committed to the violent overthrow of the government.

Changing times seemed natural to some, especially those who were part of the youth culture. To others, usually older and more traditional, the changes often seemed like a major new problem. This was also a time of progress in civil rights, science, medicine, space exploration, and global awareness. For the first time, humans saw earth's beautiful blue oceans from the perspective of space. This was a powerful inspiration for "Save the Planet" movements. Future generations inheriting a healthy earth seems doubtful today, but it continues to remain the responsibility of the seemingly helpless hands of each of us and those we choose to lead us to preserve our planet.

Owl of Minerva

When school ended in June, my students sometimes honored me with unique farewell gifts. There have been books written by their favorite authors, personal poetry, a gavel inscribed with "Judge Mac," and numerous coffee cups with inscriptions. One of the most memorable gifts was a replica of an owl. This served as a reminder of an almost inscrutable quote from the nineteenth-century philosopher Friedrich Hegel in the preface to his *Philosophy of Rights:* "The owl of Minerva spreads its wings and takes its flight only when the shades of night are gathering."

Hegel's writings at first glance were usually beyond the understanding of most of us. The historical context of this enigmatic comment is helpful. Hegel was writing in the early nineteenth century. This was relatively soon after the French Revolution, arguably the most cataclysmic event in early modern European history. The social order had been shaken from top to bottom. At least forty thousand people in Paris alone were executed by guillotine, including thousands of nobles and, most notably, King Louis XVI and Queen Marie Antoinette. This became the most horrifying example yet of what Hegel described as the "slaughter bench of history." International confusion reigned. By 1848, most major European nations had undergone violent revolutions of their own.

So what does Hegel's quote explain about the meaning of these events? The owl is a reference to Athena, the Greek goddess of wisdom, known as Minerva to the Romans. For Hegel, the owl of Minerva represented wisdom. Human enlightenment can only spread its wings many years after an epoch has ended. It is only then that the causes and effects of important historical events can be analyzed and understood.

It was years after the American conflicts in Korea and Vietnam had ended and the dust had settled before we could clearly analyze whether or not those wars were worthy of such enormous human sacrifices. Many innocent humans died. Others saw their lives forever changed. The Vietnam War placed a generation of young Americans and the people of Vietnam on the "slaughter bench." Tragically, wars and revolutions confirm another statement by Hegel: "History is not the soil in which happiness grows."

Can we gain wisdom from studying our recent past or has the owl of Minerva not yet taken flight?

Existence vs. Essence

> What is meant by 'existence precedes essence'? Existentialists mean that man first exists: he materializes in the world, encounters himself, and only afterward defines himself. He will not be anything until later, and then he will be what he makes of himself. Thus, there is no human nature since there is no God to conceive of it—this is the first principle of existentialism.
>
> —JEAN-PAUL SARTRE, *Existentialism Is a Humanism*

After the Great Depression and World War II, there was an understandable loss of confidence in the world's institutions. Governments, economic systems, and religions appeared incapable of solving the enormity of our manmade problems. Prior to that time, most people's understanding of themselves and their lives initially prioritized their "essence"—their nature—before their "existence."

This newer philosophy, existentialism, suggests that existence—what you decide in the present and choose to become—takes precedence over essence. Accordingly, you create the meaning of your life, i.e., meaning is not pre-determined. This philosophy puts the onus on the individual for his or her life-defining decisions.

Existentialism became extremely popular among intellectuals. Like the bikini, it was the new French fashion of the fifties. People were excited by these new ideas. They opened the door to greater personal freedom and independent thinking. Decisions regarding unmarried couples living together, sexual preferences, and gender choices became personal and were no longer dictated by societal rules, norms, or religious doctrines.

Explaining the premise that existence precedes essence was the task of some brilliant philosophical minds, like Jean-Paul Sartre, Simone de Beauvoir, Albert Camus, and Martin Heidegger. The philosophy of existentialism did not originate with these modern intellectuals. It had been around in Europe for at least a century. A brilliant and scholarly voice from Copenhagen, Søren Kierkegaard, reminded us that we had an important decision to make during our lives. Kierkegaard, and those who followed him, termed it the "leap of faith." Raised in a strict Lutheran home, Kierkegaard was depressed for much of his adult life. This stemmed from the phoniness he observed in his fellow man and particularly in the Christian church of his day. He criticized religion for failing to change people's values for the better. He believed that strict rationality would never lead to faith in God. He ultimately made his own hypothetical "leap of faith," choosing to believe. Still unsure and without the guarantee of a safe landing, his was not a rational move. However, it changed his life in a positive way. The atheistic implication was made by later existentialists that Kierkegaard was actually replacing the role of God by creating the existence of God for himself.

A century later, during the dark days on the eve of World War II, a frustrated, disgruntled writer at Oxford by the name of C.S. Lewis was searching for his own answers regarding God. He had several serious talks with his colleague and friend, J.R.R. Tolkien. Tolkien was a devout Catholic who decided to write a book one day while he was grading tests. He began to write in the margins and other unused parts of his students' examination booklets. This resulted in the *Lord of the Rings* trilogy.

Apparently, Tolkien's impact on Lewis was enormous. Lewis describes being alone in his room one night after a long period of agonizing, getting down on his knees, making his "leap of faith," and becoming a dedicated follower of Jesus Christ. Lewis went on to write several popular books, including the *Chronicles of Narnia* series. His nonfiction testament to his faith, *Mere Christianity,* became an important Christian apologetical work of the twentieth century.

Sartre claimed that his existential fiction *Nausea* was his best work. Written just after the Spanish Civil War and published right before the outbreak of World War II, it is the story of a French writer who is horrified and confused by his own existence. A main theme is that love is hopeless; by being a lover or the object of love, either way, one becomes enslaved. Love is a doomed relationship that always fails. The Frenchman catalogs his every feeling of despair to the sickening degree of "ad nauseam" in a diary.

Sartre's play *No Exit* is a one-act philosophical drama, first performed in 1944. It has three characters who are brought into a small, well-lit room by a mysterious valet. They realize that they are dead and locked in hell together for all eternity. The only instruments of torture in the room are each other. The play explores Sartre's idea that "hell is other people" rather than a state created by God. Sartre is honest. His atheism comes across loud and clear, leaving some feeling happily free and others unhappily nihilistic. The hopeless despair and pessimism Sartre expresses in his writings reflects his lonely childhood, as he described in his autobiography, *Les Mots (The Words)*. Sartre's parents both came from prominent families. Sartre lost his father at an early age and grew up in thc highly disciplined home of his maternal grandfather, Karl Schweitzer, a respected writer on religion, philosophy, and languages. His uncle was the renowned medical missionary Albert Schweitzer. Sartre describes himself as a young boy, "cross-eyed and small in stature," who wandered in the parks of Paris longing to find playmates and acceptance. Finally, he retreated to the sixth floor of his apartment to escape from a world that rejected him. He opted for a life of books. "The words saved the child," according to Sartre.

The book-long philosophical essay *The Myth of Sisyphus,* by French-Algerian Nobel laureate Albert Camus, was also very popular at the time. According to the Greek myth, Sisyphus' punishment was to repeat for all eternity the same meaningless task of rolling a rock up a mountain, only to have it fall back down to the bottom. Camus introduced and developed the concept of the absurd, the characteristic of man forever trying to find meaning and order in life in a meaningless and indifferent world.

Existentialism became a literary phenomenon. The play *Waiting for Godot* by Irish novelist Samuel Beckett was a smash hit. Its main characters are two men sitting on a bench near a sickly looking tree, waiting for an unspecified friend named Godot. They quarrel, make up, contemplate suicide, gnaw on chicken bones, and try to sleep. Just before the curtain comes down at the end of the first half, a young boy shows up to tell them that Godot cannot make it, but will come the next day. When the curtain rises again, it is the next day and the two bedraggled men are again sitting on the bench, waiting for Godot. The tree has sprouted a few sparse leaves, signifying there is some small hope in a despairing world. As the curtain goes down at the end of the play, the same boy appears to say that Godot will come the next day.

The two characters vainly waited for the ethereal God to rescue them from their completely useless and confused lives. In the meantime, neither man understood that he has the option to alleviate his angst by the existential choices of human freedom and responsibility. There were many plays like this in the fifties and sixties, part of a genre that was aptly labeled "Theater of the Absurd."

Death of God

Perhaps the most brilliant and controversial philosopher of the second half of the nineteenth century was Friedrich Nietzsche. Considered a forerunner of the existentialists, he was an exciting writer and as quotable as any philosopher ever was. Probably best known for his shocking phrase "God is dead," he describes it in his book *The Gay Science:*

> One morning, a crazy man carrying a lighted lantern storms into a market place searching for God. He announces to the crowd that God is dead. "We have killed him, you and I! We are all his murderers . . . Whither are we going now? . . . Do we not now wander through an endless nothingness? Does not empty space breathe upon us? Has it not become colder? Does not night come on continually, darker and darker?"

Nietzsche did not literally mean that we had killed God. He meant that our belief in the existence of God had become obsolete during his own era. Science and technological progress had exposed the lack of any further need for God. Nietzsche challenged the men of his own modern generation to stand up and become *Übermensch,* or supermen. Strong, intelligent, and bold human beings were needed to replace the void that God once filled. This became Nietzsche's goal for humanity.

He saw the ancient Greco-Roman civilizations as initially powerful and strong. However, they were eventually corrupted by the slave mentality and inferior weakness of the Judco-Christian mindset. These softer, more humanistic principles were responsible for the ultimate demise of those civilizations and only the noble races outside the old Roman Empire maintained a proud, victorious consciousness, something akin to being a god.

Why does Nietzsche omit most positive references to the Judeo-Christian cultures from ancient history up to his own times? As he said in *On the Genealogy of Morals / Ecce Homo:*

> At the center of all these noble races we cannot fail to see the blond beast of prey, the magnificent blond beast avidly prowling around for spoil and victory; this hidden center needs release from time to time, the beast must out again, must return to the wild: Roman, Arabian, Germanic, Japanese nobility, Homeric heroes, Scandinavian Vikings—in this requirement they are all alike. It was the noble races which left the concept of 'barbarian' in their traces wherever they went; even their highest culture betrays the fact that they were conscious of this and indeed proud of it.

Important questions regarding Nietzsche and anti-Semitism still linger, primarily having to do with his younger sister, Elisabeth Förster-Nietzsche. They were close in childhood, but grew apart when she married a former schoolteacher, Bernhard Förster. Förster was a fanatic racist who was planning a "pure Aryan settlement" in South America. He and Elisabeth persuaded over a dozen German families to join them in a colony, named "Nueva Germania," in Paraguay in 1887. The colony didn't survive, due to poor farming methods, illness, and mounting debt. Förster committed suicide and Elizabeth came home to

Germany just as her brother succumbed to mental illness. As a result, she became his caretaker, and took control of his unpublished writings. Hitler's political star had begun to rise, and Elisabeth Förster-Nietzsche became a devoted follower of Hitler and a member of the Nazi party. Hitler was understandably flattered by this association with the sister of the famous philosopher. After gaining total power in 1932, Hitler would have his motorcade stop at her home and personally present her with flowers, often referring to her as the "Mother of the New Germany." He attended her funeral, along with other Nazi dignitaries. It is believed that Nietzsche's sister Elisabeth altered her brother's writings to reflect her own ideology and to advance her position with Hitler and the Nazis. This is a letter from Nietzsche to his sister right after she left for Paraguay with Förster:

In the meantime, I've seen proof, black on white, that Herr Dr. Förster has not yet severed his connection with the anti-Semitic movement... Since then I've had difficulty coming up with any of the tenderness and protectiveness I've so long felt toward you. The separation between us is thereby decided in really the most absurd way. Have you grasped nothing of the reason why I am in the world? Now it has gone so far that I have to defend myself hand and foot against people who confuse me with anti-Semitic canaille; after my own sister, my former sister, and after Widemann more recently have given the impetus to the most dire of all confusions.

After I read the name Zarathustra in the anti-Semitic Correspondence, my forbearance came to an end. I am now in a position of emergency defense against your spouse's party. These accursed anti-Semite deformities shall not sully my ideal!

—FRIEDRICH NIETZSCHE, *Nice, France, 1887*

Princes vs. Pagans

About thirty years ago, in my Comparative Religion and Philosophy classes, I came up with the idea of having students role-play famous people in history debating the existencc of God and the value of religion. The classroom was set up like a courtroom. Teams of witnesses and attorneys for the opposing sides would first organize their cases. After opening speeches, each famous person could bring in "witnesses" to support their arguments and refute the opposition. My high school class of mostly seniors was divided into two groups: the theists, who argued for God's existence and that religion has been a force for good in human history, and the atheists, along with some agnostics, who presented the case that God does not exist and that religion is not only a useless waste of time, but often dangerous. Student witnesses would role-play philosophers from the past and present, as well as scholars, scientists, theologians, and notorious criminals.

Over the years of this debate many famous and infamous individuals from the past and present took the stand for their "day in court." Student attorneys would organize their cases beforehand and submit a "brief," disclosing their witnesses and qualifications. The rest of the students in the class, usually about twelve, would be required for "jury duty." They would watch, listen, take notes, and decide the verdict at the end. I would give them a score sheet for rating the effectiveness of each witness.

As the "judge," I made rulings on some of the most profound issues in human history without ever having gone to law school or taken the bar exam. In a black graduation gown, I would sit at the "bar," listening and occasionally pounding a gavel that former students had given me as a gift. It bore the inscription "Judge Mac." Oh, the power and glory of it all! Sometimes, the job was over my head because of my lack of legal background. Our best "student attorneys" were also on our school's Mock Trial Team. These bright students quickly discovered my limitations and frequently challenged me with procedural objections. I could handle obvious objections—badgering, irrelevant, leading the witness, or hearsay—but sometimes I ran into trouble over "speculation." Once, student attorneys cleverly backed me into a corner by saying: "You're allowing testimony from people in history, but they're all dead! Doesn't a ruling on their behalf show favoritism for the God side by implying that life after death exists?" They were right. The premise of the whole trial was speculative and ridiculous. Even though I agreed with their logic, I had to rule against them because the trial was already in progress and my primary objective for having it was to get the students to learn more about philosophy, religion, and history.

The theists would introduce illustrious ancient and medieval philosophers such as Socrates, Plato, and Aristotle, and saints such as Augustine, Thomas Aquinas, and Anselm. They would raise arguments we learned at Loyola as standard proofs for the existence of God: Causality, the Prime Mover, the Uncaused Cause, and Intelligent Design. The Swedish philosopher Søren Kierkegaard and the Christian writer C.S. Lewis would explain their "leap of faith." Religious leaders were put on the stand: Popes John Paul and Francis, Archbishop Desmond Tutu, and the Dalai Lama. Activists were conjured: Gandhi, Martin Luther King, Albert Schweitzer, Nelson Mandela, and Mother Teresa.

The anti-God side prepared strong cases based on history: the Crusades, the persecution of women for witchcraft in the Middle Ages, and the trial of Galileo. Then came Darwin and evolution. Nietzsche argued that "God is dead" and Karl Marx declared that "religion is the opium of the people." Freud, Jean-Paul Sartre and his mistress Simone de Beauvoir, and other existentialists made powerful and convincing arguments. The pedophile scandals of the Catholic Church and the prostitution and rape scandals of televangelists Jimmy Swaggert and Jim Bakker were cited as evidence of corruption. Dictators like Hitler, Mussolini, Stalin, Mao Tse-Tung, and Fidel Castro were sometimes presented by the student attorneys for shock value. International terrorists and criminals like Osama Bin Laden, Joaquín "El Chapo" Guzmán, and Carlos the Jackal took the stand.

If it is true that incongruity forms the basis of humor, it explains why one of the funniest incidents of my teaching career happened during this mock trial. A new student by the name of Sean had just transferred into my class a few days earlier. He was a tall, soft-spoken, slightly shy Nigerian teenager. Although he was a year younger than most of the seniors, he showed intelligence, poise, and good manners. Sean had the longest surname I had ever seen. I wouldn't attempt to spell it. It was twenty-one letters long. I asked him if his name had a particular meaning. He said it meant "prince who is a warrior for God." The name seemed to fit him because Sean exhibited a natural dignity and regal bearing. He had attended a Jesuit missionary school in Nigeria.

Due to his late enrollment in my class, there were no more openings on the pro-God side, so I assigned him to join the anti-God side in the debate. That meant he was required to go on the witness stand for the atheists. Even more incongruent, Sean was assigned to portray Simone de Beauvoir, the famous French atheist, existentialist, and radical feminist. Sean did well when answering his own counsel's rehearsed questions. The difficult part for him came with his cross-examination by the opposition. The attorneys had clearly done their research on Simone de Beauvoir and quickly tried to smear her character. Sean, representing Simone, was asked: "During the 1950s in Paris, did you and your lover Jean-Paul Sartre ever engage in a *ménage à trois?*" Sean's bright mind was working hard to understand the question. He kept his cool and in his deep melodious voice, slowly and carefully asked, "Could you please explain to me the meaning of those words 'manage of Troy'?" Before I could protect Sean from embarrassment and reject the question, the prosecution fired back: "It means a three-way!"

After that exchange, pandemonium reigned over the proceedings. The incongruity caused an eruption of laughter from around the room. I banged my gavel a few times and jumped down from my chair, crossing my hands like an umpire at home plate. "Okay, it's over. Court's adjourned!"

I thought Sean handled the situation well. He maintained the dignity of his given name in spite of the courtroom antics. The following year, I wrote Sean a letter of recommendation for college. He was admitted to the University of San Francisco. On the last day of school, I found the gift he had left for me inside my teacher's mailbox. It was a thank-you note and a coffee mug with the inscription:

> *"God is dead."* —NIETZSCHE, *1883*
>
> *"Nietzsche is dead."* —GOD, *1900*
>
> *"Thanks, Mr. Mac."* —SEAN

Fear of Death

Near the end of his life, I often visited my father. We were glad he was neither in the hospital nor on life-support. The last time I saw him, he was sitting up in bed, staring out the window. His lips were parted and his eyes were wide as if he were in deep thought. There was a pensive, distant, slightly worried look on his face. I sat on the edge of his bed as close as I could be to him. His face was clean-shaven and I could smell a familiar scent. I knew my older brother John had been there earlier. Shaving had become a tender ritual between them, which always ended with John gently slapping Old Spice aftershave on Dad's face.

Now Dad and I were alone. I didn't say anything at first because I thought my voice might break down. It was painful to see the light in him slowly fading. I took his hand and asked: "What are you thinking about, Dad?" He sounded pensive. "The Great Beyond." I asked: "Are you worrying about it or wondering what comes next?" He nodded and gave an almost inaudible "Yes."

At that moment, I thought of a book I had recently read titled *Life After Life* by Raymond Moody. Moody had interviewed hundreds of flatliners: people who had been pronounced clinically dead, some for several minutes or more, before coming back to life. They were of all ages (including children) and different cultures. These people reported remarkably similar experiences of dying. I thought this information could be a source of comfort. "Dad, I just finished a book about what happens when you die. It's not scary at all. Want me to tell you about it?" He nodded his head affirmatively. "Well, they said that you go slowly down through this tunnel but it's not painful. Then you wind up in this beautiful crystal city. There, you meet old friends and relatives who have gone before you. It's a very beautiful, peaceful, and happy place. Finally, you have the greatest experience of all. You are with God and feel His complete love for you."

Dad was listening intensely. I could see the worry and fear leaving his face and a softer, more relaxed smile taking over. "Thanks, Jim," he whispered softly as he squeezed my hand. I kissed his cheek and left.

I sat in my car trying to control my emotions. My heart was hurting. I was already feeling the deep loss that was coming. I tried to choose a perfect memory of when Dad was still strong and vibrant. I pictured him on the grand staircase of the Fairmont Hotel in San Francisco. He was holding Mom's arm and they were smiling. He had just won another award for "best salesman of the year" for his company.

The next morning, I learned Dad had died in his sleep.

God

As with other vast, incomprehensible ideas such as eternity and infinity, I'll never be able to wrap my finite mind around God. I'm okay with that because I accept the fact that I am limited at birth in ways unique to me. Like all of us, I am a complex amalgam of my genetic composition; the influence of my parents, siblings, friends, enemies, culture, education, and religious experiences; and my place in human history. However, given this to be true, we can also surmise that we are more than the influence of our gene pool and life experiences and are the carriers, creators, and salvation of the future.

I remember reading that a professor of religious studies and theology was once asked by a student if she believed in God. She replied emphatically: "Yes! Some days not so much." I admit that I too have those days. My life is made up of periods of happiness interspersed with periods of sadness. When there is joy in my life, I am reminded of the wonders of God's creation. When sadness engulfs me, I remember that I am mortal and I am humbled by God as the Infinite Mystery of Life. The consequences of my free will are determined by my listening to or ignoring God speaking to me through my conscience. I firmly believe that the truths of science should not destroy our belief in God; rather, we should acknowledge those truths as His gift.

Finding God can be a struggle. Some find Him in magnificent cathedrals in metropolitan cities; others find Him in humble country chapels. The lofty Tower of Babel was built in order to reach the heavens in search of God. The ancient Celtics looked for God in nature, the Persians in fire, and the Hindus in every place and thing. I know I cannot know God by relying on reason. Similarly to the Buddhist belief that God is within oneself, the words of Luke 17:21 ring true to me: "the kingdom of God lies within you." When I turn inside myself and connect with my heart, I find God and I am comforted.

I became more cynical about the integrity and authority of political and religious institutions during the late sixties. One reason came during graduate school while I was working on a doctorate in history at USC. I was required to do in-depth, primary source research relating to the quotation by Lord Acton, a famous English historian: "Power tends to corrupt and absolute power corrupts absolutely."

I initially thought the quotation referred to corrupt monarchies that led to the French Revolution of 1789 and various revolutions across Europe in 1848. I was wrong. It referred to Pope Pius IX's declaration of "papal infallibility." For over a thousand years, the papacy controlled most of the Italian peninsula. However, by the 1860s, a political and social movement known as the Risorgimento had unified small states across the peninsula into the new nation-state of Italy. The pope's temporal power was greatly reduced to an area of little more than a hundred acres inside Rome called Vatican City. Pope Pius was depicted in political cartoons as "the Prisoner of the Vatican." To compensate for his loss of political power, he had himself declared "infallible in all matters of faith and morals."

I've always been bothered by the patronizing position the Catholic Church takes toward women by locking them out of the priesthood in spite of the fact there are many outstandingly qualified, gifted, and pious women who could be wonderful priests. An excellent example of this to me is Mother Paula, an Episcopalian priest. My wife and I met her at a neighbor's Christmas party. She had previously been a Catholic nun. I asked her how she became a priest. She explained that although she was raised as a Catholic, she felt she had a calling and a God-given gift to give more than the constraints of the Catholic Church allowed. She had a strong desire to offer Mass, give Communion, preach homilies, and counsel people in confession. I invited her to be a guest speaker in my religion class to represent Christianity. After a thoughtful presentation, she asked for questions. One of my students raised her hand and asked: "I'm a Muslim and practice my faith every day. I read and follow the teachings of the Quran. Do you believe a non-Christian can go to heaven?" Mother Paula replied: "I don't believe God requires a passport for heaven."

After class, the student came up to me to say that she now realized in her heart that there is "only One True God of Creation and that He is described in many different forms and different names by the world's religions." Mother Paula's answer to my student's question was in stark contrast to the answers given by Christian fundamentalists to Muslim students in the past, who had asked the same question and been told they would go to Hell if they didn't convert.

My personal relationship with God is one without rigid rituals and doctrines. My church is a private one-on-one while walking alone with my Creator. In the most quiet of times, I feel God's presence.

Loyola and Lawyers

Students in my Loyola class of 1960 went into law more than any other profession. This was true for my brother John's class of 1954 and my brother Phil's class of 1948, and I would guess it is still true today. Why has this common characteristic prevailed for so long?

Loyola High was all about competition. You had to compete with other students on the entrance exam to be admitted. You competed for grades in almost every class. Test performances and GPA were usually posted. There were competitions in debate, elocution, and dramatic interpretation. I lost my first contest with a speech about crime to my classmate Dean who gave a stirring rendition of the priest's dockside eulogy in the classic movie *On the Waterfront*. Then there were the athletic events.

Whether it was George rounding the bend and winning the 440-yard dash at the Catholic League track meet, Bernie and Bill on the mound pitching hardballs to Al at the plate, John's tough rebounding under the basket, or Bill, Rich, and me at the goal line stand, those battles were intense and very real to us.

Jesuit education fostered a kind of logic-based critical thinking geared for persuasion. We were encouraged to express our opinions in forensic exercises where the goal was not just to clearly make the point, but to prove it by combining proper logic with effective argumentation. Excellent English teachers like Mr. Barnet encouraged students to have open arguments with him and the other students. The reward was your grade. This verbal sparring became popular intellectual entertainment in and outside the classroom.

It was a never-ending game of wits that continued through college. We realized at the time it was a kind of "intellectual calisthenics," as well as an enjoyable way to learn. All topics were fair game: politics, literature, philosophical concepts, and especially ethical issues. An English professor assigned us a short story to read, analyze, and discuss in class: "Two Lovely Beasts," written by Irish writer Liam O'Flaherty, a socialist at the time. The story concerned a peasant family's struggle against their community because they wanted more. Jocko and I verbally sparred for weeks over whether Colm had the moral right to own another beast.

Once on a long car ride to Las Vegas, our lofty topic of discussion was: "What is the difference between ketchup and catsup?" Silly, but it turned out to be a great way to pass the time.

Jerry

In 2010, during the process of locating Loyola High class members and reminding them about our 50th reunion, I received an email from Jerry, a former classmate. Because of a family tragedy, he didn't graduate. His father died of a heart attack during our junior year. The loss devastated Jerry and his mother. They were forced to leave Los Angeles and return to their family home in Pendleton, Oregon. Jerry's father had been a famous sports columnist for several Los Angeles newspapers and was a local celebrity with contacts throughout the city. At Loyola, I knew Jerry more as a football teammate than a close friend. I admired him for his athleticism and his major contributions to our winning team junior year. Over a decade passed before I saw Jerry again. We accidentally bumped into each other on a summer day at Laguna Beach. We were eager to catch up and reminisce.

I learned that day that we had more in common than Loyola High. In some ways we had led parallel lives. After college, while I was teaching in India, Jerry joined the Peace Corps and lived in a remote rural village in South America. There, he spoke Spanish exclusively for two years. Afterward, he had a variety of interesting jobs, including working for an oil company in Alaska and specializing in educational technology at various large school districts in Chicago and Los Angeles. Jerry's tendency to leave a job after he had mastered it was a trait we didn't share. He struck me as kind of a "rolling stone." After conquering a challenge, he always seemed to be searching for a new adventure.

Jerry told me that after his mother's and aunt's lengthy illnesses and deaths, he had taken out a reverse mortgage to handle the costs of their hospitalizations and funerals. This had placed him in permanent financial trouble. He was dealing with enormous debt.

One day, several weeks after our talk on the beach, Jerry emailed me: "Jim, do you think it's wrong to ask a friend for financial help when you're in need?" I responded with a flippant attempt at humor and a noncommittal answer: "No, I don't think there's anything wrong with asking somebody, as long as it's not me!" Jerry replied: "No, I meant Jocko." I paused to think and then said: "Well, what I can tell you is something you probably already know. Jocko has been extremely successful in the legal profession. He's also made many wise investments and is very generous. He's given a ton of money to his three alma maters: Loyola High, Loyola University, and USC. You'll have to make your own decision about asking him."

After contacting Jocko, Jerry's life quickly began to change for the better. He had three immediate needs: housing, health care, and transportation. Jerry had been living the idealistic wandering life of a Thoreau or a Kerouac without a steady means of income. His home in Oregon and Northern California was a rundown RV. The roof had rusted out in places and the ceiling was musty and full of mildew from the frequent rain. Water had seeped in between the walls and they were beginning to buckle. He was at the point where his living conditions were seriously harming his health.

Jocko is a "doer." He quickly figures out the essentials of a problem and if he can fix it, he does. He is a major philanthropist who has helped many people in need. When Jocko learned of the severity of Jerry's living conditions and poor health, he quickly provided him with the money to obtain an RV that was virtually new and free of damage. He then paid for Jerry to come down to Los Angeles, arranged for his lodging, and made appointments with his own personal physician and various specialists for extensive testing and medical treatment. After several months, Jerry began to improve. Without going into the medical details, Jocko's "rescue" saved Jerry's life. Later, Jerry moved to a rural area near San Luis Obispo and took a job as a Spanish teacher at a public school in a nearby town. It seemed as if his financial problems were solved. Things went well for a month or two until Jerry realized a different kind of problem. He was working in a corrupt school system.

Jerry wrote to me: "I gave the students writing assignments and many of them refused to do the work. As a consequence, I gave them a zero for each assignment that was not turned in. When it was time to give them their second quarter grades, I was astonished to discover that someone had changed one girl's final grade from 28 to 100! Also, I was told by the counselor to give the principal's daughter an A for Spanish II, even though she never came to class. This girl simply turned in a single sheet of notebook paper with a few vocabulary words and three con-jugated verbs." Jerry told the counselor: "Giving high grades for doing nothing in my class is something I cannot ethically do."

The principal and the superintendent were forcing teachers to change the grades of many of their students, not just the athletes but also kids whose parents were on the school board. This was clearly systemic corruption. Twenty days later, Jerry was given a layoff notice, and told that his services would not be necessary the following year. The stated reason was low school enrollment.

When Jerry told Jocko this story, the wily old barrister decided to come out of retirement for one last case. Jocko can-didly admitted beforehand that there was no realistic chance of Jerry winning the case because he hadn't been there the three years required for tenure. Despite this, Jocko and his wife Dee Dee, who had been a court reporter, went full force into the case as a matter of principle and spent several months gather-ing evidence to support Jerry's accusations. The administrative judge in the case said that she would only allow one hour for the trial as there were no real issues in contention. Jocko filed a hearing notice and demanded a full day for the hearing and the right to make an offer of proof before it began. Jocko's burden of proof was convincing in that the case was retaliation against a whistle-blowing employee and the reduction in force (RIF) was a fraud and a fiction to cover up a retaliation dismissal. The judge agreed to extend the trial.

Jerry wrote: "I wish I had been able to videotape the trial because Jocko reduced these witnesses to babbling fools." They had been coached by their own attorneys to answer "I don't recall" and "I don't remember" to each question. An example of this came when Jocko asked the superintendent: "What do you talk about when you meet with the high school principal weekly?" "I don't recall" was not acceptable to Jocko so he kept on pressing. He asked her: "Is there a disciplinary policy for administrators who break the law?" She said that there was. He then asked what the policy was specifically. She replied that it was "progressive." When Jocko kept probing for specifics, she became frustrated and just kept repeating that it was "progressive." It was apparent that the superintendent didn't know the policy. After Jocko ended his interrogation, she quickly exited the room in a shaken condition. I was surprised to later learn that this inept superintendent's salary was close to that of the Governor of California at that time.

When the librarian had to testify, he asked her if she was a credentialed teacher. She replied that she was not. He then asked how she could supervise the daughter of the principal, since she was the student's teacher of record and was required to give her a grade. The student was using the online language program Rosetta Stone. The librarian was asked how many minutes a week the girl spent using the program and how her proficiency was measured. The librarian couldn't do the math to determine the minutes per week and replied: "I don't know Spanish." Jocko then held up the single sheet of notebook paper that the girl had turned in to represent an entire quarter's worth of work. "Do you think this is valid proof of a student's proficiency in Spanish?" She replied, "I can't comment on that because I'm not a teacher."

The inept administrators and their corrupt school system were eventually exposed to the community. The superintendent was fired along with most of the others. Jerry felt vindicated. Because he lacked tenure, he did lose the case, but he redeemed his self-esteem. This seemed like a "happily ever after" ending but it wasn't, because Jerry was still out of a job and his old car was breaking down.

I wrote a letter to our fellow Loyola High classmates about Jerry's situation and asked them to donate financial help to keep him going. I described our old friend as a gifted and dedicated teacher and I pointed out the amount of good he had already done, particularly teaching in an area with so many poor Hispanic immigrants. Our classmates' response was immediate and overwhelming. The first and by far the most generous responder was Joe. He was an extremely successful personal injury lawyer in private practice. With the help of Joe and our other classmates, Jerry purchased a good certified used car and kept teaching and tutoring English to poor kids and adults in rural areas of Central California. He continues to fulfill his mission of helping others as he did long ago in South America.

Losing Our "Youth"

Pat's fraternity nickname was "The Youth." It was perfect for him because it reflected his handsome, clean-cut, Irish good looks and jovial nature. Pat loved to laugh and when he did, it was wholehearted. Jocko especially knew how to "tickle his funny bone," and frequently did just to hear Pat's unique chuckle. It started low in his gut and rippled up into a chortle. Pat's friendly manner and boyish appearance naturally made him popular with the ladies. He eventually dated and married one of the most beautiful girls in our college group.

When it came to athletic competition, Pat's affable nature changed. He became a ferocious warrior in every sport he played. Whether he was sliding in at home plate, or shoving his elbows in your face while going for a rebound under the basket, he was relentless. His teams usually took home the trophy.

As the years went by and the rest of us began to look older, "The Youth" never seemed to slow down or show signs of aging except for a little gray hair at his temples. He continued working at his finance company, long-distance running, traveling the world, and skiing with friends.

Suddenly, out of nowhere, tragedy struck our friend in the prime of his life. In 2012, he was diagnosed with a virulent form of prostate cancer at an advanced stage. At first, it was hard to tell he was sick. However, within weeks, we began to witness his physical deterioration. He was very ill.

Pat had stayed in touch with his old friends and always attended our reunions and parties. We began to receive more frequent text messages from him. Every few weeks, he'd invite us all to join him for lunch, each time at a restaurant in a different area of Los Angeles. I remember driving Fernando to a Marie Callender's in Glendale for one of the first luncheons. It was held in their small banquet room. Pat seemed to be his old self as he greeted and joked with us. I didn't yet realize how ill he was, and how brave. After we had finished eating, Pat rose up from his chair and walked over to a nearby corner where he had stashed a blanket and a pillow. As he lay down on the floor, he said: "You guys keep on telling jokes. I just want to be comfortable and listen." That moment stands out in my memory, not only for its poignancy but also for the realization that our friend was using our bonds of friendship to help him momentarily forget his terrible pain and foreboding future.

As I pulled out of the parking lot, I noticed Jocko's Navigator. He often loaded it up with food and beer for USC football game tailgate parties. Later, I learned that Jocko had his Navigator modified with a lounge mattress installed so Pat could lie down. Jocko would drive Pat to USC Keck Medical Center for his cancer treatments. In spite of the pain he endured, Pat still laughed at the old stories with all of us. Close to the end, he was staying with Julie at their home in Belmont Shores. Pete, Jocko, and I paid him a final visit. He could hardly walk. We sat down in lawn chairs out on the sand, looking at the bay. For the first time, he didn't say much. He seemed at peace watching his grandkids play football on the beach and sometimes dozing. After a bit, I gently touched his shoulder and said my last good-bye. Then we went back in the house to alert Julie that we were leaving. We lost our "Youth" a few days later. Pat had bravely accepted his terminal illness. He set an example for all of us and taught us how to die with dignity.

Father Steve "Redux"

I have always been proud of my high school and college friends because of their service to others and humanity. I would place Steve at the top of my list. I am proud of him for the man he became. The path to become a Jesuit priest is very narrow and steep, and to stay committed to a religious vocation for the rest of one's life is an exceptional achievement by any measure. Father Steve has done that. When I think of values such as courage, bravery, and commitment to a cause, I think of Steve in El Salvador. With deadly government planes circling overhead, he offered Mass in an open field for his fallen Jesuit brothers after their brutal assassinations by the military.

Steve was the principal at several schools, and worked most of his life as the president of the University of San Francisco. Currently he is the president of a unique high school, Verbum Dei, which means "The Word of God."

Verbum Dei is an all-boys Catholic high school located in Watts, the poorest area of South Los Angeles. The mission of this school is to change society one student at a time through education. A recent op-ed piece in the *New York Times* noted that the thirty-eight most selective universities in our country have more students from the top one percent of the income scale than from the bottom sixty percent. It also showed how this gap is widening. Anyone who cares about democracy, social justice, and economic stability in the United States should be concerned about this trend. What is the most effective way to change the imbalance between rich and poor in our society? Education is the answer.

Verbum Dei offers a rigorous college prep education as well as a corporate work experience for over three hundred students. One hundred percent of these students have earned college acceptance upon their graduation. The statements below speak for themselves. They were written by students who are attending or have attended this unique high school.

"Not a lot of people with backgrounds like mine make it past their teenage years. I don't want that to be my fate/destiny. I want to be someone to pave the way for generations after me."

"I stood at a fork in the road before Verbum Dei. The way to my left would lead me to a life of crime, prison, or death. The road to my right was hardly ever traveled, so I really had no idea what would come of it."

"Making my mom smile meant the world to me, so I took the leap of faith and went to the all-boys school on the wrong side of the tracks and that made all the difference."

"Growing up with two Mexican immigrant parents, work was always defined by sweat, stress, and insecurity. I got a different perception of work thanks to the work-study program. I was able to envision myself working in a corporate setting. Now that I have graduated from Loyola Marymount University, I will be actually working in the office of a large corporation. I hope to raise the bar for generations that will follow in my footsteps."

When Jeanne and I were first married, she worked for a large successful company that built and financed many shopping centers across the Los Angeles area. One day after work, she told me that a new member had joined her office team. She described him as a tall, lanky, clean-cut, extremely thin African American young man, who was bussed to their Manhattan Beach office from Verbum Dei. A memo was never sent out to explain who he was, or that he was in the school's corporate work program.

He always arrived wearing a spotless, albeit threadbare, white shirt, and a clean but somewhat rumpled jacket and slacks. When Jeanne became aware that he seldom had more than a peanut butter sandwich for lunch, she made a point to pack a nutritious and hardy lunch for him each morning. She would often sit with him at lunchtime. She wanted to get to know this young man who seemed to be an anomaly. She learned that he lived with his grandmother. He told her his favorite sport was football and that Verbum Dei had to relinquish the program because of lack of funds. He wanted to become a policeman because there was so much crime in his neighborhood. She was extremely impressed with his gentlemanly manners. He addressed people by the respectful terms "sir" and "ma'am," and always opened doors for her and others. He never failed to fold his hands and bow his head to say a prayerful blessing before eating. He expressed to Jeanne that he loved school and hoped to keep up his good grades so he could get a scholarship to college. She was impressed with his sincerity when he told her how grateful he was to be able to go to Verbum Dei.

Prayer Group

Sometimes at a party or during our Loyola lunches, I would have one-on-one conversations with Tom or Ron. These talks were never lengthy because of time constraints and interruptions.

Tom especially seemed curious about my religious beliefs.

On a beautiful Sunday afternoon a few years ago, while I was taking one of my daily walks around our neighborhood and praying for some writing inspiration, a question surfaced in my mind: "What would praying with others feel like after all these years?" When I returned home, there was an email from Tom. He wrote: "Jim, how would you like to join Ron and me in a prayer group?" I asked: "Since our previous conversations have centered more on the philosophy of religion, would it be accurate to call it a prayer group?" He insightfully replied: "God is always part of our conversation when we see each other. In my opinion, whenever you are thinking or talking about God, you are actually praying. This would give us the opportunity to share our thoughts and beliefs in more depth."

He had a good point. Because it was centrally located in the city, the three of us decided to meet at the same restaurant in Marina Del Rey where we held our Loyola luncheons. As an opening goodwill gesture, I presented both friends with a copy of Huston Smith's *The World's Religions*, the same book I used in my Comparative Religion classes. The next time we met, I was pleased that they had both read the book, which became a catalyst for discussions at future meetings. Both of these friends have a low-key style when expressing their opinions. There's never been any form of argument or contention when we are exchanging our views. It is always a joyful and enlightening experience.

These meetings began during my final year of teaching. At the same time, Tom was working hard at transitioning his pharmacy business, making important personnel changes. Ron stepped up and kept our group's spiritual focus by sending us consistent email contributions. Ron has been a steady reader of a newspaper column written by a Catholic priest by the name of Father Ronald Rolheiser. His essays deal with spiritual questions about God, morality, faith, and their relationship to contemporary issues.

In his Christmas essay "Standing on New Borders," Father Rolheiser presents the biblical story of Jesus meeting a woman on the border of Samaria, a foreign country in both ethnicity and religion. By standing on these "new borders," Jesus began to see more clearly how his role as God's son encompassed the world as a whole. Father Rolheiser writes: "I believe that this is where we are standing today as Christians, on new borders in terms of relating to other religions, not least to our Islamic brothers and sisters. The single most important agenda for our churches for the next fifty years will be the issue of relating to other religions: Islam, Hinduism, Buddhism, Taoism, indigenous religions in the Americas and Africa, and various forms, old and new, of Paganism and New Age."

In my mind, the image of the holy family, poor immigrants giving birth to the Savior in a stable in a foreign country, is analogous to the multicultural streets of Los Angeles today. I closely identify with Father Rolheiser's Christmas message because of an experience I had not long after reading it. It was during that same Christmas season. One morning I stopped to fill my tank at a gas station, and went inside to pay the man behind the counter. He was on the phone speaking in Arabic and hung up just as I walked in. I greeted him with the traditional Islamic greeting: "As-Salaam Alaikum." His face lit up as he replied "Alaikum Salaam." He asked if I spoke Arabic. I replied, "No, only that I do know that the word 'Islam' means 'peace.'" He nodded. "Yes. It means 'Peace be to you from the heart, where God is.'" As I was leaving, he bowed, thanked me, and called me "brother."

It was just a friendly conversation between two people in a time of xenophobic fear and mistrust. I don't remember our country and the world being like this. I can recall traveling through India, long before September 11, 2001, when three Muslims, noticing I was an American, came up to offer their sincere condolences to me for the death of our President Kennedy two years earlier.

Simon's Rock Experiment

My Advanced Placement European History class was made up mainly of sophomores. Most were bright, ambitious, and hard-working. Close to the end of the year, one of those students asked me for a college recommendation. I was surprised by this and asked, "Aren't you getting a little ahead of yourself? Don't you still have two more years left in high school?"

The student told me his parents wanted him to bypass his last two years of high school and apply to a special college in Massachusetts by the name of Bard College at Simon's Rock. I went online to learn more about the school before writing his recommendation. It was founded in the 1960s by a gifted professor who believed that bright high school students were not learning as effectively as they could during their last two years for various reasons. She pioneered an outstanding "early college" in rural Massachusetts near a landmark called Simon's Rock. It began as a women's college, but later became coeducational. With changes in leadership over the decades, the school has survived and expanded.

I learned that the most impressive characteristic of this school, besides allowing students to begin their college education at age sixteen, is that the student-to-faculty ratio is six to one. That means students can regularly engage in sophisticated directed research programs with the luxury of frequent individual conferencing with their professors. I wrote the letter of recommendation for my student and he was admitted to Simon's Rock.

At the beginning of the following year, I had a feeling that it might be my final year of teaching due to some medical issues.

I had already been teaching for over fifty years. I wanted to leave a legacy, so I began thinking of the best way to handle my students' final research projects in philosophy. I asked myself how they could be directed and advised by teachers with more specialized depth in certain academic areas. The answer was right in front of me—our own teachers! A small volunteer group of my outstanding colleagues at Peninsula High could play the "directive" role of the professors back at Simon's Rock. There was no question in my mind that we had the teaching talent at Peninsula for this. I had often heard our high school described as a small college.

These were the last philosophy classes I would ever teach. I hoped they would be unique for their quality, depth of insight, and new interdisciplinary approach with other teachers working along with me. If the experiment was successful, the students would gain a much wider perspective of their subjects.

Starting at the top, I paid a visit to our principal, Mitzi. I didn't know at the time that this would also be her final year at Peninsula High. I needed her permission to begin this interdisciplinary program. I knew trying something innovative would not be a problem for Mitzi, but there could be complications and it was getting late in the school year.

I wanted to design the research topics with my colleagues' different areas of expertise in mind. I knew that Mitzi had a genuine appreciation and concern for animals. I invited her to be the faculty advisor for a group of students who were working on these questions: "How intelligent are animals? How different are they from us? Should animals have the same legal rights as humans?" Mitzi immediately loved the idea. She even offered additional funding.

When my students in the "Animal Projects" group had their first meeting in the principal's office, Mitzi had assembled books and videos on animal intelligence. One video showed Koko, the well-known gorilla who had learned sign language from Francine Patterson at Stanford. The video showed the moment of realization when Koko became aware that the image in the mirror was herself. Another video showed a chimpanzee who had learned to order his food preferences from a menu on a computer image board.

One by one, I met with gifted members of our faculty to learn their interests. One was Mark, an outstanding physics teacher. He liked the question I had tailored for some of his students: "What are the future implications for our society with the narrowing gap between reality and virtual reality?" Mark accepted, but when I asked him if he wanted to serve on a committee, he responded: "Please, no committees! Committees are where good ideas go to die!" Mark worked with the students to explore the growing range of virtual reality, from games, trips to the surface of Mars, archeological digs, and even scouting future college campuses. Students also considered the downside of "VR": social isolation and desensitization.

"Why does music evoke such powerful emotions?" This was a question I gave to Fred, our music teacher and school orchestra director. He worked with a small group of students who were also outstanding musicians. Before performing some beautiful and emotional pieces with violins and cello, they illustrated their point about the power of music in a unique way. They showed a short segment of the award-winning animated film *Up* without any sound. It was a sequence reviewing an elderly couple's married life and relationship. Then they showed the same clip again, but this time with music. It brought many of us to tears, confirming the emotional power of the music itself.

My questions for Ben, our environmental science teacher, were: "At this time in history, are we capable of saving the planet from environmental destruction? If so, what are the major steps necessary for our survival and how can they be achieved?" Ben was the right teacher for this project. He had traveled all over the globe studying this subject for decades. His group came up with sophisticated and technical solutions to the serious issues of climate change, the preservation of natural resources, and the tragic environmental effects of greed, war, and poverty.

Lara, an exceptional English teacher, coached a group of my philosophy students on classical fundamentals in literature. They learned to recognize similar plots and themes, such as love and betrayal, that appear over and over again in different ages and contexts, from the original Greek tragedies, to Shakespeare, to modern culture. The students discovered that the classic 1948 film *The Treasure of Sierra Madre,* starring Humphrey Bogart, was based on *The Pardoner's Tale* by Geoffrey Chaucer. The two works shared the same classic plot line: greed. The film setting was not medieval England, but rather nineteenth-century Mexico. Three prospectors join forces to find gold and end up succumbing to paranoia and greed. Most of us who saw the film remember the Mexican actor Alfonso Bedoya, who played "Gold Hat." His delivery of the line "We don't need no stink'n badges!" is said to be the only time Humphrey Bogart was upstaged.

John, my closest teacher friend and colleague over the decades, came through in a big way by advising two different project groups. He is a kind of Renaissance man, having taught history, psychology, and economics. His primary focus these days is his popular Advanced Placement Psychology course. The questions John selected were: "Why has there always been such a disparity of wealth between the rich and poor around the world? What can be done to change that equation?" And: "What do you see as the most serious psychological and sociological problems facing people of your age in our country right now?" His groups did their research by conducting surveys among students on campus to gain a wider range of opinion. It was interesting to me that the students from both separate research groups came up with similar conclusions: the major problems are greed, self-ishness, and social isolation.

I've always encouraged students to learn through research projects. This time they demonstrated far more depth of insight and proved the "Simon's Rock" experiment to be a success. The multiple perspectives presented by the different teachers resulted in a broader understanding for my students and once again proved to me that teaching and learning should be a collective activity.

Lucky

I had been single for over twenty years and had just turned fifty. One day after teaching summer school, I drove to an apartment rental agency in my area to place an ad. I was looking for a roommate to rent the guest room in my newly constructed house near the beach. After filling out the forms and leaving my contact information, I stopped at a Lucky Market located on Pacific Coast Highway between Redondo and Hermosa beaches. I had just bought a new dishwasher, and needed some detergent. I stood in the aisle trying to decide what product to buy. I hesitated because there were so many brands.

Out of the corner of my eye, I saw a woman pushing a shopping cart. Her dark brown hair was curly and disheveled. She was casually dressed, in jeans and a light blue sweatshirt spotted with colored paint. At the time, I had no idea she was an artist and had taken a break from painting to pick up a few essentials for her dinner.

She had the most beautiful, angelic face I'd ever seen. A commanding voice in the back of my head came in loud and clear: "Say something to her. Say anything."

"Excuse me. Do you know anything about dishwasher soap?"

She smiled sweetly and said: "What would you like to know?"

"Well, uh . . . I just bought a new dishwasher . . . and . . . uh, I was wondering what kind of soap you'd recommend. The granulated or the liquid kind?"

She smiled again and replied: "I'd go with the liquid. It breaks down a little faster."

The next sentence required a creative segue to a different subject. "You seem to know a lot about dishwashers. What other subjects are you knowledgeable about?"

She laughed and said, "Well, I'm not sure. One subject I'm not familiar with is Los Angeles. I just moved here from Michigan and I'm staying with my daughter in Hermosa Beach. I'm actually looking for an apartment because she's planning to attend Pepperdine University and our place is too large for one person."

This was the best news I could hear. "I have a room to rent with a bath and a separate entrance. It's very close to the beach. Would you be interested in seeing it?" We exchanged information so we could set up a time for her to see the space. As it turned out, my one room was not large enough for her furniture and belongings, but it gave me the opportunity to ask her for a date.

"Have you ever been to the Hollywood Bowl? They have wonderful concerts there and I have season tickets. In fact, the music of George Gershwin is featured next Saturday, if you're free. I have four tickets and we could double-date with my brother and his wife." She nodded affirmatively with a friendly smile and said she would love to go.

Before the concert, the four of us had a picnic on the enormous lawn outside the "Bowl." I had picked up Kentucky Fried Chicken and John and Dee brought wine. It was rare that after decades of being single, I had finally found someone I admired enough to actually meet the members of my family.

When Jeanne left for the ladies' room, my sister-in-law Dee turned to me and began her interrogation: "She is so beautiful and sweet! So, what's up next for you and Jeanne?" I replied: "I don't know. I'm thinking of taking her for a drink at Yamashiro... you know, the Japanese restaurant up the hill above Hollywood Boulevard." "Then what?" she asked, sounding irritated. "I guess I'll drive her home? Do you want me to call you for a report afterward?" For some reason, I enjoyed frustrating her attempts at information-gathering regarding my limited social life.

Yamashiro is a beautiful and romantic old Japanese restaurant. It was built in the traditional pagoda style. It was also the location where a few scenes from the motion picture *Sayonara* were filmed. I thought it would be completely different from places she had seen in the Midwest. After martinis, we walked out on the patio and along the path that wound through tall pines. Under the full moon, we had our first kiss.

We fell in love very quickly. Kismet had worked its magic on both of us. I would call her nightly and we would talk until we were so sleepy we couldn't talk anymore. I had a deep, almost spiritual feeling that I had found my soulmate. It didn't matter if we ran out of subject matter or not, the important thing was to stay connected. To this day, we find comfort hearing each other's voices, even when there is nothing important to communicate.

By the time Thanksgiving arrived, Jeanne invited me to go to the Midwest to meet her parents and her brother's family. I was touched by the invitation. She said she didn't want me to be lonely over the holiday.

Our plane landed in Grand Rapids, Michigan, in the middle of a blizzard. Because of the driving snow and wind, we could barely see through our windshield. The icy roads made it too dangerous to drive safely. We were relieved to find a bed and breakfast that had a vacancy and decided to stop for the night. We hoped that by morning, the roads would be cleared and we could drive the thirty miles to Greenville, where her parents lived.

Our lodging was a beautifully restored Victorian home. There was a cheerful fire burning in the living room. Directly in front of it, an elderly couple sat close to each other on a comfortable sofa, enjoying the peaceful ambience. In a corner of the room, a young couple sat at a small table, putting together a jigsaw puzzle. We could smell the odor of fresh pine coming from a large Christmas tree next to the fireplace. We were greeted by the owners, who offered us refreshments from a round oak table in the center of the room. On it were trays with various pastries and carafes of hot tea and coffee. We gratefully accepted. We were weary from our long day and stressful drive from the airport. Afterward, we were shown to our second-story room. Through the frosty window we could see colorful Christmas lights on other houses, dimmed by the huge swirling flakes that blanketed everything in white.

I opened the complimentary bottle of Cabernet that was on a dresser and poured us each a glass of wine. I then got down on my knees, pulled out the engagement ring from my pocket, and asked Jeanne to marry me. She accepted with happy tears. Despite our excitement, the relaxing effects of the wine and exhaustion took over and we soon fell asleep.

We woke to the sound of snowplows. The wind had died down and the storm had subsided. We said our goodbyes to the innkeepers and stepped out into a snowy wonderland. Icy air bit into our eyes and cheeks. I sent Jeanne back inside to stay warm while I brushed the snow off of the car and defrosted the windshield. Soon we were off, still reliving the thrill of being newly engaged. It was early afternoon when we arrived at her parents' home. Jeanne's father, an immigrant and engineer, was a tough old Dutchman. He had designed bridges and roads all over Michigan. When we were alone, I decided to show my respect for him by asking for his daughter's hand in marriage. His answer touched me when I considered his situation with

Jeanne's mother, who had Alzheimer's disease. He had opted to be her caretaker, rather than place her in a special home for patients with dementia. He fed, bathed, and dressed her, and daily changed her bed linens, as she was incontinent and unable to take care of those functions herself. After affirming my request for Jeanne's hand, he said: "The way I figure it is that we should take every opportunity for as much joy and happiness as possible during our lives."

Jeanne and I were both divorced with grown children. She had two daughters and a son and I was the father of a son and a daughter. We waited a few months to marry so our families could get to know each other. We had a beautiful wedding amid a grove of towering redwood trees on the shores of the Pacific Ocean. Fernando, my dear friend from high school, was my best man. The ceremony was performed in the Wayfarers Chapel, also known as "The Glass Chapel." It is a unique stone-and-glass structure designed by the son of the renowned architect Frank Lloyd Wright.

The Power of Music

The last day of the school year was also the last meeting of my European History Advanced Placement (EHAP) class before my retirement. The first and final days of school are important in terms of lasting impressions. The final day of history class was usually a nostalgic attempt to retrace history one last time. This was especially true of the EHAP class, arguably one of the most difficult of the AP courses. Just as I was preparing to start my traditional "Farewell Address," Robert volunteered to get his violin from the music room for some musical accompaniment. I thought it was a great idea. When he returned, he began to play the haunting and melancholy score of the film *Schindler's List*. This was two weeks after my class had listened to the heart-wrenching testimonies of the guest Holocaust survivors.

I began my talk: "Okay, you guys! We've been together through some good times, but it's also been a long, painful journey through the horrors of history: the Black Death, the Inquisition, the Thirty Years' War. We've been through global depressions, world wars, and the scourge of witchcraft." I was surprised to see tears welling up in so many eyes. The emotional power of Robert's beautiful and expressive violin music had pulled at their heartstrings and brought tears of nostalgia.

The next day I asked my colleague Fred, the school orchestra teacher and director, if he thought Robert might wind up one day as the first violinist for the LA Philharmonic. He replied: "No, he'll be an international soloist!"

50th Class Reunion and Beyond

It was 2010, the year of our 50th Loyola High reunion. Jocko and I served on the reunion committee with about a dozen others. Part of the job was contacting class members to find out if they were still alive and if they would be attending, and announcing the details of the event. The reunion would be held over a two-day weekend in Los Angeles. Many of our classmates and their wives who were coming from all over the country would stay at the Bonaventure Hotel in downtown Los Angeles. That distinctive hotel holds special meaning for many of us. Trent, one of our classmates, had been a key member of the project management team that built the hotel early in his construction career. He also helped with the construction of the Skirball Cultural Center and the Los Angeles County Museum of Art.

Jocko and I, as usual, were in charge of the reunion program, to be held after Mass and dinner on the Loyola High campus. Enriching the program with nostalgia and humor at every reunion since high school was a responsibility we both took quite seriously. I had been the senior class president. Jocko was a good co-emcee. I continued as the "straight man" for his antics because it seemed to work and we had a blast.

That evening as the program began, I stood up and looked out at over a hundred men, some with wheelchairs, walkers, and canes. I began by saying: "My god, you guys really look old! We've finally matured over the last few decades." Then I asked how many classmates could still remember the first poem Father Doyle had us memorize and recite in freshman English class: "How Did You Die?" by Edmund Vance Cooke. I began to recite:

> *Did you tackle that trouble that came your way*
> *With a resolute heart and cheerful?*
> *Or hide your face from the light of day*
> *With a craven soul and fearful?*

It was a great feeling when almost all of my classmates remembered the poem and immediately joined me.

> *Oh, a trouble's a ton, or a trouble's an ounce,*
> *Or a trouble is what you make it.*
> *And it isn't the fact that you're hurt that counts,*
> *but only how did you take it?*

Holding wireless microphones, Jocko and I walked around the dining room asking our classmates to recall funny stories. Someone recounted an amusing incident regarding Tony, a beloved but now deceased classmate. Tony was small in stature, but he had the heart of a giant. Once, when Tony was faced with the wrath of a much larger and fiercer local gang and its leader, the guy challenged Tony to take back an expletive he had yelled at him. Tony quickly responded, "No, no, no. I didn't say F . . . you. I said F . . . me!"

We presented an award to George, one of our most successful classmates. He became the Paris correspondent for *Time* magazine, and eventually an editor. Then he became a successful novelist with his book *The Judgment of Paris,* which was later made into the motion picture *Bottle Shock.* It centered on a wine competition he attended in Paris in 1976, in which French judges carried out two blind tasting comparisons, one of which would determine the top Chardonnay and the other the top red wine. California wines were awarded first place in each category. George, not surprisingly, is a wine connoisseur himself. As a joke, we honored our classmate by presenting him with two bottles of Charles Shaw, the bargain wine nicknamed "Two Buck Chuck" and sold at Trader Joe's.

Father Steve, our Jesuit classmate, had been the president of the University of San Francisco for almost fifteen years. As a student, he had been the best impersonator of our teachers. Steve had us laughing nonstop with his imitations of Father Conneally, Father Saussotte, the school principal of our day, and of course, the legendary Clyde.

Stories were told of successful and unsuccessful attempts at cheating in difficult classes such as Latin. One classmate had found an interlinear Latin translation of Julius Caesar's *The Gallic War.* He cut it out and pasted it into his textbook. When he was called upon to recite, he gave a superb acting performance by pretending to be translating Latin on the spot, while he was actually reading it. "Gallia est omnis divisa in partes tres." Slowly and struggling, he translated "All Gaul . . . is divided . . . in three parts." The teacher was fooled, but most of us knew his game.

We were glad to hear from one of our old friends, an African American by the name of Wardell. He talked about his freshman year, after he had moved to Los Angeles from one of the toughest neighborhoods in South Chicago. For some reason, the Jesuits had nicknamed him "Ignatius." He said he carried a switchblade to Loyola High for two weeks as protection because he didn't know any of us or what kind of guys we were. Eventually he realized we were "nice guys" and his switchblade wasn't necessary.

He was right. Now, we are a bunch of "nice *old* guys." Something that has always intrigued me about aging is the way our friendships renew at every one of our class reunions. The same thing happens at our monthly luncheon gatherings. Our friendships and the nostalgia we share are still very real. No matter how many years have passed, when we get together the same dynamics occur. Something takes over that brings back the warmth and humor of our teenage years at Loyola, when we first met and became friends, gathering in classrooms or at lunchtime on hard wooden benches to dig into our brown paper bags. Our personality characteristics haven't really changed that much over time. They remind us why we initially became friends more than sixty-four years ago. The funny guys are still funny and whatever brand a guy's humor was then, it still is today. Jocko continues to make us laugh. I still get laughs when I do my Jonathan Winters or Jack Nicholson imitations, and now I also imitate Bernie Sanders doing his stump speech, because so many people have told me that I look like him. Steve's imitations of our teachers seem more precious to me now than ever, no matter how many dozens of times I've seen him do them. As we grow older, the bonds between us remain strong.

I must have been blessed with an unusually keen audio recall. I can still call to mind at any time the unique sound of each guy's laughter. When I was writing about Pat's terrible cancer, to cheer myself up I would frequently "dial up" the sound of his contagious guffaw. He could always be heard in a noisy crowd. Bob is a very quick-witted and creative guy who became successful in the advertising business. He is also an author who has written several books. Bob is one person whose laughter I can't wait to hear at our monthly lunch or at any occasion. I could recognize Bob's laugh out of hundreds of others. Fernando is still the Fernando we all love. He no longer drives and now lives in an assisted living center in Orange County. He rarely misses Loyola luncheons because our classmates Tom and Ken always go out of their way to drive him. Our Jesuit teachers told us that the bonding among our classmates of the Class of 1960 is stronger than it is in some other classes. They believe that Fernando's serious accident, coma, and brush with death shocked us into an awareness of our own mortality and the preciousness of life.

When I remember the old friends who are no longer with us, I think of Rich, my huge, tough football teammate, and the guy who called for a time-out when I lost my front teeth during a game. Because of his size, strength, and comedic mannerisms, we sometimes teased him as the archetypal "football player." In actuality, he was far from that. Rich worked along with Dave as an officer in the LAPD for twenty-seven years. Rich was in charge of the entire security team for the 1984 Olympic Games held in Los Angeles. Those games came off without a hitch. I was proud of Rich and the LAPD for that achievement. The last time I saw him, he was in a wheelchair. He thanked me for being his friend and his daughter's high school teacher. He passed away a few years later.

I reminisce with Bill, a football teammate, another lineman who also lost his front teeth during a game when he tried to block a kick. Tackling Bill, with all his strength and energy, was like tangling with a Brahma bull. Now, in our senior years, we both share another price of playing football, along with Jerry. All three of us have undergone double hip replacement surgeries.

Now we are approaching our sixtieth class reunion. I'm looking forward to participating in this occasion with as many of my old classmates as possible. One of them is Jocko. Over the years, he came to realize that his high school education contributed in a major way to his successful life and that his friends are his "real wealth." He decided to express his gratitude. In 2015, Jocko committed ten million dollars to Loyola High, the largest single endowment gift in the school's history. Initially, he attached two requirements to his donation: First, the money was to fund scholarships with a preference for students from single-parent or sole-provider homes whose families might not be able to afford Loyola. Second, he wanted to remain anonymous. No publicity, announcements, or honors were to connect him to the gift, other than that it came from a member of our Class of 1960.

Of course, speculation began immediately as to the identity of the anonymous donor. Jocko was one of several prime suspects but there was no proof. Over two years later, the Loyola administration approached Jocko asking his permission to reveal his identity in order to encourage further major scholarship donors. This idea has been successful and now many more inner-city youth will have the life-changing opportunity to receive the kind of quality education at Loyola that we did.

After my long career as a teacher and knowing Jocko's antics in high school, I can only guess what a handful he must have been for the nuns who taught him in elementary school. Lately he has been in a payback mode for his youthful behavior. Jocko had his legal firm's investigator track down an elderly former nun who had been his grade school teacher. When he learned she was destitute, he wired her money anonymously. When she found out and called him to return the money, he replied: "Whatever you get is sent from God . . . so send it back to Him."

Recently, in Palos Verdes near where I taught, I noticed a major renovation project at an old convent. Among the many improvements, they were installing elevators to make it possible for the elderly nuns to reach the second floor without having to climb the steep stairs. I found out from one of the nuns that their benefactor had been her former student many decades ago. It was Jocko. When he handed her the check for the project, she exclaimed: "I always knew you weren't a bad boy, nor a good boy either. You were sort of a good-bad boy!"

That was a keen observation about his character and was actually true of many of us growing up. It explains why during our first years at Loyola High, we needed Clyde's tough terror tactics to reel us in from self-destruction and expulsion.

In his second year as president of Verbum Dei High in Watts, Father Steve continues to expand his work for the inner-city kids there. Many more will gain the opportunity to take a better path in life. Besides the work-study program, he has initiated an ambitious adopt-a-kid program involving many more people from the affluent suburbs of Los Angeles.

One of my favorite high school friends is Tom, our "prayer group of three" founder. We never played on the same sports team but we were actually in a play together: Gilbert and Sullivan's classic *The Pirates of Penzance*. One evening after a rehearsal, Tom treated me to my first-ever "Tommy's hamburger." The taste of that delicious burger dripping with chili sauce changed my culinary preferences for decades.

After earning his pharmaceutical degree, Tom has owned and managed several pharmacies in the Hollywood area since the midsixties. I've always thought of him as a very busy businessman. Yet why was it Tom who called me about starting the prayer group with Ron? My dad frequently said: "If you want to get something done, ask a busy man." Tom is a good example. I recently learned he is the president of a major charity, the Mission Doctors Association, a Catholic organization that sends doctors to serve in some of the poorest countries all over the world. Tom works with others to figure out the areas of greatest medical need and then sends doctors on assignments ranging from one month to three years. Their mission statement states: "Following Christ's call to heal the sick, Mission Doctors

Association provides lifesaving medical care for the poor and training for local health care professionals around the world." They serve people of all different faiths while respecting each individual's personal faith. They are a very "catholic" organization in the best sense of that word by sharing "universal" human values.

Most of my old friends share those values because of the early Jesuit education we received. AMDG—*ad majorem Dei gloriam,* meaning "for the greater glory of God"—is still a common thread interwoven in different "colors" inside each one of us. Another slogan I hear frequently is the Loyola High School motto which defines its students as "Men for Others." These influences continue to play a formative part in our lives and the lives of other Jesuit-educated young men and women.

Since my retirement almost two years ago, my life has changed in certain ways but not completely. I'm excited to return to the classroom in the role of a substitute teacher. It's a way to keep my hand in. Many of the teachers are my former students. They are kind enough to "let Mr. Mac get back into action," leading discussions on comparative religion, philosophy, history, literature, and even physics. They know how much I love being around teenagers, sharing ideas and preparing them for university education and life beyond school. Teaching continues to be a source of entertainment and joy.

> *What is the point of this story?*
> *What information pertains?*
> *The thought that life could be better*
> *Is woven indelibly*
> *Into our hearts*
> *And our brains.*
>
> —PAUL SIMON, "Train in the Distance"

I first met Jim Maechling in 1969 when I was enrolled in his sophomore Western Civilization class at Miraleste High School. It was the end of a tumultuous decade that forever changed our nation. We were a confused generation trying to make rational decisions about our direction in life despite existing in an irrational world of assassinations, riots, protests, racial injustice, and a war in Vietnam. The way we dressed, our music, and our behavior were a rejection of our parents' social norms and expectations. We were searching for answers and an eccentric, brilliant, humorous, animated teacher, fondly referred to as "Mr. Mac," was the perfect person to put our troubled times in historical perspective and give us hope for the future. A decade earlier, he was a student in a Western Civilization class at Loyola High School, soaking up Father Conneally's fascinating stories about history, mesmerized by the person who encouraged his love of the subject and set the stage for the student to eventually become the teacher. Although I never met Father Conneally, his memory lives on in Jim, just as Jim's influence lives on in all of those he has worked with in the past fifty years. That is the legacy of an exemplary teacher.

I lost contact with Mr. Mac until my daughter attended Miraleste High School in 1989 and was enrolled in his Western Civilization class. Every night at dinner, she would enthusiastically share what she had learned that day in Mr. Mac's class.

Twenty years had passed since I sat in his class, yet he still had that special ability to relate to his students and inspire them to think, observe, analyze, and question. I was fortunate to have had him as a teacher, and fortunate again that he had become my daughter's teacher. And before long, I would be fortunate to call him my colleague.

In 1995 I joined the faculty at Peninsula High School and for the next twenty-two years, I had the honor of working alongside Mr. Mac—and for seventeen of those years, ironically, I was his boss. As a school administrator, there are always going to be days that are tougher than others. On those days, I often found my way to Mr. Mac's Comparative Religion class to observe the magic of his Socratic discussions that had lifted me through questioning times decades earlier and continued to reinvigorate my sense of purpose as an educator.

Teaching religion in a public school can be filled with landmines, but Mr. Mac magically avoided controversy with his steadfast mission to treat all religions, people, and cultures fairly and with respect. Students often tried to guess, but Mr. Mac never divulged his own religious beliefs. As I read the student vignettes in this book, it brought back fond memories of the thousands of students who were impacted by his passionate commitment to them. These stories are just the tip of the iceberg of lives enriched by Mr. Mac.

Mr. Mac sparked my lifelong desire to witness history, experience cultures, and explore the world. His words resonated while I was walking into the Roman Coliseum, climbing the slippery stones of the Parthenon, musing over the Moai on Easter Island, waiting for the sun to rise through mountain peaks at Machu Picchu, silently dining in the evening shadow of Uluru, observing the faithful pilgrims in Lourdes, scaling the steps of the Dalai Lama's Potala Palace in Tibet, experiencing tears at Auschwitz, hearing the stillness of Hiroshima, contemplating the mysteries of Stonehenge, visiting the battlefields of great wars, and sailing the oceans on the same paths as great explorers. I am forever grateful for Mr. Mac's role in my life and can testify to generations of students who would say the same.

With respect and gratitude,

> *—Mitzi Cress*
> *Retired Principal*
> *Palos Verdes Peninsula High School*

As a teenager, Mitzi Cress was one of Mr. Mac's students in the late 1960s at Miraleste High School in Palos Verdes, California. An outstanding student, she thrived in the new school's innovative Humanities program. The "Flex Program" featured a team-teaching, flexible-schedule learning program that coordinated history and literature. Nearly three decades later, she became Mr. Mac's colleague as a counselor on the staff of Palos Verdes Peninsula High School. Soon she became head counselor, school vice-principal, and ultimately principal. In that capacity for nearly a decade she continued to foster team-teaching and innovative learning programs across the curriculum. Peninsula High School was consistently rated academically as one of the most outstanding high schools in California and in the United States.

ACKNOWLEDGEMENTS

Sincere thanks to my editor, Ruth Mullen, for her initial encouraging comments regarding the book's depth and value and for her intellectual contribution. I am especially grateful to my publisher Susan Shankin of Precocity Press, who not only designed the cover and interior layout but contributed much value by her keen insight and always cheerful guidance. Both professionals worked in coordination to address the challenge of integrating the stories of friends, teachers, and students with the intellectual concepts accumulated over my education, teaching career, and life experiences into one cohesive story.

This book could not have been possible without my wife Jeanne, and her daily assistance, ongoing faith in me, and unending patience and encouragement throughout what became a three-year odyssey for both of us.

Also, thank you to our dear daughter Jennifer, who as an award-winning teacher contributed much with her boundless wit and wisdom.

Special thanks to Jacques for his outstanding suggestion to include what I taught and my teaching methodology. This was a tremendous direction-finding boost that helped me develop the initial subject material involved, particularly in Comparative Religions and Advanced Philosophy.

I wish to thank Ron Russo and Dave Nichols, two loyal classmates and life-long friends who provided valuable input.

Jim Maechling was the youngest child in a Catholic family. In grade school, he was the questioning kid with his hand usually stuck in the air. Could these fantastic stories in the Bible be true? After a strong classical education from his Jesuit teachers in high school and college, he wanted to study the real world at close range.

While his friends entered law, medicine, and business, he gathered $75 in cash, his passport, and his seaman's papers, and took a job as a deck boy on a Norwegian freighter bound for Asia. After 'an eventful voyage, including a typhoon and a visit to Hiroshima, he landed in Madras, India, where a more realistic education began. At the Jesuit college, he wandered into the office of a French priest, Father Pierre Ceyrac, SJ, a humanitarian legend who had saved over two hundred thousand lives during droughts in India and Thailand. Jim then traveled north on rickety trains to Jamshedpur, where he found a job teaching history at a Jesuit school. On holiday vacations, he visited remote jungle regions, waded across rivers, and interacted with people from an isolated culture. While self-touring Calcutta with an outdated guidebook in his hand, he climbed the steps of what he thought was an ancient temple dedicated to the Hindu goddess Kali. He was surprised to be greeted at the door by a tiny nun wearing a white habit and speaking with a European accent. This was Mother Teresa whom the world did not yet know.

She had transformed the abandoned Hindu temple into a hospice home for the dying, free to the poor and accepting of all religions. Perhaps regarding Jim as a potential volunteer, she gave him a tour. During their discussion, her answer to one of his questions changed the direction of his life. By the end of that school year, Jim had fallen in love with the teaching profession as well as with a teacher at his school. She was a bright and beautiful colleague, an Indian of Persian descent. At the end of the school year, homesickness and illness influenced his decision to return home. In gratitude for his service, the Jesuits paid for his long journey home.

Back in California, Jim's next two years were about graduate school, teaching credentials, and some interesting odd jobs, including directing a play. Ultimately, he decided to forego the business paths of his father and older brothers for a teaching career of fifty years in the public schools of Palos Verdes, California. A popular teacher whose elective courses were always packed, Jim was a pioneer in introducing Eastern religious concepts and practices, such as mindfulness and meditation, to American high school students.

Jim was the recipient of many awards over his long career. In 2000, his Comparative Religion class was featured on PBS's *NewsHour with Jim Lehrer*. The following year, after the tragedy of September 11, Jim was distinguished with the "Educator of the Year" award in Palos Verdes, California.

Made in the USA
Las Vegas, NV
27 December 2021

39560349R00185